A History of the American People:
An Interpretation

THE
AMERICAN
REVOLUTION
1763-1783

HERBERT APTHEKER

INTERNATIONAL PUBLISHERS • NEW YORK

Library of Congress Catalog Card Number: 60-9948
ISBN 0-7178-0006-7, ISBN 0-7178-0005-9 (pbk)

PUBLISHERS NOTE

The author has supplied a list of significant works dealing with the American Revolution which appeared in the period, 1960-66, in the Additional Bibliography on page 297.

Sixth printing   1985

PRINTED IN THE UNITED STATES OF AMERICA

Contents

A History of the American People:
An Interpretation

The American Revolution

1763-1783

Chapter I

The Nature of the Revolution

Τ H E D O M I N A N T trend in recent American historiography—though by no means uncontested—so far as the American Revolution is concerned, is to treat it as quite unique in that it was either no "revolution" at all, or, if a "revolution," then a conservative one. This interpretation, while not new, as we shall show, clearly does form part of the general pattern of the "New Conservatism" that has been so significant an ideological phenomenon in the United States in the years since World War II.

Among the more explicit of this school is Professor Daniel J. Boorstin, whose work (*The Genius of American Politics,* 1953) may be used as characteristic of its views. Boorstin finds: "The most obvious peculiarity of our American Revolution is that, in the modern European sense of the word, it was hardly a revolution at all." He notes that this view is the one promulgated for generations by the Daughters of the American Revolution; but he refuses to allow anything, even this coincidence, to keep him from announcing the result of his scholarly pursuits. Hence: "The more I have looked into the subject, the more convinced I have become of the wisdom of their [the Daughters'] naiveté."

As a matter of fact, Boorstin ends up slightly to the Right of the Daughters, for while they had always insisted that the American Revolution was not a revolution but merely a colonial rebellion, Boorstin adds that it was a "conservative colonial rebellion" since it was "notably lacking in cultural self-consciousness and in any passion for national unity."

9

The new feature in this conservative revisionism, of which Boorstin's work is so striking an example, is its abundance and its starkness. Its essence may be found in the observations of De Tocqueville, made a century ago, to the effect that the United States was democratic without ever having had a democratic revolution. It is present, too, in the writings of some professional historians of earlier generations; for example, of John Fiske, in the late 19th century, and of G. A. Koch and Reginald Coupland, in the 1930's. The latter, an English historian, in his stimulating study of *The American Revolution and the British Empire* (1930), found the Revolution remarkable in that it was made by a "prosperous, not on the whole ill-governed, largely indeed self-governing people" and so he could only explain it as being "almost entirely a matter of theories and principles."

Similarly, in the present period, writers like Louis Hartz and Robert E. Brown see the revolution as coming not because of oppression but because of freedom; the American revolutionists sought stability, not change. Indeed, if there were any "revolutionists"—*i.e.*, any who sought drastic change—they were the inept, deluded and misinformed British King and his Ministry. Hence, as Hartz says in *The Liberal Tradition in America* (1955), "this makes radicalism irrelevant to the American Revolution." The Americans did not "join in the great Enlightenment enterprise of shattering the Christian concept of sin" and "did not share the crusading spirit" that one finds in real revolutionists as those of France and Russia.

This, again, is similar to the earlier view of Charles M. Andrews who insisted that the Americans were seeking nothing but the "rights of Englishmen," that these rights "had nothing to do with democracy and represented nothing that was in advance of the age in which the colonists lived" and that therefore the (so-called?) revolutionists "contributed little or nothing to the cause of progressive liberalism or to the advancement of those democratic ideals."

Robert E. Brown, in his effort to prove that the colonists sought to preserve and not to change, made of colonial society an advanced "middle-class democracy" and so pictured the Revolution purely in terms of separation from an England which was seeking to destroy an already existent democratic social order. Where he offered detailed evidences of the considerable advances that had been made towards elementary political democratic forms in some of the colonies, Brown's study is important —though hardly as new as he would have the reader believe, for very much the same point may be found in Edward Channing's study of the Revolution published in 1912, and even earlier in W. E. H. Lecky's work on 18th century English history.

But in affirming the "middle-class democratic" character of colonial America, Brown exaggerates to the point of absurdity: "Except for the inhabitants of a few towns, the people from Nova Scotia to West Florida were farmers. They were motivated by a spirit of industry which was unfettered and unrestrained because each person worked for himself, not for others."

Such a view is remarkable not only for its ignoring of such basic colonial enterprises as commercial trading, fishing, fur-trading and land-engrossing; it is even more remarkable for its ignoring of the entire Indian population and the 35 per cent of the non-Indian population which consisted of chattel slaves and of indentured servants. Surely they would have been astonished to learn that they were "unfettered and unrestrained" and that they "worked for themselves." And, of course, ignoring the unfre ignores the classes that owned them and profited from their labor.

A variant in the effort to take the revolution out of the American Revolution consists of ascribing the outbreak to errors in judgment and failings in temperament. That is an essential thesis of Charles R. Ritcheson's *British Politics and the American Revolution* (1954)—mutual misunderstanding and bungling by the respective leaders produced the fighting. Similarly, Richard B. Morris, in his *The American Revolution* (1955), after announcing that his subject "refuses to conform to the Marxist pattern," makes its occurrence depend upon the existence in Britain of an insufficiently astute administration which did not know how "to reconcile the demands of imperial security with that measure of self-government which colonial maturity justified."

Another reflection of the impact of conservative revisionism is writing which does not go so far as to deny the revolutionary content of the Revolution, but which apologizes for its existence. John Richard Alden, for example, in his *The American Revolution* (1954), guardedly writes that "he believes that the thought and conduct of the American patriots are ultimately defensible, that the Declaration of Independence is in the last analysis justifiable." And Max Savelle described the event in 1952 as though it were a supreme example of human failure:

> The American Revolution was one of the great tragic events of human history. Two societies, each led by a body of able and sincere men, and each motivated by the highest ideas it knew, came to an impasse over the question of the true nature of the Imperial constitution. When they finally arrived at this impasse neither side could retreat without the sacrifice of its highest political ideal. It is difficult to imagine a more colossal example of the tragic consequences of sheer misunderstanding and stubborn unwillingness, in the name of principle, to compromise.

No matter how the Revolution is evaluated, however—and we shall, of course, offer our own views on this matter in due course —there remains the related, but yet distinct problem of accounting for its occurrence. On this question there is truly an enormous literature, the most significant features of which we shall now summarize.

A still widely prevalent view is that which may be characterized as economic determinist, a view subjected to severe buffeting in the past generation and one which, in its time, made important contributions. Emory R. Johnson, in his *History of Domestic and Foreign Commerce of the United States* (1915), expressed this succinctly:

> The Revolution in America was fought to secure commercial and industrial freedom through the establishment of political liberty. . . . The Revolutionary War was fought to secure freedom of trade and to obtain home rule in the levying of taxes for the support of the government.

Similar is the conclusion of J. Franklin Jameson in his very significant study, *The American Revolution Considered as a Social Movement* (1926):

. . . of the deep underlying causes, which for a generation had been moving the American in the direction of independence, none was so potent, according to all the best testimony, as the parliamentary restrictions on the trade of the colonies.

Other writers, taking the economic determinist view, add emphases on different economic conflicts, as those involving heavily indebted planters, threatened land speculators, thwarted manufacturers, and harassed investors in fur, fish or forest.

A view very much like that of Johnson and Jameson was held by Edward Channing, the young Charles A. Beard and the young Louis M. Hacker. Here the essence remained economic determinist but the expression was Madisonian and redolent with terms suggesting conflicts between different propertied groups and classes. Thus Channing opened the third volume of his monumental *History of the United States* with these words:

> Commercialism, the desire for advantage and profit in trade and industry, was at the bottom of the struggle between England and America; the immutable principles of human association were brought forward to justify colonial resistance to British selfishness. The governing classes of the old country wished to exploit the American colonists for their own use and behoof; the Americans desired to work their lands and carry on their trade for themselves.

The Beard-Hacker version did not differ substantially from this, though its use of words like bourgeoisie and its concentration upon conflicting needs of British mercantilism and rising American capitalism led some, like Charles M. Andrews, to confuse their views with the outlook of historical materialism—a confusion expedited, at least in the case of Hacker's work, by the fact that the author himself then fell victim to such confusion.

There is also a substantial body of literature, clustering about the names of scholars like George L. Beer, Lawrence H. Gipson, Lawrence A. Harper, Oliver M. Dickerson, and Curtis P. Nettels, which offers differing views as to the actual impact of the Navigation and Trade Acts, the weight of restrictions upon manufacturing and currency, the period when these and other mercantile measures began to adversely affect the colonial economy. These writings are of great consequence, and some of their

findings will be reflected in later pages, but in terms of fundamental causative analysis, similarities are greater than differences
and in that sense they add little to the schools already sketched.

Some historians deny that economic conflict between the
propertied groups of England and the colonies was significant
in producing the breakaway. A good example is Eric Robson's
posthumously published study of *The American Revolution*
(1955). This scholar found himself unable to discover "any in-
exorable economic forces which were inevitably drawing the
colonies towards revolution"; he thought, rather, that "conflicting political ideas, not tea or taxes, caused the secession of the
colonial peoples from the British Empire."

In rather lonely splendor stands Thomas J. Wertenbaker. He
found in his study of the Revolution in New York, *Father
Knickerbocker Rebels,* (1948), that: "When the colonists placed
themselves outside the British Empire they were sacrificing far
more in an economic sense than they gained, and they all knew
it. In other words, the Americans rebelled in spite of the economic situation, not because of it."

Wertenbaker joins some other historians in his view that the
revolution was due to politics—"the Americans rebelled against
Great Britain because they insisted upon governing themselves";
but he is unique in maintaining that the economic pull was all
the other way.

There are many scholars who take an eclectic approach to the
origins of the Revolution and attribute it to the existence of a
myriad of discrete and separate "factors"—the economic, the
political, the social, the religious, the climatic, the psychological,
and others. Through the infinite multiplication of "causes,"
cause itself is liquidated.

On the other hand, there have been some scholars who have
taken a more dialectical view and in doing so have offered fresh
insights. A pioneer work in this regard was Charles H. Lincoln's
Revolutionary Movement in Pennsylvania, 1760-1776, published
in 1901. Lincoln noted—and this fact was especially marked in
Pennsylvania—that the revolutionists "were more eager to obtain
independence within their own state than to throw off the
British connection." He continued:

> The national movement furnished the opportunity for which
> the dissatisfied people throughout the province had been wait-
> ing, and the result was a double change of government. . . .
> The purpose of this work has been to show the interdependence
> of the colonial and national revolutions.

Elsewhere in the same volume, Lincoln added another component, though he nowhere developed this thought, namely,
that in the 17th and 18th centuries a highly variegated peoples,
although predominantly English, came to the colonies and that
they found here "utterly dissimilar environments" from those at
home and so developed needs and institutions unlike those in
Europe.

Lincoln did see clearly an inter-imperial struggle and an intra-
colonial struggle and he sensed the merging of the two in the
nature of the Revolution—at least so far as Pennsylvania was
concerned—and this marked a pushing forward of historical
comprehension.

This thesis was stated more pointedly and applied more generally in the first book from the creative pen of the late Carl
L. Becker. In his *History of Political Parties in the Province of
New York, 1760-1776,* published in 1909, Becker pointed out
that there were two questions central to the revolutionary ferment
prior to 1776: (1) home rule, and (2) who was to rule at home.
Later writers, notably Arthur M. Schlesinger in his *Colonial
Merchants and the American Revolution* (1918), and the more
recent work of Merrill Jensen, have added fresh evidence and
substantiation of this view, which, despite some attacks in the
past and most recently in the work of Robert E. Brown, remains
illuminating and basically sound.

In the enormous range of writing by Charles M. Andrews,
dealing with the colonial and Revolutionary periods, one can
find significant expressions of the dialectical quality of history.
Though, as we have seen, Andrews insisted—mistakenly, I think
—that the Revolutionary effort had nothing to do with the
question of democracy, he did express very interesting views as
to the nature and origin of that effort.

Thus, in an article in the *American Historical Review* (January, 1926) he found an inherent contradiction in the position
of England and its colonies as at the root of the separation:

On one side was the immutable, stereotyped system of the mother country, based on precedent and tradition and designed to keep things comfortably as they were; on the other, a vital dynamic organism, containing the seed of a great nation, its forces untried, still to be proved. It is inconceivable that a connection should have continued long between two such yoke-fellows, one static, the other dynamic, separated by an ocean and bound only by the ties of a legal relationship.

Though Andrews does not spell out here why one system was "static" and the other "dynamic," he does, in this passage, suggest the maturing of a revolutionary social process which is more helpful than the "infinite-factor" school of narration, and much richer than the mechanical, economic determinist views.

Again, certain analytical passages in his *magnum opus* reflect the same awareness of social-developmental processes. Thus, in the second volume of Andrews' *Colonial Period of American History* there is this paragraph:

The separation from the mother country was more than a matter of revolutionary warfare for eight years. It was a century long process, without dates and without boundaries, whereby little by little, features of English law, constituted authority and precedent, land tenure, and other conditions ingrained in the minds and habits of Englishmen at home, such as were neither needed nor wanted in the colonies, were being one by one altered, reduced, or eliminated altogether. In that way and for that reason independence of the mother country had been won in many directions before the Treaty of Paris of 1783.

In the fourth volume of his work, Andrews has more exposition of the details of this "separation." Furthermore, he places the matter more clearly in terms of social contradiction and antagonistic interests, though he one-sidedly confines the matter exclusively to the question of England versus the colonies:

England's determination to centralize authority at Whitehall and Westminster; to maintain her colonies in a permanent state of subordination, politically as well as commercially; to deny them the status of self-governing communities, refusing privileges asked for and denying many that were already enjoyed; to consider her own prosperity and security before the welfare of her outlying dependencies, whose "rights" as we call them today, she neither recognized nor understood; and to belittle protests from America as the work only of agitators and radicals—all these things must be taken into consideration by anyone who wishes to understand the circumstances that brought on the American Revolution.

Andrews clearly felt that ideas and considerations such as are expressed in the paragraphs that I have quoted were beyond the ken of the Marxist writer. This was due to the fact that he did not comprehend historical materialism—a failing made crystal-clear in the concluding sentences of the last volume of his *Colonial History*.

There Andrews attacked what he thought was "the Marxian doctrine" as enunciated by Beard and Hacker, but actually was an economic determinist view. Andrews felt it was "untrue to fact to say that there was any one grievance common to all [colonies] and that grievance solely commercial or industrial." He saw more to history than "a clash of economic interests" and concluded:

> To emphasize the economic aspects to the exclusion of all else is to interpret human affairs in terms of material things only, to say nothing of the spiritual power necessary to use these material resources for human welfare, to ignore the influence of sentiment and morality, and to underrate the rich and varied stuff of human nature, the distractions of statesmen, and the waywardness and uncertainty of events.

Marxism ignores none of the forces mentioned by Andrews. Marxism does not see the American Revolution "exclusively" in terms of "commercial or industrial," or, one might add, agrarian, grievances. Marxism does deal with "England" more realistically than did Andrews, for even Disraeli acknowledged that there was more than one "England" and the class differences in England were certainly of the greatest consequence in the origins, conduct, and conclusion of the American Revolution. Marxism sees "the colonies," also, more realistically than did Andrews, for these colonies were themselves class-stratified societies (as so much of Andrews' own *narrative* makes clear) and this fact, too, is of decisive consequence in comprehending the nature of that society and the changes therein and the demands raised by different classes and groups within the colonies. Without this as a base, nothing in colonial history, and certainly not the struggle to achieve independence from Great Britain, makes sense.

Marxism, in viewing the economic factor as ultimately decisive, does not think of "economic factor" in the narrow sense as this or that particular economic conflict or economic interest. The economic factor in the Marxist outlook, is itself the offshoot of the basic economic foundation—the mode of production, the resulting relations of production, and the social superstructure arising from them, bulwarking them, and effecting them. In this sense, is the economic factor ultimately the decisive one in the historical process, a process which manifests itself, of course, through the activities of human beings. This lies at the heart of historical materialism, its view of class roles and of historical dynamics. It is quite different from considering any particular economic item or "factor" as determinant; and it insists upon the interpenetrating, complex—dialectical—quality of life and history.

It will not be amiss to quote Marx' own definition of historical materialism, where he gives this in the fullest form. This is the philosophical outlook of the present work's author; moreover, in present-day American scholarship it is usual to combat "Marxism" without having ever really studied it, let alone extensively quote from Marx himself. The passage occurs in the preface which Marx wrote for his book, *A Contribution to the Critique of Political Economy* (1859):

> In the social production which men carry on they enter into definite relations that are indispensable and independent of their will; these relations of production correspond to a definite stage of development of their material forces of production. The sum total of these relations of production constitutes the economic structure of society—the real foundation, on which rises a legal and political superstructure and to which correspond definite forms of social consciousness.
>
> The mode of production in material life determines the social, political, and intellectual life processes in general. It is not the consciousness of men that determines their being, but, on the contrary, their social being that determines their consciousness.
>
> At a certain stage of their development, the material forces of production come in conflict with the existing relations of

production, or—what is but a legal expression for the same thing—with the property relations within which they have been at work before. From forms of development of the forces of production these relations turn into their fetters. Then begins an epoch of social revolution.

With the change of the economic foundation the entire immense superstructure is more or less rapidly transformed. In considering such transformations a distinction should always be made between the material transformation of the economic conditions of production which can be determined with the precision of natural science, and the legal, political, religious, aesthetic or philosophic—in short, ideological forms in which men became conscious of this conflict and fight it out.

Just as our opinion of an individual is not based on what he thinks of himself, so can we not judge of such a period of transformation by its own consciousness; on the contrary this consciousness must be explained rather from the contradictions of material life, from the existing conflict between the social forces of production and the relations of production. No social order ever disappears before all the productive forces for which there is room in it have been developed; and new higher relations of production never appear before the material conditions of their existence have matured in the womb of the old society itself.

The most notable recent sustained efforts to deal with the American Revolution from a Marxist viewpoint have come from Herbert M. Morais and William Z. Foster. In both cases very much more richness is apparent than Andrews would grant could come from this outlook.

Morais, in his splendid brief survey of the first two-hundred years of American history (*The Struggle for American Freedom,* 1944) devotes eighty pages specifically to the Revolutionary War. His analysis is summarized in this paragraph:

> The first American Revolution was the product of two general movements: the struggle for self government and national independence and the struggle among the American people themselves for a more democratic order. The Revolution therefore had an external aspect, the colonial war of liberation against Britain, and an internal aspect, the mass upsurge against anti-democratic elements. It ushered in the modern era of revolutionary struggles and became the prototype of a whole series of bourgeois-democratic upheavals in Europe and colonial uprisings throughout the world.

Foster's views are given, with somewhat different emphases, in his two volumes, *Outline Political History of the Americas* (1951), and *The Negro People in American History* (1954).

In the later volume, Foster quotes the well-known estimate of Lenin—in his *Letter to American Workers* (1920)—that the American War for Independence was "one of those great . . . really revolutionary wars of which there have been so few." Foster goes on to say that the revolution "dealt a mighty blow to feudal reaction and greatly stimulated democracy all over the world." He characterizes the Revolution as "a bourgeois revolution, with strong democratic currents within it." Earlier, in the same book, he spells out certain of its features in this manner: "The first American Revolution was a violent economic, political, and military collision between the young colonial capitalism striving to grow and acquire independence, and the dominant British capitalism, which sought to stifle and restrict it."

In his earlier volume, Foster added the very stimulating view that the American Revolution was the first and the major one of "the American hemispheric revolutions" that continued on into the next century. He presented it as a revolt for colonial national liberation against burdensome domestic conditions and pressing grievances; and he emphasized its international character. Moreover, Foster placed this hemispheric revolution within the larger world revolution against feudalism, or the world-wide movement from feudalism to capitalism, and he saw the development of political democracy as a central feature of such a change. He recognized, of course, national differences in revolutionary development, depending upon local variations in conditions, but saw the above aspects as basic and present to a greater or lesser degree throughout the Americas.

The American Revolution was the result of the interpenetration of three currents: The fundamental conflict in interest between the rulers of the colonizing power and the vast majority of the colonists; the class stratification within the colonies themselves and the resulting class struggles that marked colonial history which almost always found the British imperial power as a bulwark of the reactionary or the conservative interests in such struggles; and the developing sense of American nationality, transcending class lines, which resulted from the varied origins of the colonies' peoples, their physical separation from England, the different fauna and flora and climate of their surroundings, their different problems and interests, their own developing culture and psychology and even language, their own common history, and from their own experience of common hostility— varying in degree with place and time—towards the powers-that-be in England.

These currents were inter-related; each reacted upon the other. Of course, to have a colonial revolt one must have a colony and in this sense the American Revolution, which was centrally a war against the colonizing power, rested ultimately upon the antagonism of interests between the rulers of England and the American colonists as a whole. And basic to that antagonism was the conflict between a rising bourgeoisie in the colonies and a restraining bourgeoisie in England.

Adam Smith, in his classical *Wealth of Nations* (1776), put the matter this way: "To prohibit a great people from making all that they can of every part of their own produce, or from employing their stock and industry in a way that they may judge most advantageous to themselves, is a manifest violation of the most sacred rights of mankind."

This struggle between two conflicting national propertied interests is not one to which the Marxist can be indifferent. The colonial bourgeoisie was the young and straining one which sought control of its national market as a necessary preliminary to its growth; it was exactly this control and this growth which the British rulers would deny. They would deny it because they themselves had control through a monopoly on trade, the processing of finished goods, credit facilities and world-wide marketing know-how.

The denial inhibited the fullest growth of productive forces and was therefore reactionary. In this sense, also, the banner of the young, colonially-restrained American propertied interests with the notable exception of the slaveowners, bore the democratic emblem.

Again, in democratic mass struggles which were so central a feature of colonial life, it was characteristic—from Bacon's Re-

volt in 1676 to the Massachusetts Land Bank War of the 1740's
—to find the British power as the last resort of home-grown and
British-fed reaction. Hence in these struggles, of such great concern to large numbers and involving questions of bread and
butter—civil liberties, taxes, land, debts, suffrage, representation
—invariably there appeared a dual aspect, against England
and against home-based tyranny, and invariably these were
intertwined.

Furthermore, as the 18th century proceeded, a definite sense
of American nationality appeared and developed; this encompassed all classes. The desire for the right of self-determination
of this new nationality, which was at the heart of the revolutionary effort, was confined to no class, and most certainly was not
a monopoly of the well-to-do. On the contrary, in the American
Revolution, because of its nature, and because of the progressive
character of the American bourgeoisie then, the active involve-
ment of the masses of workers and farmers was notable. Again,
one has an inter-related phenomenon—the progressive and democratic content of the effort attracted the masses; the participation of the masses helped guarantee and enhance the democratic
content of the effort.

True it is, of course, that the American Revolution was fundamentally a colonial one, and hence it did not have the profoundly
transforming quality that more basically social ones have—as, for
example, the deep anti-feudal upheavals of the English and
French Revolutions of the 17th and 18th centuries, not to speak
of the anti-capitalist revolutions of our own century. And its
thorough-going nature was limited further by its compromising
with and then acceptance of the pre-feudal form that did charac-
terize American colonial society, namely chattel slavery—something to be undone in a future revolution. Nevertheless, the
American Revolution, in its opposition to colonial fetters, in its
impetus to democratic political and social innovations, and in its
assertion of the right of national self-determination, carried along
with it enough to justify Lenin's characterization as "one of those
great . . . really revolutionary wars."

It is necessary to emphasize, too, the radical quality of the
dominant revolutionary ideology. This will be examined at length

later; here let it be said, that ideology represented a fundamental break with feudal and monarchical thinking and in this respect had the widest international ramifications as it had had the widest international sources.

In evaluating the quality of the Revolution it is also necessary to remember, if one is to get its full contemporaneous impact, that it was the first successful colonial revolution in history. The imperial powers from Spain to France to Holland to Portugal had all faced colonial insurrections and they had all been put down. But the American succeeded and that fact itself, quite apart from the resulting political and social institutions, had an enormously revolutionary influence upon the peoples of the world.

Chapter II

The Origins

CHARLES THOMSON, native of Ireland, Philadelphia merchant, leader of the radicals in that city—called by John Adams, "the Sam Adams of Philadelphia"—wrote a letter to Pennsylvania's London agent, Benjamin Franklin, on September 24, 1765. In it is well summarized widely-held colonial feelings as to the distressing present and the portentous future:

> There never was any mention aiming at independence, till the ministry began to abridge them [the colonies] of their liberties. . . .
> The Sun of Liberty is indeed setting fast, if not down already, in the American colonies. . . . They are in general alarmed to the last degree. The colonies expect, and with reason expect, that some regard shall be had to their liberties and privileges, as well as trade. They cannot bring themselves to believe, nor can they see how England with reason or justice could expect, that they should have encountered the horrors of the desert, borne the attacks of barbarous savages, and, at the expence of their blood and treasure, settled this country to the great emolument of England, and after all quietly submit to be deprived of every thing an Englishman has been taught to hold dear.
> It is not property only we contend for. Our Liberty and most essential privileges are struck at: Arbitrary courts are set over us, and trials by juries taken away: The Press is so restricted that we cannot complain: An army of mercenaries threatened to be billeted on us: The sources of our trade stopped; and, to compleat our ruin, the little property we had acquired, taken

from us, without even allowing us the merit of giving it; I really dread the consequences.

The parliament insist on a power over all the liberties and privileges claimed by the colonies, and hence require a blind obedience and acquiescence in whatever they do: Should the behavior of the colonies happen not to square with these sovereign notions, (as I much fear it will not) what remains but by violence to compel them to obedience. Violence will beget resentment, and provoke to acts never dreamt of: But I will not anticipate evil; I pray God avert it.

This was a conflict derived not from human bungling or stubbornness but from social contradiction. The failure to resolve the conflict by compromise was not due to weakness or stupidity, but rather to the fact that the contradiction was not subject to compromise; only elimination of the antagonism at the root of the contradiction could remove it—transformation, not reformation, was needed.

I

The eighteenth century was the century of the rise to world hegemony of Great Britain. It was a rise whose culmination appeared to come with France's acknowledgment of defeat and her signing the peace treaty of 1763. By that treaty Great Britain stood forth as by far the greatest economic, naval and colonial power; she then set out to consolidate her holdings and revivify her imperial system throughout the world. Not least among these holdings and central to that imperial system were the possessions in the New World, including much of the West Indies and, on the Continent itself, everything from Nova Scotia through Florida and from the sea to the Mississippi River.

Simultaneously, the home economy of England, in considerable part because of the consolidation of world power and the resources and market the colonies already meant and clearly promised, underwent so startling a quantitative growth as to result in a qualitative shift—the industrial revolution. As Frank E. Manuel has commented, in his *Age of Reason* (1951): "After 1760 . . . the basic character of the English economy was altered; it became evident that England's wealth was no longer founded primarily upon agriculture, but upon the manufacture and exchange of industrial products."

Ten years later contemporaries observed that the bulk of the population of Wales and England was engaged in manufactures and commerce, not in agriculture. Works by Adam Smith and Jeremy Bentham, appearing in 1776, were to provide ideological systems reflecting this transformation; turmoil in Parliament and increasing demands for the renovation of the Parliamentary system and the amendment of the Crown's relationship to that system were to provide the political reflections of this transformation.

Similarly, the whole nature of the colonial system was being questioned, and with it, mercantilism itself. Increasingly, politicians like the Whig leader, Shelburne, were thinking in terms of "trade not dominion." Geographers like Alexander Dalrymple were writing (in 1769) "that if colonies are aiming at independence" the best way "of securing the power and prosperity of the Mother Country must be by extending its commerce to distant nations who have no connexion with those dissatisfied colonies." Explorers like James Cook, in his voyages of 1768-71, 1772-75, 1776-80, were extending British interest to the Pacific coast of America, the South Seas and to Australia and New Zealand. Economists like Adam Smith, Richard Price and Josiah Tucker were attacking mercantilist economics as a barrier to the fullest development of British manufacturing.[1]

II

While the British empire had reached its greatest dimensions, and the English economy was being drastically changed; while mercantilism was fundamentally challenged, and the Parliamentary arrangements were being sharply attacked, in the midst of this and in part as a response to this, the British Crown and Ministry sought to centralize the administration of the colonies and to intensify the efficiency with which they were exploited. Meanwhile, the colonies, especially on the Continent, were responding in their own way to momentous changes.

Those colonies were numerously settled, unlike Canada and

the maritimes; they were not surrounded by the sea and so were not thoroughly dependent upon Great Britain, unlike the West Indies, Newfoundland, and Nova Scotia. In addition, the English continental colonists did not find themselves in the midst of an area the greatest part of whose population was made up of slaves, unlike Jamaica, and so were not especially dependent upon British power for purposes of police.[2] Where all this was true, the response to the developments of the 18th century was bound to be challenging to continued subordination to England. It was true in the thirteen colonies (least so in Georgia, last to be settled).

Moreover, England's victory of 1763 meant for those colonies that a hostile Spain no longer held Florida, and a hostile France was removed from the North and from the West. Hence, thereafter, as almost all contemporaries warned, English presence could be more a cause for resentment than for relief. An exception was Benjamin Franklin who, in 1766, wrote that had France's presence remained on the North American continent, it might have offered a force to which the American colonies might have tended and that therefore "Parliament would not have dared to oppress them." Yet, with all due respect to the enormous wisdom of Franklin, he was here referring only to the opposition to the Stamp Act; in that one particular he may have been correct. But surely, in the long run, the removal of France served to invigorate colonial resistance to British pretensions.

The colonies by this time, also, had among their white population over a third who were not English in origin—among whom were some, especially the Irish and Dutch, with significant anti-English hostilities. And, above all, these colonies had grown so that their numbers were pressing on three millions, and while England had been busy subduing her rivals and conquering the world (with some help from the colonies), those colonies had developed rather considerable economies and viable political entities and clear feelings of solidarity connoting rudimentary nationality.

In the midst of this swift growth and mounting pride, this release from enemies to the south and the north and the west, this mounting separateness, in the midst of a situation wherein even ancient fetters were increasingly resented, came the post-war British policy of centralization, consolidation, and intensified exploitation. Restraint evoked resistance; resistance produced punishment; punishment caused resentment. Resentment was met by forcible repression; forcible repression led to revolution. Moreover, the British effort to centralize the administration had the effect of generalizing the resistance and thus uniting the colonies.

There was no area of American colonial life that went unaffected by the British policies and interests. Merchants, manufacturers, planters, farmers, debtors, professionals, urban workers, fur traders, land speculators—all found particular legislative or administrative acts especially burdensome or restraining. And masses of people, quite independent of their particular role or place in the economy, found cause for concern in British policy as reflected in the areas of religion, civil liberties and political rights.

As a result, up to 1775, there was very near unanimity among the colonists in their view that British policy was ill-advised and hostile to their best interests. The differences that did exist revolved around degree—how ill-advised and how hostile were the measures; did they reflect a *policy* antagonistic to colonial needs; were they subject to redress by this kind of method, or that, by this kind of argumentation, or that?

Let us repeat the broad outlines of British colonial policy: to monopolize the market for British manufactured goods, hence to restrain local manufacturing; to favor British fur-traders, land-speculators, fishermen, lumbermen; to channelize shipping within the orbit of the British dominion and to monopolize the economic benefits from commerce; to dominate as much as might be the merchandising of colonial commodities; to control the credit and the finances of the colonial economy; to inhibit the westward settlement of the colonial population; to centralize the political machinery of the colonies, throttle democratic developments, and diminish home rule, especially in terms of the purse and the judiciary; to increase the role of the military in colonial life; to raise the revenue needed to run the colonies from within the colonies themselves and, even more important, to protect British capital invested within the colonies.

Certain of these aims have been elucidated earlier. Let us turn to some of the other main features of this policy and see how the effort was made to implement them.

III

We turn first to the Southern planter and farmer. They were in economic bondage to the merchants of England. Thomas Jefferson often cursed the thraldom of himself and his fellow-Southerner planters. "These debts," he once wrote, referring to what was owed the English, "had become hereditary from father to son, for many generations, so that the planters were a species of property, annexed to certain mercantile houses in London."

Earlier, William Byrd, one of the wealthiest men of the South, lamented his own similar position. He found that the plantation economy—based upon slave labor, devoted to the raising of a single crop, and generally unscientific in its conduct—ate up the fertility of the soil with great speed. Hence, expansion into new lands was a pressing requirement, and heavy borrowing to pay for this was customary. This was one reason for the indebtedness to the British merchant capitalist; the interest charges were such that Byrd complained, in 1736, that he was "selling off land and Negroes to stay the stomach" of his creditors. Similarly, Washington, another large-scale Virginia planter, wrote, "certain it is, that our whole substance does already in a manner flow to Great Britain."

The Southern planter took all risks; the British merchant took much of the profits. The planter paid import duties in England. He paid the merchant for hauling his commodity; he met insurance costs; the merchant normally not only transported the commodity but sold it for the planter in the British-dominated market and for this service received a commission. All warehouse, inspection and carting fees were met by the planter; all damage costs were met by the same source.

The planter bought the finished products that he needed from the merchant, who deducted the costs and the service charges from the payment for the planter's shipment. And the merchant, in selling the planter's goods, might or might not get as good a deal for him as he could. If the planter's indebtedness was very great, then the merchant knew that he could trade nowhere else and might well allow him less for his tobacco than some others. In any case, the British merchant dominated the marketing of the colonial planter's crop.

Finally, of course, for all debts incurred, very large interest rates were charged. The planters were, indeed, "a species of property" controlled and milked by the English mercantile houses.

As a class, the planters, particularly the more affluent among them, sought to recoup their fortunes, or hedge against bad crops, by intensive land speculation. Indeed, Thomas P. Abernethy, in his *From Frontier to Plantation in Tennessee* (1932), declared that "speculation in lands was the most absorbing American enterprise" in the pre-Revolutionary generation.

The greater productivity of new lands was another major attraction to the planters, particularly in view of the exhausting nature of tobacco. As a result, in the South, as Isaac S. Harrell has written, "the demand for land was insatiable, but the supply east of the line fixed under the Proclamation of 1763 was exhausted by 1774."

Moreover, this Proclamation Line, barring further American westward movement, (temporarily, the British promised) sought to favor British land speculators (as well as fur-traders), and had blasted the hopes of the Ohio Land Company—in which George Washington, Richard Henry Lee, and George Mason were major investors—in favor of the British Vandalia Company. This cutthroat competition continued down to the days of Revolution, so that, for example, Virginia land claims to acreage in present Kentucky and Ohio were threatened, in 1774, by the Walpole Company, in which such figures as Lord Camden and the Earl of Hertford had invested and which had been sponsored by George Grenville, himself, the same man who was Prime Minister from 1763-65.

IV

Turning from the Southern planters and farmers in particular, to the remainder of the colonial population, one finds that British imperial policy was contrary to the best interests of the vast majority amongst them. The essential nature of this antagonism was indicated in two "New Fables" with which Benjamin Franklin, writing anonymously, favored the readers of the London *Public Advertiser* in January, 1770. These, like their Aesopian models, illuminate through indirection, and taken together they tell as much as volumes concerning the developing estrangement between England and her American colonies. The first fable went this way:

> A herd of cows had long afforded plenty of milk, butter and cheese to an avaricious farmer, who grudged them the grass they subsisted on, and at length mowed it to make money of the hay, leaving them to shift for food as they could, and yet still expected to milk them as before; but the cows, offended with the unreasonableness, resolved for the future to suckle one another.

And here is the second fable:

> A Lion's whelp was put on board a Guinea ship bound for America as a present to a friend in that country: It was tame and harmless as a kitten, and therefore not confined, but suffered to walk about the ship at pleasure. A stately, full-grown English mastiff, belonging to the Captain, despising the weakness of the young lion, frequently took its food by force, and often turned it out of its lodging box, when he had a mind to repose there himself. The young lion nevertheless grew daily in size and strength, and the voyage being long, he became at last a more equal match for the mastiff; who continuing his insults, received a stunning blow from the lion's paw that fetched his skin over his ears, and deterred him from any future contest with such growing strength; regretting that he had not rather secured its friendship than provoked its enmity.

The immensity of the colonies, their tremendous resources, the swiftness of their population growth—its "young lion" character —impressed many, especially after the Seven Years' War, with the inevitability of their breaking loose from England. Typical was the comment of a French traveller through America in 1765:

> This country cannot be long subject to Great Britain, nor indeed to any distant power; its extent is so great, the daily increase of its inhabitants so considerable, and having everything within themselves for (more than) their own defence, that no nation whatsoever seems better calculated for independency.

While Professor Wertenbaker believes that economic interest favored continued subjection to Great Britain and while other historians have taken similar, though less extremely stated positions, this was not the view of such contemporaries as John Adams and Thomas Jefferson and Alexander Hamilton.

John Adams held that he who wanted to comprehend the American Revolution had to pay particular attention to the whole mercantilist system, basic to which were the Acts of Trade —without this, "the causes, feelings, and principles of the Revolution" were incomprehensible. In these regulatory acts, asked John Adams, was there "the smallest consideration of the health, the comfort, the happiness, the wealth, the growth, the population, the agriculture, the manufactures, the commerce, the fisheries of the American people?" No, he said: "All these are sacrificed to British wealth, British commerce, British domination, and the British navy, as the great engine and instrument to accomplish all."

Thomas Jefferson's *Summary View of the Rights of British America* (1774) offered this as its central argument:

> We are willing on our part, to sacrifice everything which reason can ask to the restoration of that tranquillity for which all must wish. On their part, let them be ready to establish union on a generous plan. Let them name their terms, but let them be just. Accept of every commercial preference it is in our power to give for such things as we can raise for their use, or they make for ours. But let them not think to exclude us from going to other markets to dispose of those commodities which they cannot use, or to supply those wants which they cannot supply. Still less let it be proposed that our properties within our own territories shall be taxed or regulated by any power on earth but our own.

Alexander Hamilton published his first work also in 1774—
A Full Vindication of the Measures of the Congress—and the
heart of his theme was in this paragraph:

> The colonies contain above three millions of people [sic.].
> Commerce flourishes with the most rapid progress throughout
> them. This commerce Great Britain has hitherto regulated to her
> own advantage. Can we think the annihilation of so exuberant
> a source of wealth, a matter of trifling import? On the con-
> trary, must it not be productive of the most disastrous effects?
> It is evident it must. It is equally evident that the conquest of
> so numerous a people, armed in the animating cause of liberty,
> could not be accomplished without an inconceivable expense
> of blood and treasure.

The fact is that the continental colonies had outgrown the
tight British mercantilist system by the sixth decade of the 18th
century. By that time the British colonies in the West Indies were
unable to supply the mainland with its needs in terms of sugar,
rum and molasses, and they were far from capable of absorbing
anything like all the commodities, both finished and raw, that
the continent needed to export. Indeed, the Empire as a whole
was insufficient to absorb all this production, especially since it
revolved around regulations favoring England.

The excess of imports from England over exports from the
colonies rose throughout the pre-Revolutionary decades, and for
the first 70 years of the 18th century the unfavorable balance of
trade, for the colonies, totalled about 20 million pounds, a
colossal indirect tax and a significant source of the wealth of
the British ruling classes. Indeed, this balance of trade, which
had to be paid in gold and silver, was the main economic problem confronting the Empire, and the American colonists bore
the brunt of the load.

Continually the English creditors pressed their colonial debtors
for payment in specie, but when the colonists sought to meet their
debts with specie through increased trade outside the confines of
the Empire or through manufacturing, they met restrictions and
prohibitions. If they sought to pay off their debts through inflationary devices, they met Royal vetoes and then blanket
Parliamentary bans.

Meanwhile, in England, as we have remarked, an industrial revolution was simultaneously under way and this required an outlet quite beyond the absorbing capacities of the West Indies or even of the plantation-crop producing colonies south of the Mason-Dixon line. Thus, at the close of the 17th century, seven-eighths of England's colonial trade was with the colonies from Maryland on south, including the islands, while all the remaining American colonies, including Newfoundland and Hudson's Bay, accounted for the remaining one-eighth. But by the 1750's one-half, and by the end of the 1760's, two-thirds of English colonial exports went to the areas *north* of Maryland. This decisive shift—the colonies being valued more as markets than as producers of raw materials—clearly carried with it the idea that the colonists were to be forced forever to buy more than they sold, which meant that the colonial merchant, manufacturer and farmer and planter—generally speaking, for there were significant exceptions—had a united interest in getting rid of British domination.

Hence it is that even so moderate a proponent of colonial rights as John Dickinson authored resolutions adopted by a meeting of Philadelphia merchants in April, 1768, which protested English laws prohibiting the making of steel or the erection of steel furnaces, or the building of plating and slitting mills; those restraining hatters and prohibiting the exportation of hats; those banning colonial trade in wool and woolens, and the whole range of enactments that required exports to Europe to go through England.

The exacerbations were aggravated or alleviated by fluctuations in business conditions. In the 1750's, prior to the Seven Years' War, there was a recession in the colonies; with the war, until 1763, an upturn. Recession followed, to the point of rather severe depression from 1764 through 1769, an upturn starting in 1770 lasted for about two years; then from 1772 to the outbreak of actual hostilities in 1775 the colonial economy was in the grip of recession. Of course, depression then, as now, meant unemployment, falling prices for farmers and merchants, special hardships for debtors, increased bankruptcies—all of which reflected itself politically in increased restlessness and sharpened dissatisfaction with the status of subordination to the interests of the British rulers.

The colonists felt the weight of British policy in very concrete and provoking ways. They saw increased centralization of administration; enhanced militarization of colonial life and the stationing of thousands of soldiers in America; increasing British restrictions upon established civil rights. They saw efforts to establish an Episcopate in America; whittle away the political democracy that had been established in certain of the colonies and inhibit its appearance elsewhere; make the judiciary in the colonies quite independent of the colonists or their legislatures; vitiate the powers of the colonial legislatures in additional ways, particularly by curbing their power over the purse; confine the colonists within a narrow strip of land hugging the seacoast; rigidly enforce the commercial and manufacturing restrictions. They saw an ever more prominent role being given to the British navy; trials without jury established in certain colonial cases; swarms of officeholders moving in from England to take over the American civil service; writs of assistance being issued and the sanctity of their homes violated; coveys of informers crowding the ports and being paid for bringing misery to others; new and burdensome systems of taxation concocted and levied; new restraints placed upon their economic development, and monopolies given to favored English companies or individuals. It summed itself up, in the opinion of Thomas Jefferson, expressed in 1774, as "a deliberate and systematical plan of reducing us to slavery."

V

A chronological summary of the highpoints in the legislative and administrative efforts of Great Britain to accomplish the effective subjection of the colonies will give substance to Jefferson's view.

The year marking the peace treaty between France and Great Britain witnessed the serious beginning of this effort. Notable was the promulgation in 1763 of the Line across the crest of the Appalachians beyond which settlement by the colonists was forbidden. In that same year the Royal Navy was assigned to coastal patrol work in order to assist in the enforcement of the Acts of Trade, and an Order in Council provided that naval officers were entitled to half the value of all seizures made in the course of enforcing those laws. Simultaneously, the burden of proof, as to the payment of duties and the country of origin of goods in question, was placed upon the owner. In addition, holders of colonial customs jobs were required to take up their posts in the colonies, rather than treating them, as in the past, as sinecures to be filled by hired men.

The British policy of vigorously enforcing the trading acts was accomplished; thus, while the revenue from American customs in the early 1760's equalled some £2,000 per year, from 1768 to 1774 it averaged over £30,000 a year.

In 1764, additional measures of the Grenville ministry pursued its policy not only of tightening the bonds of mercantilism but of raising a revenue in the colonies which would relieve the Crown of any administrative costs and simultaneously enhance the Royal administration's independence from the provincial legislatures. Thus, an American Revenue Act, generally called the Sugar Act, renewed duties on molasses and refined sugar, placed new duties on wines, silk, indigo, coffee, and non-British textiles and banned the importation of foreign rum and of French wine altogether, and prohibited trade with the French and Dutch West Indies. It was required that the duties be paid in silver. Also in 1764, provision was made for the trial of offenders against the Acts of Trade before Vice-Admiralty courts, which sat without juries. Finally, that same year the Currency Act was passed. This applied to all the colonies that which, in 1751, had been applied only to New England—namely, prohibiting the issuance of legal-tender paper money. This, let it be noted, was passed at the same time as the Sugar Act which demanded the payment of all duties in silver. The reader is reminded, too, that in 1761, writs of assistance—general search warrants—were made applicable to all the colonies; these were, of course, to be used in the enforcement of the stiffer trade policy then inaugurated.

The next year, the Grenville government rounded out its colonial policy. The appointment of the Superintendents of Indian Affairs—key officers in the fur trade and in the handling of Indian diplomacy—hitherto largely in the hands of colonial governors and legislatures, was placed in the permanent control of the Crown. Enumerated articles under the Acts of Trade— those which though destined for European markets, had first to land at London, pay duties and pass inspections—were extended to include lumber, hides and skins, pig and bar iron, pot and pearl-ashes.

Meanwhile, still in 1765, a Quartering Act was passed at the request of General Thomas Gage, commanding British forces in America. By this time, and with the intent of enforcing the laws lately passed, about 6,000 British troops formed a standing army in the colonies. The Quartering Act, effective in March, required colonial civilian authorities to provide barracks and supplies for these troops.

And, just as the Sugar Act of 1764 was the first Parliamentary statute specifically aimed at raising moneys in the colonies for the use of the Crown, so in 1765 was passed the notorious Stamp Act, the first direct tax ever placed upon the colonies by Parliament itself.

This Act provided for quite burdensome taxes, aiming at the realization for the Crown's treasury of £60,000 annually, as compared with some £45,000 hoped for from the Sugar Act. All taxes under the Stamp Act, as all duties under the Sugar Act, were to be paid in silver. The Stamp Act provided for taxes on all deeds, bonds, leases, licenses, articles of apprenticehip, all newspapers, advertisements, pamphlets, hand-bills, almanacs, and calendars, cards and dice.

The Stamp Act was widely held by the colonists to be especially dangerous to freedom of the press and freedom of political agitation. It dealt a heavy blow to lawyers in particular and was onerous to all who conducted businesses of any kind, urban or rural. To enforce the law, heavy fines and forfeitures were provided, and informers were overtly encouraged by handsome rewards. Moreover, prosecution might be conducted before vice-admiralty courts, thus once again undercutting the precious right of trial before a jury of one's peers.

The Stamp Act became effective in November, 1765, but the

enactment of a law is not synonymous with its enforcement. The fact is that this act produced unanimous opposition in the colonies—a story to be amplified in subsequent pages. Its taxes were high and payable in silver only but, as Benjamin Franklin, Pennsylvania's London agent, told Parliament in February, 1766, the colonists did not have enough specie to honor the Act even if they wanted to.

Repeal of the Stamp Act was enacted in March, 1766. On the same day that this act was repealed, however, Parliament passed the Declaratory Act. This made quite clear that the rulers of England, in repealing the Stamp Act were doing so not because they were abandoning the policy which produced it but because they believed it was actually unenforceable and hence would not serve to further that policy.

The full title of the new act tells its purpose: "An Act for the better securing the dependency of His Majesty's Dominions in America upon the Crown and Parliament of Great Britain." Its substantive sentence was a verbatim copy of the Irish Declaratory Act of 1719, and the completeness and ruthlessness of British domination of Ireland added portentousness to this parallel. The 1766 act declared that Parliament "had, hath, and of right ought to have, full power and authority to make laws and statutes of sufficient force and validity to bind the colonies and people of America, subjects of the crown of Great Britain, in all cases whatever."

The news of the Declaratory Act tempered considerably the great rejoicing with which the colonists had greeted the repeal of the Stamp Act. A somber mood began to return with the end of the year 1766, for in November there took effect additional changes to the Trade Acts which, while cutting the taxes in a few cases, had as their major result the addition of every colonial export to the enumerated goods list. That is, thenceforth *all* American products destined for Europe, north of Cape Finisterre (in northwestern Spain, at a latitude equal to southernmost France), first had to clear through British ports.

Colonial resistance to the Quartering and Stamp Acts of 1765 provoked increasing resentment among those members of Parliament who were for tight control over the colonies. The failure of the New York Assembly to make what the King felt were adequate provisions for his troops (the colonial military center was New York City) led to bitter struggles through 1767. At the same time, British efforts to enforce the total enumerated list policy provoked increased illicit trade by colonial merchants, especially with the Dutch.

This is what Lord George Sackville had in mind when he wrote in February, 1767: "These matters must come into Parliament, and will afford matter of triumph to those who foretold the fatal consequences of yielding to riot and ill-grounded clamour." Furthermore, the defeat of the Stamp Act had cut a large hole in the expected revenues of the Crown and this was intensified when, early in 1767, the British land tax was drastically cut, diminishing home revenue by as much as half a million pounds a year.

How better to fill this hole than by taxing the colonists, especially if by so doing one simultaneously taught a needed disciplinary lesson to unruly agitators and their deluded followers?

Several acts with these motives in mind were passed by Parliament in 1767, to take effect October and November of that year. The new Chancellor of the Exchequer, Charles Townshend (who, because of the illness of the Prime Minister, Lord Chatham, was actually the head of the Government) decided to honor the colonists' denunciation of the Stamp Act as *internal taxation*. His system was confined to customs duties and hence was purely external in nature—which, far from making the colonists give up their opposition, made them shift it. If in the past they had denounced as unjust and illegal Parliamentary internal taxes, they now—faced with external taxation—moved to the position of denouncing Parliamentary taxation of the colonies altogether, that is, to the immortal slogan, No Taxation without Representation.

The Townshend Act placed duties, calculated to bring in about £40,000 annually, upon imported glass, lead, painters' colors, paper and tea. It stated that this money was to be used not only for the colonies' defense but also for "the administration of justice and the support of civil government" inside the colonies —that is to say, it threatened the power of the provincial assemblies. Parliament explicitly reaffirmed the power of royal justices to issue writs of assistance throughout America for the purpose of enforcing these duties; it set up additional vice-admiralty courts for prosecutions resulting from such enforcement; and it established an American Board of Commissioners, to sit in Boston, to supervise the Act's enforcement but to be directly responsible only to the Treasury Board in London.

Simultaneously, Parliament issued a Restraining Act suspending the legislative privileges of the New York Assembly until "provision shall have been made [by it] for furnishing the King's Troops with all the necessaries required by [the 1765] law."

The next eighteen months did not witness the production of new Parliamentary measures aimed against the colonies—they were taken up rather with British efforts to enforce those on the books and with American resistance to such enforcement. There was, however, an Address to the King adopted by Parliament in 1769 which had a more perturbing effect upon American public opinion than most current history works indicate. In that year, at the suggestion of Lord Mansfield, the British Chief Justice, both Houses joined in urging the King to bring the leaders of colonial unrest *to England to stand trial for treason,* something the King himself was not to attempt for several years.

VI

When Lord North assumed the Prime Ministership in 1770, a re-examination of the policy towards American was undertaken. This, backed by the intense and organized resistance to the Townshend Acts in the colonies and growing opposition by a powerful segment of the English merchant class to the Acts because of their devastating effects on the American trade—New York City imports totalled £482,000 in 1767-68; they totalled £74,000 in 1768-69—led to sharp changes. All duties provided for in the Townshend Acts were repealed, effective December, 1770, with the single exception—again made largely in order to maintain the principle of Parliamentary supremacy over the colonies—of that on tea. Of course, this repeal in no way affected older duties, as those on tobacco, wine, sugar and molasses, nor did it affect the administrative and enforcement machinery that had been created, particularly since 1763.

It was the enforcement machinery that provoked the next major crisis. Specifically, a British revenue schooner, the *Gaspee*, ran aground near Providence, Rhode Island, while giving chase to a colonial vessel. Several score men, led by John Brown, a Providence merchant, overpowered the British crew, put them ashore and then set fire to the ship. In August the King, by proclamation, offered a reward of £500 for information leading to the apprehension of the lawbreakers, but such was the feeling of the colonial inhabitants that no one turned informer. As a result a Commission of Inquiry—consisting of very distinguished figures, including the Governor of Rhode Island and chief justices of several other colonies—was appointed in September, 1772. With the appointment of this body it was announced that any accused by it were *to be sent to England for trial*. The Commission held public sessions early in 1773, but so great was the hostility of the populace that it turned up no information, named no one, and dissolved in June.

At the same time that the King was acting, in 1772, in accordance with the Parliamentary recommendation of 1769—that colonial law-breakers be sent to England for trial—the Royal Governor of Massachusetts, Thomas Hutchinson, let it be known that henceforth his salary would come not from the provincial assembly but directly from the Crown; three months later, in September, 1772, an identical announcement was made in behalf of the judges of Massachusetts.

The next year, 1773, was, of course, the year of the Tea Act. By this Act the British Parliament sought to dump some of the problems accumulating in one portion of its colonial world upon another portion—just as by the Stamp Act it had sought to make up in revenue what it had lost by cutting the land tax at home. But the dumping of the tea by the Boston patriots—which John Adams described in his diary as having "a dignity, a majesty, a sublimity" and as marking "an epocha in history"—indicated that the Parliament was something less than omnipotent even within the British realm.

British India had been governed and fed upon by the East

India Company ever since the early 1600's. By the 1760's, war with France, wars of suppression against the inhabitants, fearful exploitation of the laboring masses, and the colossal dimensions of graft brought the sub-continent to the verge of utter chaos and devastation. The climax came with one of the most terrible famines in the history of humanity, starting in 1770 and within a year wiping out millions of people, numbering perhaps one-third of India's total population.

The East India Company was near bankruptcy, its stock early in 1773 having fallen almost one hundred percent on the London exchange. The Company sought relief and the Government felt the necessity of intervention not only in order to afford relief but also to take over some of the administration in India, lest that colony be lost. Hence, in 1773 a Regulating Act was passed having the effect of beginning to place the government of India under the direction of Parliament. At the same time, the Government sought to help the Company financially by assisting it in getting rid of some seventeen million pounds of tea that it had in British warehouses.

In April, 1773, Parliament remitted all duties and taxes on teas exported to America, and permitted the Company to sell its tea to its own selected agencies in America—those selected were merchants who had refused to join in the colonial non-importation agreement—rather than, as hitherto required, by public auction in England. The only duty left was the three penny one to be paid in America, as provided in the original Townshend Act. With this it was clear that the agents of the East India Company would be able to undersell all other merchants seeking to sell tea in America, and so would have a virtual monopoly of that important trade.

It is this question of monopoly, and not the question of the petty duty (which, in any case, had been in force ever since 1767) which was at the heart of the excitement in America over the Tea Act. And it was the granting of a monopoly which was behind the Act so far as Parliament was concerned, intent as it was on affording effective financial relief to the politically powerful East India Company. When to this is added the fact that that Company also controlled the trade in chinaware, drugs, calicoes, spices and silks to England—and if this monopoly in the tea trade with America could be established then a similar monopoly by the same company might be established in all the other goods —when this consideration is borne in mind then the struggle against the Tea Act as a struggle against British monopolization of the American trade becomes real. Certainly this is the way it was viewed by the majority of Americans at the time.

The Company consigned its tea to the ports of Charleston, Philadelphia, Boston and New York, but mass opposition made its sale impossible. In New York and Philadelphia the tea was turned back to England; in Charleston it was placed under lock and key, in a warehouse (to be sold three years later for the benefit of the Revolutionary Army); in Boston, the royal officials absolutely refusing to send the tea back to England, the offensive commodity was dumped into the waters of the harbor.

The British government responded with force, and in the course of several months in 1774 passed a series of laws known to the colonists as the Intolerable Acts. It was decreed that until the town of Boston paid damages to the Company and duties to the customs officers, it was to be closed to ordinary trade. The capital of Massachusetts was moved, by Royal order, from Boston to Salem. The members of the upper house of the provincial legislature—that is, the Council—hitherto chosen by the lower House, were now to be appointed by the King and were to hold their seats subject to his pleasure. The Governor—already, as we have seen, made completely subject to the Crown—was empowered to appoint all law enforcement officials, including sheriffs, and juries were now to be selected by the sheriffs, rather than elected by the people of the towns, as hitherto. Provision was made for trials to be held outside of America for any Royal officials arrested for any crimes, including capital crimes, committed while in the exercise of their duties. Henceforth, it was also provided, town meetings—so important in the real governing of Massachusetts and such effective instruments of democratic pressure—were to be held only with the written permission of the Governor, who, also, was to determine their agenda.

At the same time a new Governor was appointed for Massachusetts—General Thomas Gage, commander-in-chief of His

Majesty's forces in America. Moreover, an act was passed, applicable to all the colonies, which provided for the quartering of troops not only in vacant buildings and in taverns (as done by the law of 1765) but also in occupied homes.

In the same fateful year of 1774, Parliament passed the Quebec Act, and this was viewed by the American colonists as part of the whole "intolerable" program of repression and constriction. This Act, it is clear (especially from Professor Chester Martin's *Empire and Commonwealth*) had as a prime consideration the British desire to make of Canada a place from whence to launch coercive and repressive measures against recalcitrant American colonists. Also, by extending the borders of Canada (the size of Quebec, as established in the year 1763, was tripled) as far south as the Ohio river so that it encompassed all of present-day Michigan, Illinois, Indiana, Ohio, Wisconsin, and part of Minnesota, the Quebec Act served as a severe restraining device on the growth of the thirteen colonies and represented a heavy blow against American fur-traders and land-speculators.

Moreover, several of the colonies—Virginia, Massachusetts, Connecticut—had land claims in this area. It is true, as A. L. Burt has pointed out, that a provision of the Act declared, "Nothing herein contained shall in anywise affect the boundaries of any other Colony"—but the Act *did* include within Quebec large masses claimed by other colonies.

The Act, giving Quebec its first constitution, provided an exceedingly autocratic form of government, while taking account of the French nationality of the vast majority of its inhabitants. The Canadian Marxist historian, Stanley B. Ryerson, put the matter thus:

> On the one hand it granted recognition of the national character of the French-Canadian community on the St. Lawrence, and thereby secured its loyalty and allegiance; on the other hand, it sought to make that national survival conditional upon the denial of democracy and the maintenance of the feudal absolutism that had characterized New France.

What the restless colonists in the overwhelmingly Protestant settlements from New England through Georgia saw was an act which denied the vote to most of the inhabitants, which made

Catholicism the established religion, which set up a Council to exercise legislative power, whose members were appointed by the King, which established a judicial system wherein civil cases were to be tried without juries, and which established a taxation system entirely dependent upon Parliament. And the size of the Province to be governed in this manner was tripled so that it now reached down to the Ohio and Mississippi Rivers.

The colonists refused to abide by these Acts. They reflected a condition and a relationship that was becoming more and more intolerable to ever greater numbers of the Americans. The rulers could not rule in the old way; the ruled would not endure the new way. The irresistible met the immovable; the meeting ground was Lexington and Concord.

Chapter III

Class Divisions and Revolution

THE LATE Professor Henry A. Myers, of Cornell University, in his *Are Men Equal?* (1945) wrote of the "many disadvantages" flowing from the colonial status. Perceptively, he observed: "Chief among these to a multitude of ordinary Americans was the way in which the mother country fortified the social prestige of the wealthy and powerful, threatening to establish in the new world the fixed and unalterable hierarchies which had driven many of the colonists out of the old."

The weight of the most recent historical writing on the Revolution, being of the conservative-revisionist type, is directed counter to the view of Professor Myers. It holds that internal class pressures were either completely absent or were of distinctly minor significance in explaining the onset and the character of the American Revolution. The Myers' view, however, has received very substantial support from the pens of Carl Becker, Edward Channing, E. B. Greene, Arthur M. Schlesinger, Charles A. Beard, Allan Nevins and Louis Hacker (early in the careers of the last three), and from Winfred T. Root, Herbert M. Morais, Merrill Jensen and Curtis P. Nettels.

In the preceding volume of this work was demonstrated the class-stratified nature of American colonial society; it was shown that, as a result, class struggles marked the history of that society.

46

It also was shown that in these struggles the weight of British power was applied unfailingly on the side of the status quo.

Furthermore, the contemporary evidence certainly does substantiate the view that large sections of the colonial population saw in the struggle against British domination a continuation of the pro-democratic struggles that had formed so central a part of colonial history as a whole. Certainly, too, the Right-wing of American political life saw an indissoluble connection between the battle against British imperial restraints and that against the limitations of the political, economic and social rights of large segments of the colonial population.

One of the earliest reports to the Treasury in London made by the American Board of Customs Commissioners, newly-appointed to sit in Boston and oversee the enforcement of the Townshend Acts, commented with alarm about the town meetings because of their manifest "political purposes." "At these meetings," said this report of February, 1768, "the lowest Mechanics discuss upon the most important points of government, with the utmost freedom."

Tory publicists ridiculed Patriot meetings and committees with rhymes that did nothing to hide the class-venom:

> *From garrets, cellars, rushing through the street*
> *The new-born statesmen in committee meet.*

Or:

> *Down at night a bricklayer or carpenter lies,*
> *Next sun a Lycurgus, a Solon doth arise.*

Others pledged eternal enmity "to *Cobblers and Tailors*" when they so far forgot their proper place in society as to "take upon their everlasting and immeasurable shoulders the power of directing the loyal and sensible inhabitants" of the New World. One South Carolina minister dared preach a sermon, in 1774, declaring "that mechanics and country clowns had no right to dispute about politics, or what kings, lords, and commons had done." He soon found himself without a congregation and a colonial paper praised his dismissal with the words: "All such divines should be taught that mechanics and country clowns (infamously so-called) are the real and absolute masters of king, lords, commons, and priests."

A little later, in upper New York, one of the great patroon landlords, Henry Van Shaack, who looked to the might of England for the security of his holdings, wrote his brother that all about him "levelling principles are held up." Chaos impended, he was sure—"the country is convulsed"—and he knew not what to do—"God knows what the end will be."

At about the same time, Governor Wright of Georgia wrote his superiors in London of the appearance of local and colony-wide revolutionary organs. He described their make-up in this manner:

> In this province we are more unhappily circumstanced than in any other, for there are very few men of real abilities, Gentlemen, or Men of Property, in their Whig Tribunals. The Parochial Committee are a Parcel of the Lowest People, chiefly carpenters, shoemakers, blacksmiths, etc., with a Jew at their head [Mordecai Sheftall, a merchant]; in the General Committee, and Council of Safety, there are some better sort of Men, and some Merchants and Planters—but many of the Inferior Class, and it is really terrible, my Lord, that such people should be suffered to overturn the Civil Government.

All the well-to-do were troubled by the problem of how far was the Revolution to go, a problem that stemmed out of the class-divided nature of colonial society and the bourgeois hegemony of the Revolution itself. With some, as Joseph Galloway of Pennsylvania, this consideration moved him, at the final choice, to go with the King; as his biographer, E. H. Baldwin, puts it: "He feared the tyranny of mob rule more than the tyranny of Parliament."

Others, as Gouverneur Morris of New York, felt the tyranny of Britain could be overcome and the rule of the "rich, able and well-born" still could be maintained. But they recognized this as a delicate operation, and one which might require considerable concessions. "The sheep," wrote Morris, referring to the masses of people, "simple as they are, cannot be gulled as heretofore. In short, there is no ruling them; and now, to change the metaphor, the heads of the mobility grow dangerous to the gentry, and how to keep them down is the question."

At another time and more in keeping with their obviously increasing powers, Morris called the masses reptiles rather than sheep. "The mob begins to think and reason," he wrote in May, 1774. "Poor reptiles! it is with them a vernal morning; they are struggling to cast off their winter's slough, they bask in the sunshine, and ere noon they will bite." Morris did not mean to be bitten, if he could help it. If the present trend of events continued, he wrote:

> Farewell aristocracy. I see, and I see with fear and trembling that if the disputes with Great Britain continue, we shall be under the worst of all possible dominions; we shall be under the domination of a riotous mob. It is to the interest of all men, therefore, to seek for reunion with the parent state.

He, of the moderate Right, did so seek, but, with the final choice at hand, unlike Galloway of the far Right, decided to cast his lot not with the King but with his country and to attempt, at the same time, to minimize the revolutionary changes.

In several of the colonies, notably in New York and Pennsylvania, there was the closest tie between the colonial rich and the imperial power and the sharpest antagonism between the colonial poor, on the one hand and the local oligarchy and the British dominators on the other. The momentous social relationships, then, implicit in the question of independence from Britain become clear. Curtis P. Nettels, in his valuable study, *George Washington and American Independence* (1951), put this very well:

> British authorities, after 1763, shuddered at the idea of democracy and could be counted on to oppose levelers and reformers in every conceivable way. If the colonies should declare independence, they would be obliged to establish governments on a new basis of authority. Since the resistance was a popular movement, it was inevitable that new governments would rest directly on the people as a whole. To base government on popular sovereignty was to invite its complete democratization. Then farewell to the political power of the aristocracy, which owed its origin to acts of an English monarch and which had long been upheld by anti-democratic arts and practices.

The nature of the colonial movement gave great impetus to the democratic argument. For if the colonial argument rested on the injustice of the arbitrary power of Parliament to rule, did not the same argument apply to those who, wherever they might be, were ruled by others over whom they had no control whatsoever? Thus, British apologists heaped ridicule on the colonial argument that Parliamentary taxation was tyrannical since the Americans had no representation in that body, by declaring that whole cities and boroughs and whole classes of British society also had no direct representation in Parliament or could cast no vote for its Members (note that they were not called Representatives). But these British apologists had logic on their side only assuming a static quality to the political and social order. Nothing, however, is static and certainly not political and social orders. For what happened was that, in the colonies, the masses who had been deprived of the suffrage or had suffered underrepresentation (as those in the West) now demanded fuller political rights on the basis of the very arguments used by provincial assemblies *vis-á-vis* Parliament, and the British masses likewise raised the same demands.

Here are two typical examples of such argument, and that they were published is at least as significant as the fact that they were developed. A Philadelphia mechanic contributed the following letter to the *Pennsylvania Gazette,* September 27, 1770:

> It has been customary for a certain company of leading men to nominate persons, and to settle the ticket, for Assemblymen, Commissioners, Assessors, etc., without ever permitting the affirmative or negative voice of a mechanic to interfere. . . . This we have tamely submitted to so long, that those gentlemen make no scruple to say, that the mechanics (though by far the most numerous, especially in this country), have no right to be consulted; that is, in fact have no right to speak or think for themselves. Have we not an equal right of electing or being elected? . . . I think it absolutely necessary that one or two mechanics be elected to represent so large a body of inhabitants.

And here is a letter in the *Pennsylvania Journal,* April 5, 1776:

> Do not the mechanics and farmers constitute ninety-nine out of a hundred of the people of America? If these by their occupations, are to be excluded from having any share in the choice of their rulers, or forms of government, would it not be best to

acknowledge the jurisdiction of the British Parliament, which is composed entirely of GENTLEMEN?

So far as the masses in the colonies were concerned, "their [democratic] desires," correctly wrote Allan Nevins in his pioneering study, *The American States During and After the Revolution* (1924), "were among the springs which gave the revolutionary movement its irresistible power."

In showing the keen class interest of the masses in the movement for independence—in making the point that this movement was related to their efforts to overcome debts, to increase their political power, to better their economic conditions—we have not sought in any way to demean their patriotic fervor. This is stated because one finds such scholars as James Bert Loewenberg, Samuel J. Brockunier and Ray A. Billington, in their editors' notes to the account of a mass political struggle in pre-Revolutionary Virginia, writing:[1] "The lower classes . . . were no less anxious [than the planters] to raise their voices against England's measures. But their motives were only partially patriotic; they saw an unusual opportunity to improve their own social and economic position."

There is no contradiction between such desires and patriotism. Rather, patriotism surely revolves around the desire and the effort to improve the social and economic position of the masses of people. Surely, too, patriotism is not a sentiment exclusive of, or apart from, the needs and the welfare of the broadest masses of a country's population. Rather it was the real interests of the vast majority of the American people which impelled them to separate from Great Britain; in serving such interests the independence of the American republic was established. This is identical, not conflicting, with patriotism.

Chapter IV

Was the Revolution a Majority Movement?

THE PREDOMINANT view in the existing historical literature holds that the American Revolution was the work of a minority of the American people. Thus, Dora M. Clark, in her *British Opinion and the American Revolution* (1930), wrote: "The statement that a minority fought and won the Revolution has become a commonplace." And she continued to register her agreement. Again, John B. Brebner, in his *The Neutral Yankees of Nova Scotia* (1937) declared: "It is now generally believed that in most of the thirteen rebellious American Colonies the majority of the population was passive, but that the radicals formed the larger of two active minorities." Lynn Montross, in his valuable study of the Continental Congress, *The Reluctant Rebels* (1950), concurred that the Revolution was a minority movement, and even went on to generalize, "it is the rule of history that revolutions in their early stages are imposed upon the bulk of the people by an organized and determined minority."

I

Usually, when dealing with the American Revolution in particular, writers declare that one-third the population was Whig, one-third was Tory, and one-third was indifferent or neutral.

52

This has been repeated so many times—it goes back at least to Sydney George Fisher's *True History of the American Revolution,* published in 1902—that now it is offered as a self-evident truth, needing no documentation. For example, so very careful and learned a scholar as the late Evarts Boutell Green, in his study of *The Revolutionary Generation* (1943) simply asserted: "Roughly speaking, possibly a third of the population was Loyalist, a third definitely Whig, and a third not active on either side."

As the touchiness on the general subject of revolution has grown, one can observe an effort to reduce further the percentage of the American population which actually did support the revolutionary effort. Crane Brinton, for instance, in his *Anatomy of Revolution* (1938) announced that not over ten percent of the population fell into that category.

Popular authors of such different outlooks as W. E. Woodward and Leo Huberman in accepting the dominant view on the minority nature of the Revolution adorn it by informing their readers that those masses who did participate in the movement were gulled into doing so by the propertied and well-educated. Such views are grounded in reports by British officials and leading Tories who naturally saw the Revolution in terms of pawn-like masses being manipulated by their betters. But their vision was suitable to their class; it was not an accurate view of what actually happened.

Among present-day academic writers on this subject only one serious dissident appears, but it is one whose marked competence lends great weight to his opinion, exceptional though that opinion is. John Richard Alden, in *The American Revolution* (1954), declares that the patriot element outnumbered the Tory from 1775 on, and "that a substantial majority supported the patriot cause after the Declaration of Independence."

Professor Alden adds that those who affirm the one-third, one-third, one-third proposition do so on the basis of a misreading of *The Works of John Adams,* citing as they do a letter by him in 1815. Alden refers to a letter which John Adams wrote to James Lloyd in January, 1815, and he quite rightly declares that in that letter Adams is not discussing the attitude of the American people towards their own Revolution, but rather their attitude towards the French Revolution. *In that regard* Adams believed that an equal three-part breakdown of the American population would accurately reflect their feelings.

It is necessary to point out, however, that there is another letter which John Adams wrote, also in 1815, in which he did make reference to the attitude of the American people towards their own Revolution and this does offer some substantiation of the one-third school of interpreters. On December 22, 1815, John Adams wrote a long letter to Dr. Jedediah Morse, in which he stated that after 1765 and until 1775 Great Britain unleashed an intensive propaganda drive in order to win over segments of the colonial population and that, to a considerable degree, it succeeded. Specifically, says Adams: "In the course of these ten years, they formed and organized and drilled and disciplined a party in favor of Great Britain, and they seduced and deluded nearly one third of the people of the colonies."

Here, in a letter written in 1815, one finds that John Adams thought that there was something under, but close to, one-third of the colonial population which, after 1765, favored England. He says nothing at all about indifference and neutrality; rather the *inference* from his letter would appear to be that he felt that (approximately) seventy percent of the American population favored the Revolutionary cause.

My own view would go along with that kind of a reading of this Adams letter, and I agree with Professor Alden that a clear majority of the colonial population favored the revolutionary effort. It is further evident, that a reading of the letters of John Adams (and of other Revolutionary leaders) written contemporaneously with the event shows that they themselves believed they had the support of the vast majority of the population.

For example, John Adams wrote his wife, from Philadelphia, July 3, 1776—referring to the advisability of the Declaration of Independence—that "the whole people, in every colony of the thirteen, have now adopted it as their own act." George Washington, writing January 15, 1781, to John Laurens about the "calamitous distress" affecting the Army and "the inquietudes prevailing among the people," nevertheless stated: "A large majority [of the people] are still firmly attached to the independence of these States, [and] abhor a reunion with Great Britain."

Contemporary American historians of the Revolution took majority support for granted. David Ramsay, for instance, wrote in his *History of the American Revolution* (1789): "As the war was the people's war, and was carried on without funds, the exertions of the army would have been insufficient to effect the revolution, unless the great body of the people had been prepared for it, and also kept in a constant disposition to oppose Great Britain."

This, however, possibly may be rejected as subjective and "self-serving." We would add the following considerations. First, we deny the proposition—assertedly "the rule of history"—expressed by modern writers like Dennis W. Brogan, Crane Brinton, Lynn Montross and others, that revolutions are minority efforts. On the contrary, we think there is nothing more democratic than a revolutionary movement and we believe that the success of such a movement can be explained to a decisive degree on the basis of its representing the desires of the overwhelming majority of the inhabitants of the society being revolutionized. We say this because of the immense power ordinarily held by the vested interests against whom the revolutionary movement is directed, as well as because of the normal inertia afflicting people in terms of acting outside of the ordinary routine—and certainly revolutionary conduct is extraordinary behavior, involving enormous risks and burdens.

Further, specifically with the American Revolution, and still confining ourselves to some general principles, the actual success of that Revolution after several years of sustained effort despite great hardships, enormous handicaps and a very powerful and persistent foe, is the best evidence that the majority of the population desired to carry on the effort to a successful conclusion. For despite all the difficulties England faced, internally and internationally (and we shall consider these in due course), and despite the distances involved, the fact is that she was the greatest naval and military power on earth, that she had never before been bested in war, and that she was brought to defeat by the American Revolutionists. If those Revolutionists had not had the support of the majority of the American people it is very doubtful that England would in fact have been forced to recognize their independence, no matter what the developments in Europe.

II

Let us, however, turn from these rather theoretical propositions and consider some additional contemporary evidence as to the sentiments of the American people in the decade preceding Lexington.

Among the measuring rods of public opinion in 18th century America were elections. It is true that suffrage was restricted as compared to the present—although it was not as restricted, especially in the northern colonies, as some historians have asserted—but it is also true that a considerable segment of the adult male population, perhaps as much as 70 to 75 per cent, could vote in certain areas. In legally conducted elections held in the late 60's and early 70's in such areas as Philadelphia, New York City, Boston, Baltimore, and much of Connecticut and in Georgia, the results invariably showed overwhelming support for the patriot party. Thus, there were 410 voters in a Boston election in 1771 and though these voters faced a choice between Whigs and Tories, there were 410 votes cast for Hancock, 403 for Sam Adams, and 399 for James Otis—*i.e.*, very near unanimity for the whole Whig slate. Again, in the election of 1772, when the Royal Governor, Thomas Hutchinson, extended himself to beat the patriots in a Boston election, out of the 723 votes cast, 699 went to each of two patriot candidates—Thomas Cushing and John Hancock. In Connecticut elections in 1775 and especially early in 1776 the results were about the same—nearly a unanimous electorate behind the rebel candidates.

The last election in Maryland under the Proprietor was held in 1773. Here, also, the triumph of the radical or patriot party was overwhelming, and in certain areas, notably Annapolis and Baltimore, the Court candidates did not even dare to appear in public. In the 1768 elections in Georgia, of 25 members of the lower House, 18 were what the Governor called "violent Sons of Liberty." Thereafter, all the evidence from that area shows, the anti-British feeling continued to grow so that by June, 1775,

Governor Wright told London that there was near unanimity for rebellion and that he could not, therefore, hold on to the Province.

In the New England Town Meetings, where practically no restrictions on the voting rights of adult males existed, throughout the late 1760's and early 1770's the results of elections, on people and policies, always ran practically unanimously in favor of the patriot cause, so that the British government could see no end to this embarrassment except to forbid the holding of the Meetings.

In mass meetings and in demonstrations, both in cities and in rural areas, assemblages totalled thousands and not infrequently every adult of a community actively participated in some protest aimed at British rule or policy. Examples abound—the struggles led by the Sons of Liberty against the Stamp Act, those in favor of freedom of the press and supporting such champions of that battle as the jailed Alexander McDougall, those opposed to the Quartering Act, those protesting the Boston Massacre, supporting the opposition to the Tea Act, denouncing the Intolerable Acts, and the truly remarkable intercolonial solidarity shown for the people of Boston when their port was closed by one of those latter acts.

Thus, when in September, 1774, it was rumored—falsely, it turned out—that General Gage's troops had killed six people in Boston, very nearly every ablebodied man in Massachusetts took a gun and set out for the city. Edward Channing, a historian not given to exaggerations, stated that some 80,000 men actually started out for Boston, each carrying a weapon. This helps explain General Gage's report to Lord Dartmouth in London, October 30, 1774: "A ferment throughout the continent united the whole in one common cause . . . the country people . . . [were] raised to such a pitch of phrenzy as to be ready for any mad attempt they are put upon."

In these efforts, remarkable leaders whose names are household words in the United States, came forth. But their leadership represented, sprang from, and drew strength from the will and courage of the vast majority of the American population. These leaders functioned through indigenously-created organizations—

Sons of Liberty, Committees of Correspondence, Associations, and others (of which more will be said later)—whose creation reflected mass desire and whose continued effective operation depended upon that mass will.

"The temper and wishes of the people supplied everything at that time," wrote John Adams in one of his autobiographical memoranda, having reference to the years leading up to Revolution. Contemporaneously, Adams, in the papers signed "Novanglus" and published in the *Boston Gazette* from December, 1774, to April, 1775, said that the people were "infinitely in favor" of the patriots and that "there are 19 on one side to one on the other."

There are not only overwhelming evidences of mass support of the Revolutionary leadership; there also exists good evidence that that leadership frequently trailed behind the masses and had to be pushed forward by them. Thus, for example, it is a fact that the colonial leaders were opposed to the Stamp Act, but it is also a fact that most of them were surprised at the sweep and the vigor of the mass opposition that the Act aroused. This was true of Franklin in England; and of Richard Henry Lee in Virginia, who, once the Act was passed, actually applied for a position as a collector, an application he hastily withdrew when the extent of the mass opposition became clear to him.

In April, 1776, Joseph Hawley, a Revolutionary leader in Massachusetts, wrote to Sam Adams, then in Philadelphia as a member of the Continental Congress: "The people are now ahead of you [*i.e.,* Congress] and the only way to prevent discord and disunion is to strike while the iron is hot. The people's blood is too hot to admit of delays."

That same spring, John Adams, also a member of the Congress, reported the mounting mass will: "Every post and every day rolls in upon us independence like a torrent."

George Mason wrote truly, in a letter to John Mercer, dated October 2, 1778, when he condemned the efforts of the British government to put forward the lie

> that this great Revolution has been the work of a faction, of a junto of ambitious men against the sense of the people of America. On the contrary, nothing has been done without the

approbation of the people, who have indeed outrun their leaders, so that no capital measure has been adopted until they called loudly for it.

There is a significant exception to this thesis of the mass support of the Revolutionary effort; it is so often reiterated as to need separate, if brief, treatment. This concerns the members of the Regulator Movement in North Carolina from 1768 through 1771. In *The Colonial Era* we touched on this movement and need but reiterate here that it may be characterized as being pro-debtor, pro-democratic, pioneer West versus settled and planter East. There has long persisted the idea that the members of this movement, incensed at its suppression by the East, turned against the Revolution and became Tories and active supporters of the Crown.

This idea persists despite the fact that its falseness has been conclusively demonstrated in the most thorough and careful study yet made of the Regulators, that by Elmer D. Johnson—possibly because that study, for some reason, has never been published. This work, completed in 1942, showed that exactly the opposite of the widely-held view actually was correct. Johnson demonstrated that "many of the men who opposed the Regulators became Tories in the Revolution." And he showed further that "the majority of the Regulators fought on the side of the Whigs during the Revolution." Specifically, Johnson discovered and listed the names of every known Regulator—to a total of 883. Of these, the Revolutionary status—whether Tory or Patriot—of 323 can be positively ascertained, and of these, 289 are known to have actively fought in the Revolutionary army and 34 to have fought as Tories. In the face of this study, one still generally finds the Regulators classified as Tories, with the classifier usually adding that this shows the "unpopular" character of the American Revolution!

The fact is that the American Revolution, in its origins, had the fervent support of the overwhelming majority of the American people. That this was a popular war had profound effects, as we shall show, upon its conduct and its repercussions.

Chapter V

The Development of Revolutionary Institutions

ONE OF THE most interesting features of the Revolutionary epoch is the formation of extra-legal and illegal organizations for purposes of agitation and political activity. These sprang out of protest movements such as those connected with the Land Bank War in Massachusetts of the 1740's and the agrarian outbreaks in New York and the Carolinas twenty years later. In the cities, too, dissident groups of mechanics, artisans, laborers, storekeepers and merchants had come into being by the 1750's and had even formed more or less distinct political parties, certainly by the 1760's.

Thus, in New York City at least as early as 1752 there was a Whig Club whose politics were quite radical and some of whose members were later to be leaders of the Sons of Liberty. Again, at about the same time, in Hartford and in New Haven, men who described themselves as "true sons of righteous Liberty" united politically and had a club organization that met more or less regularly.

Traditionally, these Left-wing groups, both rural and urban, concentrated their opposition upon either a Conservative-controlled provincial legislature and/or Governor. But with the '60's it became more and more clear that the opponent was the British Parliament itself; this became sharper as the Parliament promulgated a policy that was aimed at all the colonies together. In such a situation the normal legislative modes of battle—such as with-holding the Governor's purse, refusing appropriations needed to implement hated regulations (as the Quartering Act), presenting petitions—clearly were inadequate.

If such measures, for example, as the Sugar Act or the Stamp Act or the Quartering Act or the Townshend Acts were to be effectively opposed—and opposed at once—what was required was the interposition of mass action. Thus, resistance to the Quartering Act required not only legislative resolves; it required also that the people, in whose homes the soldiers were to be quartered, oppose the measure. Resistance to the Stamp Act naturally resulted in provincial petitions and declarations con-demnatory of the measure; but meanwhile the stamps were printed and the agents were appointed and questions arose for immediate *decision:* Should the stamps be distributed or not? Should business go on illegally without the payment of the Stamp tax? Should men be suffered to accept the position as Stamp Act agents? The same kinds of questions arose with the Townshend Acts: Should the duties be paid? What should be the attitude towards the British informers whose presence went with the Acts? Should all trade in taxable commodities be boycotted until the taxes were repealed?

Political action could no longer be confined to the provincial legislatures and to the particular seasons when they were in ses-sion; nor could political action be confined only to those who were able to meet whatever requirements might exist for voting or for being elected to office. The questions placed on the agenda for immediate resolution by the post-war British policy demanded mass participation and full-time activity and some kind of disci-pline so that the effect was not dissipated in anarchistic or purely individualistic acts.

I

Organizations expressive of mass opposition to Parliamentary policy made their appearance—their names varied, as Vox Pop-uli, the Sons of Neptune (indicative of the importance of the maritime workers in the resistance to Britain) and, most important, the Sons of Liberty, and the Daughters of Liberty, too. Generally these began as secret organizations, but once they became numerous enough to make legal persecution unwise and unlikely they gave up their secrecy.

As seamen's organizations, like the Sons of Neptune, had their beginnings in the resistance to unpopular British laws and then continued as forerunners of welfare and later trade union groups, something similar happened with the merchants. Thus, at the root of the founding of the New York Chamber of Commerce, in 1768, was the rather seditious banding together of merchants in resistance to the Townshend Acts and their agreeing not to trade in the enumerated articles.

Of all the organizations, the broadest, most numerous and most widespread was the Sons of Liberty,[1] founded as part of the effort to force the repeal of the Stamp Act. In it were merchants, lawyers and urban workers and its policy was often split in accordance with its multi-class character, but the Left-wing—which generally coincided with those of more moderate means—was generally dominant and the organization was a leading force propelling the colonies towards independence.

It is the Sons of Liberty, in existence from New England to South Carolina, that first launched the idea of inter-colonial solidarity in resistance to England, of basic importance in the holding of the Stamp Act Congress. It, too, was the germinating force behind the Committees of Correspondence—which, in turn, became the actual engines of revolution.

The Stamp Act Congress, as an organization, is of extreme interest. It was suggested in June, 1765, in the Massachusetts Assembly by James Otis. The idea was for each of the Provincial legislatures to appoint committees to consult jointly on the problem raised by the Stamp Act. A letter from the Assembly urging such a meeting to be held in New York City in October was sent to the other colonies and in a remarkably short time positive responses were received from most of them. Meanwhile, in Massachusetts and Connecticut, there appeared Committees of Correspondence in various towns whose functions were to inform each other and to unite each other in the face of the crisis.

Twenty-eight delegates met in the New York City Hall on

October 7; they represented nine of the colonies—only Virginia, Georgia, New Hampshire and North Carolina had been unable to send delegates.[2] Six of the colonies were represented by committees of their Assemblies, but since New York, Delaware, and New Jersey had failed to take formal action, these colonies were represented by men informally designated by various popular organizations and mass meetings. All 28 were treated as equals and the "First Congress of the American Colonies in Opposition to the Tyrannical Acts of the British Parliament"—popularly known as the Stamp Act Congress—began its deliberations.

At this Congress was represented all colonial opinion, radical, moderate and conservative; only the view of direct Crown agents was missing. The Congress adopted unanimously, after days of discussion, three documents: A Declaration of Rights, a Petition to the King, and a Memorial to Both Houses of Parliament. Neither the King nor the Parliament would acknowledge the existence of this upstart and extra-legal organization called a Congress, and the Petition and the Memorial were not received.

But all were published and were well received by public opinion, a growing power with which both King and Parliament would have to reckon. The Declaration of Rights was a frank presentation of the colonists' point of view and represented a new instrument of political struggle reflective of the new institution of such struggle—a Congress of popularly designated or chosen delegates.

This Declaration, issued October 19, 1765, started out by acknowledging allegiance to the Crown and "due subordination" to Parliament. It then insisted that the colonists were "entitled to all the inherent rights and liberties of his [the King's] natural born subjects" within Great Britain. Among these rights, said the Declaration, was that of being taxed only by freely-given consent, either in person or through one's representatives; that the colonists were not and, because of geography, could not be, represented in Parliament and that therefore taxes could be imposed upon them only by their own colonial legislatures.

Further, the Declaration insisted that trial by jury was an "inherent and invaluable right" and that those portions of recent laws which denied such a right in particular cases "have a mani-

fest tendency to subvert the . . . liberties of the colonists." The
burdensomeness of the taxes and the Acts of Trade were complained of, and, as to the restrictions of the latter, it was emphasized that they curbed the colonists' capacity to purchase British
manufactured goods.

The Declaration closed by urging the repeal of the Stamp Act,
of those acts setting up Admiralty courts, "and of the other late
Acts for the restriction of American commerce."

The Stamp Act Congress adjourned October 24, 1765. One
week later, 200 leading merchants of New York City made public
the first of the non-importation agreements. These were new
revolutionary instrumentalities and were to be of recurring consequence in American history for half a century.

These merchants unanimously agreed upon two things: "In
all orders they send out to Great Britain for goods or merchandise of any nature, kind, or quality whatsoever, usually imported
from Great Britain, they will direct their correspondents not to
ship them unless the Stamp Act be repealed"; and "no merchant
will vend any goods or merchandise sent upon commission from
Great Britain that shall be shipped from thence after the first day
of January next," unless the Stamp Act be repealed. At the same
time, the leading storekeepers and retailers of the city obliged
themselves, in a public announcement, "not to buy any goods,
wares, or merchandise of any person or persons whatsoever that
shall be shipped from Great Britain after the first day of January
next"—unless the Stamp Act be repealed.

Meanwhile, many mass meetings, delegations and demonstrations, with the inter-colonial Sons of Liberty in the lead, were
held. Through this pressure, sometimes reaching the point of violence, every stamp agent in every colony had resigned his post by
November 1, 1765, the date set for the Stamp Act to take effect.

So effective was the Sons of Liberty in this period—with regular meetings, efficient committees, elected delegates to enforce
decisions, a press to make the decisions quickly known—that
Professor Lawrence H. Gipson, having in mind Connecticut,
wrote in his life of *Jared Ingersoll,* that its government "virtually
passed out of the hands of the legally constituted authorities; in

place of these was substituted a species of control in public affairs essentially revolutionary in character."

II

Other forms of mass pressure and other expressions of popular discontent recurred during these years. There were, for example, clearly political strikes, as that of New York maritime workers against unloading British transports in 1768, and that of Boston construction workers against building fortifications for the British in their city. Sometimes strikes occurred as part of the rising sense of exploitation and malaise, with New York tailors in 1768 and New York building-trades workers in 1769 striking for improved conditions and higher wages.

Minor squabbles and pitched battles between the urban workers and the armed British soldiers (who were encouraged to compete for jobs with the native laborers) recurred, especially in New York City and in Boston throughout the '60's. Several workers were wounded and killed in these outbreaks before their culmination in the Boston Massacre of March 5, 1770, when five workingmen, one of them a Negro, were shot dead by English troops.

It is this background that lends substance to the remark of the Tory minister, Jonathan Boucher, in 1773 that:

> Both employers and the employed, much to their mutual shame and inconvenience, no longer live together with anything like attachment and cordiality on either side; and the laboring classes, instead of regarding the rich as their guardians, patrons, and benefactors, now look on them as so many overgrown collossuses, whom it is no demerit in them to wrong.

It is worth nothing, too, that the college population was overwhelmingly anti-Tory in its sentiments. Professors Hofstadter and Metzger, in their invaluable study of *The Development of Academic Freedom in the United States* (1955), make the point: "In nationalist and colonial revolutions college and university students have always played an aggressive part, and to this the American college students were no exception."

This student feeling manifested itself in the college papers and addresses dealing with such inflammable subjects as the right of resistance to a tyrannical chief magistrate; the natural rights of man; the compact theory of government; the question of female equality; the justice or injustice of Negro slavery; the question of taxation without representation. Measures of repression, which in colleges of the 18th century tended to be more brutally physical than in those of the 20th century, evoked extraordinary and vigorous opposition.

A notable example of both the repressive efforts and the resistance is offered by Yale, in the 1760's. President Thomas Clap, seeking to eliminate the "exuberance" of the student body, instituted in 1765 exceedingly tight discipline, heavy fines for its infraction, increased tuition, poorer meals, and a policy of quick expulsion. He was repaid with visitation from most of the student body who expressed their feelings towards him by breaking the windows in his home and nearly breaking several bones in his body. When President Clap showed no improvement in the 1766 term, practically all the students and most of the tutors withdrew from the college and let it be known that the college could have its Clap and no students, or students and no Clap. In 1766, President Clap resigned and Yale continued.

The broadest and most firmly established of the popular organizations in New England was the inimitable Town Meeting. These were therefore more radical and more completely representative than the provincial assemblies, or than the Stamp Act Congress itself. These town meetings were busily adopting resolutions supporting the boycott proposals and demanding the repeal of all obnoxious laws.

These resolutions generally contained governmental theories and political proposals that were further to the Left than that of the Congress and that, in many instances, were harbingers of the Declaration of Independence.

Thus, the Town Meeting of New London, Connecticut, unanimously adopted resolutions on December 10, 1765 that, among other things, declared:

> Whenever those bounds are exceeded, the people have a right to reassure the exercise of that authority which by nature they had before they delegated it to individuals.

> That every tax imposed upon English subjects without consent is against the natural rights and the bounds prescribed by the English constitution. . . .
>
> That it is the duty of every person in the colonies to oppose by every lawful means the execution of those acts imposed on them, and if they can in no other way be relieved, to reassume their natural rights and the authority the laws of nature and of God have vested them with.

This Town Meeting did not rest with the pronouncement of these highly seditious sentiments; characteristically it proceeded to spell out a program of recommended action. The program had three parts, expressed in directives that were short, sweet and straight to the point:

> 1st. That every officer in this colony duly execute the trust reposed in him, agreeable to the true spirit of the English constitution [as above defined, of course] and the laws of this colony.
>
> 2nd. That every officer neglecting the exercise of his office may justly expect the resentment of the people, and those who proceed may depend on their protection.
>
> 3rd. It is presumed no person will publicly, in the pulpit or otherwise, inculcate the doctrine of passive obedience, or any other doctrine tending to quiet the minds of the people, in a tame submission to any unjust imposition.

The agitation against the Stamp Act plus the consequent appearance of the Sons of Liberty lie at the root of the formation of the earliest political groups and parties of the mechanics and artisans as such. One of the first of these is the Mechanics' Party of Charleston, South Carolina, certainly in existence by 1766 and led by Christopher Gadsden. Gadsden, one of the most prominent of the Sons of Liberty in the South, had been a delegate to the Stamp Act Congress and a spark-plug there in calling for inter-colonial unity, in urging "there ought to be no New England men, no New Yorker, etc., known on the continent, but all of us Americans."

This Charleston Mechanics' Party lasted for several years and from time to time elected its candidates to public office. It played a particularly prominent part in leading the resistance to the Townshend Acts in South Carolina, and in supervising the device of economic boycott which was revived and extended towards the end of 1767 to fight those Acts. By the early 1770's there was no major town in the colonies that did not have its Mechanics' Party or Association or its Committee of Mechanics. These were new instrumentalities representing the Left in the American revolutionary coalition, most scrupulous about non-importation, most diligent in serving various Committees of Correspondence and of Safety and of Inspection. They were pioneers—as the Committee of Mechanics in New York City was the first—to raise the perspective of independence from England.

III

In the resistance to the Townshend Acts the colonists could draw on the experience gained and the forms erected to battle against the Stamp Act. As a result, the non-importation movement was more extensive in this case, and again took its lead from the Left within the colonial protest movement.

The device of Committees of Correspondence was revived. It was employed by the Massachusetts House of Representatives, which in February, 1768, sent a "circular letter," drawn up by Samuel Adams, to each of the other twelve colonies protesting the Townshend Acts, and other recent British acts limiting the power of the House, and reiterating sharp objection to taxation without representation. In April, this "letter" reaching England, the Ministry ordered that the Massachusetts House repudiate it or face dissolution and also ordered that all the other colonial legislatures refuse to receive it. Their orders were disobeyed in every particular: Massachusetts refused to repudiate and the other Houses refused to reject. Thus, the "letter" and the tyrannical response it brought from the British, resulted in more fully uniting the colonies and further estranging them from Great Britain.

A result was the ordering in June, 1768, of the stationing of British troops in Boston and this in turn led directly to still another new revolutionary instrument—the provincial convention. News of the troops order resulted in a Boston Town Meeting resolution, in September, for the calling of a provincial convention. This did assemble, with delegates from almost a hundred Massachusetts towns; it met for five days, protested British policy, and adjourned on September 28, 1768, the day the troops landed in Boston.

Provincial conventions appeared elsewhere (as in Maryland in June, 1769), the non-importation association spread throughout the colonies, and very strong anti-Parliament resolves, written by George Mason and introduced by George Washington, were adopted by the Virginia House of Burgesses (in May, 1769). From 1768 to 1769 colonial imports from England fell by half.

It is noteworthy that even after the British repealed the Townshend Acts—with the fateful exception of the tea tax—the popular leaders and the mass organizations and parties wanted to retain the boycott until all obnoxious legislation was repealed and the principle of no taxation without representation was conceded. It was the merchants who first reneged and insisted that, with the partial repeal of the Townshend Acts, the boycott should end. It did—but now only a spark was needed to start the whole revolutionary apparatus into high gear again.

That spark came with the *Gaspee* incident (previously discussed), and with the British effort to take control of the colonial treasury away from the provincial legislature. The result was the reconstitution of the Association movement in 1772 and the establishment on a mass scale throughout the colonies of Committees of Correspondence.

These committees developed from two main stems, both having a common root—opposition to unfettered British domination. As we have seen, the device appeared as part of the Sons of Liberty agitation of the 1760's, and in this form had no official or legal existence. In addition the provincial legislatures generally had standing committees whose duty it was to carry on a correspondence with colonial agents in England while the legislatures were not in session.

With the fresh resistance engendered by the *Gaspee* affair, legislatures began to direct their standing committees to enlarge their duties by corresponding with similar committees in other colonies. This was formally done in March, 1773, by the Virginia House of Burgesses, which invited other colonies to do the same.

The Massachusetts House of Representatives followed this example in May, for, as it said, it "was fully sensible of the necessity and importance of a union of the several colonies in America . . . in order that the joint wisdom of the whole may be employed in consulting their common safety." By 1774 all the colonial legislatures had such committees.

At the same time, the committees set up by the Sons of Liberty were reconstituted as the need arose, and town meetings throughout New England and local governments elsewhere also set up similar committees. Thus, by 1774 all the communities in the colonies were knit together by one or another form of official and unofficial Committee of Correspondence.[3]

The revolutionary handling of the tea question, the resulting Intolerable Acts and the resistance to those acts, again was done through the revolutionary forms already made familiar—Committees of Correspondence, boycotts, provincial conventions. The culmination came in a revival of the Stamp Act Congress on a grander and more highly organized form, known to history as the First Continental Congress—a culmination forecast by Sam Adams in 1771 and by Franklin in 1773. This Congress consisted of 56 delegates from 12 colonies (all but Georgia) meeting from September 5 through October 26, 1774, in Philadelphia.

Meanwhile, a revolutionary re-organization was going on of the colonial militia. In 11 of the colonies (the exceptions were Rhode Island and Connecticut) the officers of the militia had received their commissions from the Royal or Proprietary governors and so tended to be Tory in politics and highly unpopular with the rank and file. Therefore groups of "minutemen" were organized by the Whig parties, clubs and organizations, whose officers were elected and were leaders of the movement to resist Parliament. As late as the Battle of Bunker Hill (June 17, 1775) it is this loosely associated, illegally established people's militia that formed the heart of the colonial armed resistance.

IV

We turn now to a consideration of the Continental Congress,[4] the greatest of the American-made revolutionary instruments and one whose very name struck terror in the palaces of all Europe.

The direct precipitant of the Continental Congress was the Intolerable Acts, and particularly the Boston Port Act. The latter closed the port of Boston because "divers ill-affected persons" there had "fomented" "commotions and insurrections." Trade was to remain interdicted until the city paid damages to the East India Tea company and until "reasonable satisfaction hath been made to the officers of his Majesty's revenue." It became law March 31, 1774, reached Boston May 10, and was to take effect on June 1, 1774.

Organized resistance began at once. The Boston Town Meeting instructed its Committee of Correspondence to send a letter to the other towns and colonies protesting the Act, pledging Boston's determination not to yield and asking for support. On May 13, such a letter, drafted by Samuel Adams, was on its way throughout the Continent, being carried as fast as riders like the Son of Liberty, Paul Revere, could go. "This attack," said the Boston Committee, "though made immediately upon us, is doubtless designed for every other colony who will not surrender their sacred rights and liberties into the hands of an infamous ministry." It urged that "*all* should be united in opposition to this violation of the liberties of *all*" and recommended that trade with Great Britain be suspended.

In the major cities the immediate response of the populace was favorable to resistance, boycott and unity with the Bostonians, but the wealthier inhabitants directed all their influence towards "moderation." The result, in both Philadelphia and New York City, was the enlargement of committees already in existence and replies to Boston (on May 21 and May 23 respectively) which avoided any agreement to boycott England (Philadelphia's letter even suggested that the dumped tea be paid for) and urged the meeting of delegates from all the colonies at a general congress in order to consult together and achieve a redress of grievances. At the same time, Providence (May 17) and Newport (May 20) town meetings also proposed a general Congress, and the Connecticut legislature, on May 24, resolved in favor of a Congress.

It is interesting to observe that with the United States still in an embryonic state, conservatism tended to rely on some kind of a federated center as a dilutor of local radicalism; it is also worth noting, however, that conservatives, even this early, did not have a monopoly on desiring federation.

The New York and Philadelphia replies did not satisfy the majority of the Bostonians, but they encouraged some of the more timid and conservative merchants of that city. At a Town Meeting of May 30, called to consider the responses, the "moderates" turned out in unusual numbers and sought to capture it, but, as General Gage sadly reported to the British Ministry, they were "outvoted by a great majority of the lower class." Boston stood firm for no compensation, no compromise and a full boycott. To enforce the boycott a "solemn league and covenant" was adopted and a committee appointed to get signatures from every Boston household in support thereof.

Decisive support for a policy of firm resistance came from Virginia, the most populous colony. Its House, on May 24, at the suggestion of Thomas Jefferson, set apart June 1 as a "day of fasting," promised it would oppose "every injury to American rights" and referred to the present situation as threatening America with "the evils of civil war." As a result, Governor Dunmore dissolved the House and announced he would issue no writs for a new election.

On May 27, 25 members of the dissolved House met, denounced the Boston Port Act, recommended that all payments of debts to England cease and that court orders for their payment be disregarded until the colonial grievances were remedied. Further, this rump session of a dissolved House recommended that a Provincial Congress meet in August in Williamsburg for the purpose of electing delegates to a Continental Congress.

Meanwhile, masses of people were making their sentiments known collectively and clearly. Typical of the popular gatherings held throughout the colonies in the spring and summer of '74 was the assemblage of "near one thousand people" on the green of Farmington, Connecticut, on May 19. Here a 45-foot Liberty Pole was erected, the Boston Port Bill was burned and five resolves were adopted by acclamation: "every American" was happy to remain united with England "while our liberties are duly secured, maintained and supported by our rightful sovereign, whose person we greatly revere"; the present Ministry, made up of men with "wicked and corrupt hearts," were seeking "to enslave us forever"; the Boston Port Act "is unjust, illegal and oppressive" and injures "every American"; that "those pimps and parasites" responsible for such a measure had earned "the curses of all succeeding generations"; and, finally, that "we are the sons of freedom" and shall forever despise all efforts to load us with "the chains of slavery."

Leaflets appeared, appealing directly to the man and woman on the street and in the fields, as the one issued the end of May, 1774, in Newport. It was headlined: "Join or Die," invoked memories of the successful battle against the Stamp Act, denounced the Boston Port Bill and said the British closing of the city "ought to be viewed in the same odious light as a direct, hostile invasion of every province on the continent." Relief, too, flowed into Boston from every part of the colonies. Cattle and fish came from New England; wheat from Quebec; rice from the Carolinas. A typical notice of this practical kind of solidarity is this modest little paragraph from the *Pennsylvania Journal* of September 14, 1774:

> The farmers in and about Allen-Town and Freehold, New-Jersey, having opened a subscription for the relief of Boston, in a very short time collected as much grain as loaded a sloop, which sailed from Elizabeth-Town Point last week for Salem.

In September, 1774, General Gage wrote his superiors in England: "This province [Massachusetts] is supported and abetted by others beyond the conception of most people, and foreseen by none." Encouraged by and encouraging this response was the magnificent conduct of the Bostonians themselves. Thus, when Gage sought workers to build barracks for his troops, none in Boston appeared, though unemployment was rife. Sabotage hindered Gage's preparations too—straw for the soldiers' bedding was burned; conveyances hauling building materials for their barracks were destroyed.

By June several of the colonies began selecting delegates to meet at a Continental Congress scheduled to gather in Philadelphia early in September. The Connecticut House, on June 3, empowered its Committee of Correspondence to pick the delegates, which it did on July 13. The Rhode Island General Assembly chose its delegates on June 15; the Massachusetts House did its selecting two days later, behind locked doors (the key was in Sam Adams' pocket) while a messenger from Governor Gage, with orders dissolving the body, tried vainly to enter. By August, the legislature of Pennsylvania had picked a delegation; that from South Carolina was selected by a mass meeting held in Charleston and then approved by the Provincial House.

The New York Assembly was dissolved, hence delegates were chosen from New York City and the counties of Westchester, Dutchess, Albany, Orange, Suffolk and Kings by rather irregular and certainly illegal elections held under the auspices of various *ad hoc* committees, the Sons of Liberty, and other organizations. In New Hampshire, New Jersey, Maryland, Delaware, North Carolina, and Virginia delegations were elected by illegal provincial congresses convened for that purpose.

These provincial meetings, in turn, had had *their* delegates selected by local—usually countywide—conventions so that in the creation of the main inter-colonial revolutionary instrument, the Continental Congress, there was truly grass-roots participation. The Virginia Convention, meeting August 1-6, 1774, was characteristic of the several held that summer. It had two accomplishments: The selection, with instructions, of seven delegates to the general Congress, and the adoption, in the name of the Colony, of an Association, or agreement to boycott British goods and, somewhat later, to ban all exports to Great Britain, and to ban the slave trade, from all points, after November 1, 1774. This Association required the signed pledge of all merchants and traders, with provision for county committees to inquire into its enforcement and to publish, "as inimical to this country," the names of any breaking the Association.

The instructions to the Virginia delegation included a reiteration of the basic American position on the nature of the imperial relation, an affirmation of the need for economic sanctions, and a denunciation of Governor Gage for having branded as treasonous the holding of conventions in Massachusetts. Should the Governor act to enforce his decree of treason, warned Virginia, it would prove him a "despotic viceroy . . . bound by no law" and such action would justify, on the part of the colonies, "resistance and reprisal."

These illegal provincial assemblies were doing more than selecting delegates to a Continental Congress; they were, in fact, taking upon themselves at least the rudiments of political sovereignty. Another example of this development is offered by Maryland. In Baltimore, on May 31, 1774, a town meeting recommended the holding of a province-wide Congress whose members were to come from each county and were to be empowered to take such action as the emergency might require. Less than a month later, 92 elected delegates assembled in Annapolis and thereafter actually wielded colony-wide power. The formal assumption of revolutionary power by this Congress did not come until July 26, 1775, but by then it had in fact held power for 13 months.

V

This was the manner of the selecting and this the setting for the meeting of the 56 delegates from 12 dissatisfied colonies in Philadelphia beginning September 5, 1774 (efforts in Georgia to dispatch delegates were not successful). Only one of these 56 had not been born in America (he was from Wales); more than half (30) were lawyers, 18 planters and merchants (nine each), three political office-holders, three millers, and there was one surveyor and one carpenter.

The radical and conservative divisions of the Congress, which had been present in the projections of its founding, appeared in the earliest arrangements. Thus, as to a place of meeting, Joseph Galloway, a wealthy merchant and land speculator—Speaker of the Pennsylvania Assembly and leader of the Right grouping—urged that the Congress use the State House. But the Left looked with favor at the offer made by the city's carpenters of their meeting hall, and argued that its acceptance would be "highly agreeable to the mechanics and citizens in general." The Left won, and Carpenters' Hall was immortalized.

The Right were of the opinion that the assemblage should

have a name more high-sounding than that of the purely func-
tional term, "The Congress"; but the simplicity seemed a virtue
to the Left, and Congress it remained. The Right strongly urged
that the Congress' presiding officer, selected by the delegates,
have a name in keeping with the traditions of prominence, such
as His Eminence, or His Majesty, or the like. The Left thought
the chosen presiding officer was simply the President and that
that title would go very well with the Congress, and "the President" it was.

Particularly heated, in the organizational phase of the First
Congress' meeting, was the question of who was to serve as its
Secretary. Joseph Galloway supported a conservative Connecticut lawyer, Silas Deane, for the post,[5] while the Left wished to
appoint Charles Thomson, though not a delegate, for he was
the outstanding mass leader of Philadelphia. Thomson it was,
and he held the post until 1789 when the Congress formed by
the new Constitution came into being.

These defeats of the Right on rather technical questions
heralded its defeat on the major substantive questions before the
body. Again this took the form of the consideration of a proposal
from Galloway, for a "union between Great Britain and the
Colonies." Basic to this proposal was the creation of another
Parliament for External Affairs, as it were, to be administered
by a "President General" appointed by the King. This Parliament, to be chosen each three years by the Assemblies of all the
English-American colonies, was to have full control over "all
the general police and affairs of the colonies," civil, commercial,
criminal, where those affairs were inter-colonial or related to
Great Britain and any one or more of the colonies. Regulations
or laws pertinent to the colonies might originate either in this new
Parliament, or in the old one, but the assent of both was required
for the validity of such acts.

The Galloway plan was warmly debated and finally rejected
(by one vote) largely on the grounds of cumbersomeness and the
fact that it left too much power over the colonies in the hands of
the King and Parliament.

While the colonial representatives, in provincial conventions
and the Continental Congress, were debating and organizing,

the British government was, of course, not passive. It set about for the strict enforcement of the Intolerable Acts and sent ships and regiments to reinforce General Gage in Boston.

In response to these activities and particularly the military reinforcements, the people of Massachusetts were meeting on a town and county-wide basis to gather their own strength and determine collectively their own course. Just prior to the meeting of the Continental Congress, significant meetings of this kind were held in Middlesex and Suffolk Counties and their resolutions were sent to the newly-assembled Congress.

The Middlesex document, affirming a determination to resist the Intolerable Acts, reached Philadelphia nine days after it had first met, and created excitement. But two days later, on September 16, Paul Revere rode into Philadelphia with the "Suffolk Resolves" and these made history. They were the work of Joseph Warren and Samuel Adams, men of continental repute, and this attracted attention, but above all, Boston was in Suffolk County and so these resolves brought fresh word directly from the martyred city.

These Resolves took the position of the Left in Congress and were immediately pressed upon Congress for approval by the Massachusetts delegation. They affirmed the County's intent not to obey the Intolerable Acts. They grounded the disobedience to King and Parliament on "the law of nature" and the compact theory holding that the Sovereign degenerates to tyrant where he rules without or in contravention of that law. Finally, in retaliation, the Resolves urged a complete stoppage of all trade with Great Britain. To Joseph Galloway, as he wrote in 1780, this meant in fact the open expression of treasonous intent. But to the majority at the Congress it meant what they desired by way of asserting the rights of the colonies, and the Resolves were approved.

The rejection of the Galloway plan and the approval of the Suffolk Resolves set the stage for the actual declarations and actions of the Congress itself. Though the Congress sat altogether only from September 5 to October 26, it often began work at 6 in the morning and concluded 10 in the evening, and it accomplished a great deal.

It adopted a "loyal address" to the King; an address to the people of Great Britain; another to the people of those English-American continental colonies not represented at the Congress—Quebec, Nova Scotia, Georgia and (East and West) Florida. It agreed to reconvene if American grievances were not remedied by May 10, 1775; adopted a "Declaration of Colonial Rights and Grievances"; and worked out a plan of Association.

The Declaration and the Association were of particular consequence. The former, adopted unanimously October 14, 1774, claimed for the colonists all the rights and privileges of Englishmen, demanded the repeal of the Intolerable Acts, reiterated the doctrine of no taxation without representation and, basing itself on "the immutable laws of nature," insisted that the colonists were "entitled to life, liberty and property" and that they had "never ceded to any sovereign power whatever, a right to dispose of either without their consent." It closed by announcing that they have "for the present only resolved to pursue . . . peaceable measures," the most important of which was "to enter into a non-importation, non-consumption, and non-exportation agreement or association."

VI

The Association of the First Continental Congress, adopted October 20, 1774, belongs among the ten or twelve most consequential public documents in American history. More than any other official declaration, the Association actually launched the Revolution.

"His Majesty's most loyal subjects," at great pains to reiterate their "allegiance to his Majesty," announced themselves sorely aggrieved by "a ruinous system of colony administration" instituted by his ministers, especially since 1763. The document saw this system as "evidently calculated for enslaving these colonies, and with them, the British Empire."

To remove the grievances and to resist enslavement, the Congress announced "a non-importation, non-consumption, and non-exportation agreement" which it pledged to enforce "under the sacred ties of virtue, honour and love of our country." From

December 1, 1774, the delegates agreed that all importations from Great Britain and Ireland should cease and that no goods originating there but exported from elsewhere would be imported. They agreed to import no East India tea, no indigo and no slaves from anywhere and to boycott most of the important products of the British West Indies.

As "an effectual security for the observation of the non-importation" agreement, the delegates agreed to the non-purchase and non-consumption of the commodities listed above. Further, they agreed that if the laws complained of were not repealed, they would export nothing, after September 1, 1775, to Great Britain, Ireland, or the West Indies.

The Association then enumerated, in the most specific manner, how its agreements were to be honored. It provided explicit modes of conduct for merchants, ship-owners and retailers, called for the development of local industry and urged the abandonment of all luxury. It warned against raising prices and declared that anyone charging more for goods than he had in the previous year was himself to be boycotted thereafter.

It provided, also, the machinery for enforcement, thereby setting into operation what became, second only to the Army, the actual instrumentality of revolution. This was done in two paragraphs:

> That a committee be chosen in every county, city, and town by those who are qualified to vote for representatives in the legislature, whose business it shall be attentively to observe the conduct of all persons touching this Association; and when it shall be made to appear to the satisfaction of a majority of any such committee that any person within the limits of their appointment has violated this Association, that such majority do forthwith cause the truth of the case to be published in the gazette; to the end that all such foes to the rights of British America may be publicly known, and universally condemned as the enemies of American liberty; and thenceforth we respectively will break off all dealings with him or her.

> That the committee of correspondence, in the respective colonies, do frequently inspect the entries of their custom houses, and inform each other, from time to time, of the true state thereof, and of every other material circumstance that may occur relative to this Association.

The Association closed by recommending in addition that the provincial conventions and committees "establish such farther regulations as they may think proper, for carrying into execution this Association."

The creation of the Association justifies Burnett's estimate:

> Beginning as a consultative assembly of the several colonies, the medium through which they voiced their common grievances and common desires, the Congress presently became the active head in the promotion of that movement whereby those several dependent political entities were drawn into cooperation for the attainment of their common aims.

VII

The work of the extra-legal Continental Congress was approved by equally extra-legal conventions and provincial congresses. And in every colony—except Georgia which had not been represented in the Congress, and New York which had been only partially represented—local committees of inspection or of safety or of observation (the name varied in different regions) came into being with the sanction of either the provincial assembly, or a rump assembly, or a general committee of correspondence. Even in Georgia and in New York such committees appeared in numerous communities and went ahead on their own with the enforcement of the Association.

These committees were, in fact, bodies of government, for nothing less could enforce the sweeping provisions of the Association. In the act of carrying out that prime obligation, these committees also undertook—especially as British and Tory activity intensified—the protection of the entire colonial struggle.

Governor Dunmore of Virginia, writing to Lord Dartmouth December 24, 1774, described the situation as follows:

> A committee has been chosen in every County, whose business it is to carry the Association of the Congress into execution, which committee assumes the authority to inspect the books, invoices and all other secrets . . . of merchants; to watch the conduct of every inhabitant . . . to interrogate them respecting all matters . . . and to stigmatize . . . such as they find trans-

gressing what they are now hardy enough to call the Laws of Congress. . . . Every County is now arming a Company for the avowed purpose of protecting their Committees, and to be employed against government, if occasion require.

The enforcement of the non-importation, non-exportation and non-consumption provisions of the Association required detailed and continual supervisory and administrative work. Much of this was done in a very rough and ready sort of way and none of it had any legal sanction if one viewed the colonies legally—and narrowly and unrealistically—as still fully subordinate to King and Parliament.

Of this enforcement procedure, Professor Burnett remarked: "What a pity we could not have escaped this sordid chapter of our 'Glorious Revolution'!" Many later historians have evinced the same tender emotions by drawing a veil completely over this "sordidness."

But how to enforce the Association without enforcing it and how to resist the British policy of military subjugation without resisting it are problems which such historians do not explain. The American colonial population, however, was quite in earnest. It posed and met these problems, and the solutions, in life, were often indelicate, sometimes quite arbitrary, and occasionally even brutal.

Rural and urban communities throughout the colonies entrusted the organization of the huge boycott movement to local committees of outstanding patriots. Where resistance was met to the boycott it was countered by individual visits and discussions, mass delegations, publicity—especially in the vitalized newspapers—by refusing to have any dealings with the guilty party, and, on more than one occasion, by some kind of physical punishment, directed against either property or person or both. Happily, death seems to have resulted very rarely from this activity. Even during the Revolution itself, the execution of political opponents by the Revolutionary governments, while it did occur (a few executions of Tories were even carried out after the Revolution) was limited to a small number. More will be said of this in subsequent pages.

Some joined the Association effort not because of agreement, but out of fear or for tactical considerations. Reflecting this kind of reaction was the diary entry of James Allen, scion of a leading Philadelphia merchant: "My inducement principally to join them is that a man is suspected who does not; & I chuse to have a Musket on my shoulders, to be on a par with them; & I believe discreet people mixing with them, may keep them in order."

For those who persisted in opposition to the popular movement, other forms of persuasion or neutralization or domination were employed. Again, some typical examples will be offered. Thus, in Worcester, Massachusetts, late in 1774, all the blacksmiths—there were 43 of them—publicly pledged themselves not to "do or perform any work, or business of any kind, for any person or persons commonly known by the name of tories."

An example of another kind is offered by a paragraph in a Tory-inclined New York City newspaper, *Gaine's Mercury* of February 27, 1775:

> Some time ago, Dr. Clarke, of Reading [Conn.], a gentleman distinguished by a firm attachment to the king and the constitution, was seized in the township of Hartford, and to the indelible disgrace of their police, carried upon a rail about the parish, under which cruelty he several times fainted. When dismissed by his tormentors, and examined by Dr. Tidmarsh, he was found to be injured in a manner unfit for description. The doctor was menaced with the same treatment for his humanity to the sufferer, whose only crime was speaking in terms of respect of the king, and of his government.

Dr. Clarke got off rather easily, for people in his circumstances often were treated to a bath in tar and a sprinkling with feathers, after or before the rail-ride, and there was little to choose between these for discomfort and danger.

Another kind of case involved one identified only as R.H., of Kent County, Delaware. This gentleman achieved some notoriety as the author, early in 1775, of the so-called Kentish Letter. Published in *Humphrey's Ledger*, it maintained that most of the people of Kent County were opposed to the revolutionary proceedings.

The county committee of correspondence contacted Mr. R. H.,

persuaded him of the error of his ways and urged him to manifest his persuasion by sending a letter acknowledging his mistake
to the committee. On May 2, 1775, R. H. submitted such a
letter to the committee. Here he declared that, as published, the
letter was "some altered from the original"; that he had "had
no intention to have it published" and that he was "sincerely
sorry I ever wrote it, as also for its being published." R. H. concluded by hoping, "I shall be excused for this, my first breach
in this way, and I intend it shall be the last."

The president of the Committee of Correspondence, after consulting with some other members of the committee, submitted this
letter to the county committee of inspection. That committee
then informed R. H. that it had taken his letter into consideration "and have unanimously resolved that it is unsatisfactory."
The committee was not particularly interested in the soul-
searching of R. H.; it was interested in his assertion as to the
sentiments of the majority of the people of Kent County. That
assertion had been published and was false and was not re-
tracted in R. H.'s letter. Hence, said the committee's reply to
R. H., "you are requested to attend the committee at their next
meeting on Tuesday, the 9th inst. at French Battell's, Dover, and
render such satisfaction to the committee, as will enable them to
clear the good people of this county from the aspersions of that
letter, and justify them in the eyes of the public."

R. H. did "attend the committee" at the time and place indicated but no minutes of that meeting have survived. But it did
result in another, and quite different, letter to the committee
from R. H., dated May 9, and soon published to the world. This
time R. H. "with sorrow and contrition for my weakness and
folly" "confessed" himself the author of the so-called Kentish
letter, which had been "published without my consent, and not
without some alterations." And this time R. H. announced
himself.

> now convinced that the political sentiments therein contained
> were founded on the grossest error; more especially that malig-
> nant insinuation, that "if the king's standard were now erected,
> nine out of ten would repair to it," could not have been sug-

gested, but from the deepest infatuation. True indeed it is, the people of this county have ever shewn a zealous attachment to his majesty's person and government, and whenever he raised his standard in a just cause, were ready to flock to it: but let the severe account I now render to an injured people, witness to the world, that none are more ready to oppose tyranny or to be first in the cause of liberty, than the inhabitants of Kent county.

R. H. concluded by begging forgiveness and by promising that he would "never again oppose those laudable measures, necessarily adopted by my countrymen, for the preservation of American freedom."

Of this letter it was "resolved unanimously, that the committee do think the above recantation fully satisfactory."

VIII

While the whole spirit and form of colonial government was being transformed at this local, grass-roots level, similar developments were proceeding not only in terms of the Continental Congress, but also in each of the colonies as a unit.

Thus, in Massachusetts, the Governor, General Gage, issued the necessary writs for an election of the House of Representatives in September, 1774. The election was held, but, its results displeasing the Governor and most of the royally-appointed members of the Council rejecting their seats, he refused to meet the new House and ordered it dissolved before it had even assembled.

Most of the elected members, not intimidated by the Governor, assembled as a provincial congress and proceeded to pass resolutions—in fact, laws, since the people acted on them—providing for the armed defense of the colony.

The Governor issued a proclamation, November 10, 1774, saying that

> Whereas, a number of persons unlawfully assembled at Cambridge, in the month of October last, calling themselves a Provincial Congress, did, in the most open and daring terms, assume to themselves the powers and authority of government, independent of, and repugnant to his majesty's government legally and constitutionally established within this province, and tending utterly to subvert the same . . .

all decent and loyal subjects of the King were warned that this was treason and support to it would warrant the penalties of treason.

But it was the proclamation and not the Congress that went unheeded. The Association was supported, local manufacturing was undertaken, generals were appointed, militia companies were organized, military stores gathered, and in village and hamlet, volunteer armed bodies, calling themselves "Minute Men," came into being. Here, for example, is the agreement of the voluntary armed body of the men of Ipswich, Mass., adopted January 24, 1775:

> We whose names are hereunto subscribed do voluntarily enlist ourselves as minutemen, to be ready for military operation upon the shortest notice. And we hereby promise and engage that we will immediately, each of us, provide for and equip himself with an effective fire-arm, bayonet, pouch, knapsack, and round of cartridges ready made.

These men promised to drill at least twice a week, to elect their own officers and to render them obedience. Further, they provided for a fine—"of two shillings lawful money for the use of the company"—to be imposed on any officer or soldier who neglected his duties. And this footnote was appended to their agreement: "It is to be understood that when nine companies of fifty men each are enlisted, that then the said officers of the minute companies proceed to choose their field officers, agreeable to the proposal of the provincial congress."

While revolutionary committees and conventions were providing for the arming of the patriots, they were also undertaking to disarm the Tories. A typical newspaper account of this effort occurs in the *Pennsylvania Packet* of June 5, 1775—the story itself dated May 24:

> It having been thought highly expedient, at this exigency of our public affairs, that every person among us who is known to be an enemy to the rights and privileges of this country, and has been aiding and abetting the cursed plans of a tyrannical ruler, and an abandoned ministry, should be disarmed and rendered as incapable as possible of doing further material mischief, the Tories in Worcester, Mass., were notified to appear with their

arms and ammunitions on Monday last. They accordingly appeared, and after surrendering their arms to the committee of correspondence, and being strictly ordered not to leave town, or to meet together without a permit, were dismissed.

In Maryland, the Governor refused to call for elections or to validate the meeting of any assemblies; hence a revolutionary provincial congress made up of illegally elected delegates proceeded to govern, in fact, the colony from 1775 on. In New York a Provincial Congress took over the government and in New York City a Committee of 100 ruled. From that city the Royal Governor fled to Long Island; the British officer in charge of the troops there—the Royal Irish regiment, heavily hit by desertions of his men to the patriots—moved them aboard naval vessels in the harbor.

In Pennsylvania, from January, 1775 to June, 1776—when a completely new government was established—there was in fact a dual government. A Provincial Convention with a standing committee of correspondence existed simultaneously with the old Assembly, and the extra-legal body served as a force moving the Assembly to democratize itself and to align itself with the patriots. But this going too slowly resulted in the elimination of the old Pennsylvania government and its replacement by another created under the very advanced 1776 Constitution.

In 1774, as we have seen, a Provincial Congress had already come into all but legal power in Virginia. In December of that year Lord Dunmore, the Royal Governor, announced the King's authority at an end and took himself to warships off Norfolk. Early in 1775 elections were held throughout Virginia for a second provincial convention; it assembled in March, 1775, becoming in fact the Virginia revolutionary government. It was this convention which was stirred by Patrick Henry's "as for me, give me liberty or give me death!" and it is this convention that undertook to prepare Virginia for armed resistance, while reiterating its desire for reconciliation with England.

By 1775 provincial congresses were being held even in remote and sparsely-settled Georgia. Indeed, three were held in that year and delegates to another met in January, 1776. These congresses became, in fact, the government of Georgia, and in the periods when they were not in session, a Council of Safety acted for it, on a province-wide scale, and so-called Parochial Committees, on a local scale. Through these institutions legislative, executive and judicial duties were carried out, militia organized, Indian relations conducted, money raised and issued, revolutionary propaganda broadcast, and the Tories checked.

Thus was government conducted in Georgia, until April, 1776, when a more formal, but still provisional, apparatus was established, to give way, in 1777, to republican government as provided for in the state constitution then adopted.

These provincial conventions not only heard magnificent speeches, such as that by Patrick Henry, and did not deal only with such grand questions as electing and instructing delegates to the Continental Congress. They also—as functioning governmental organs—listened to the pleas of the ordinary inhabitant and dealt with questions of individual livelihood. Again, a single example may illustrate the point.

The journal of the Maryland Provincial Convention for July 28, 1775, contains this entry:

> The petition of Patrick Graham of Charles County, Taylor [tailor], praying "remission of the sentence of the committee of Charles County, and that he might be restored to the privileges of a Citizen" being read and considered, It is thereupon ordered that the said Patrick Graham be allowed to exercise his former trade of a Taylor, and that he also be permitted to buy provisions and other necessaries for the use of his family; And that the said Patrick Graham be allowed and permitted to collect, and receive all just debts due to him; and that all persons be permitted to employ the said Patrick Graham as a Taylor, and to sell him provisions and other necessaries for his Family. But that the said Patrick Graham be not allowed to carry on any Traffic or merchandize, until it be otherwise resolved by this or some future Convention.

Thus had the revolutionary committees and conventions and parties and societies developed into local and provincial and continental revolutionary organizations and finally, organs of government.

So it was that when, in the evening of April 18, 1775, General

Gage sent out (secretly, he falsely believed) a strong contingent of troops to confiscate military stores at Concord and to take prisoner two political refugees, John Hancock and Samuel Adams —whose hiding place in the home of a minister had been revealed to Gage by Dr. Benjamin Church, one of the half-dozen top patriots of Massachusetts, and a British agent—those troops met effective resistance.

IX

Thus, it was, too, that by the time the battles at Lexington and Concord had been fought, delegates to the Second Continental Congress, due to assemble on May 10, were already on their way to Philadelphia. The delegates this time were selected not by provincial assemblies but rather by the revolutionary congresses or conventions already mentioned. This time delegates were present from all thirteen colonies, with New York officially represented by a strong delegation including George Clinton, Robert R. Livingston and Philip Schuyler. Georgia was represented by but one delegate, Lyman Hall of St. John's parish, but, it will be remembered, that colony had had no delegate at the 1774 Congress. Other delegations were strengthened as compared with the earlier Congress. Thus, from Virginia came Thomas Jefferson, from Massachusetts, John Hancock, and now among Pennsylvania's delegates was Benjamin Franklin.

The instructions of the delegates were simpler and more direct in 1775 than they had been the previous fall. Generally, they were empowered, in the words of Massachusetts, to "order such farther measures as shall to them appear to be best calculated for the recovery and establishment of American rights and liberties, and for restoring harmony between Great Britain and the colonies."

This Congress remained the Congress of the United Colonies and then of the United States until the First Congress held under the provisions of the present Constitution assembled in New York City in 1789.

In its first few weeks in the spring of 1775 its transformation from a revolutionary consultative body into a revolutionary central government, which had already begun in the first Continental Congress, was pushed further ahead.

For now hostilities had begun and all the colonies already had rallied to the support of Massachusetts when news of Lexington and Concord spread, as it did with extraordinary speed through the agency of the hundreds of committees that knit the continent together. Now insistent questions pressed for immediate answers. Should the British be resisted by arms? If so, how should the armies be organized, equipped, paid, officered? How formulate the purposes of the resistance? How raise the funds to sustain it?

To answer these questions meant to create a continental army, to make the most experienced and most distinguished colonial military man—George Washington of Virginia—the commanding general, to issue a currency, to reject Lord North's terms for "conciliation," to begin the regulation of trade, to consider—and postpone—Franklin's proposed "Articles of Confederation."

Everything flowed out of the British decision that the agitation in America was actually treason and was the result of the mischievous activity of a handful of fanatics and bandits who had terrorized or browbeaten or gulled a sufficient number of the "mob" into supporting them. For this the British Empire had a standard operating procedure: Forcible repression; stern "justice"; continued subordination.

In reply, the subversive leaders of the misguided rabble, in Congress assembled, issued on July 6, 1775, a "Declaration of the Causes and Necessity of Taking up Arms" drafted by the chief representatives of the Left and the Right in that Congress, Thomas Jefferson and John Dickinson.

Here, yet again, were the grievances of the colonists and the oppressions of the Crown enumerated. These, said the Declaration, culminated in the aggressions at Lexington and Concord, the burning of Charlestown in Massachusetts, the seizure of vessels and the issuance (on June 12, 1775) of a proclamation of martial law by General Gage which declared the patriots "either by name or description, to be rebels and traitors, to super-

sede the course of the common law" and to promise them the
hangman's noose.

Hence:

> We are reduced to the alternative of choosing an uncondi-
> tional submission to the tyranny of irritated ministers, or re-
> sistance by force. The latter is our choice. . . .
>
> Our cause is just. Our union is perfect. Our internal resources
> are great, and, if necessary, foreign assistance is undoubtedly
> attainable. . . .
>
> We mean not to dissolve that union [in the Empire] which
> has so long and so happily subsisted between us, and which we
> sincerely wish to see restored. Necessity has not yet driven us
> into that desperate measure. . . .
>
> In our own native land, in defence of the freedom that is our
> birth-right . . . for the protection of our property, acquired
> solely by the honest industry of our fore-fathers and ourselves,
> against violence actually offered, we have taken up arms. We
> shall lay them down when hostilities shall cease on the part of
> the aggressors, and all danger of their being renewed shall be
> removed, and not before.

This, plus a final petition to the King, dated July 8, 1775,
pleading for redress and reiterating loyalty, were replied to on
August 23, with the Crown's issuance of a Proclamation for
Suppressing Rebellions and Sedition. Subjects in America, "mis-
led by dangerous and ill designing men" had "proceeded to open
and avowed rebellion," said the Royal Proclamation. All His
Majesty's officers were ordered to "suppress such rebellion, and
to bring the traitors to justice," while all loyal subjects were required "to disclose and make known all traitorous conspiracies
. . . in order to bring to condign punishment" the outlaws distressing His Highness.

The forging of revolutionary institutions was complete. The
traitors or the patriots—they were one and the same, depending
on the viewpoint—now could sink or swim in their stormy voyage
on a turbulent sea. They had "resolved to die freemen rather
than to live slaves" and the might of the hitherto undefeated
British Empire was pledged to test that resolve.

Chapter **VI**

The Movement Toward Independence

INDEPENDENCE WAS NOT declared until more than 15 months had passed after Lexington and Concord. The Revolutionists were united in seeking the redress of grievances; they differed amongst themselves as to how best to assure such redress. Far from explicitly calling for separation from England, they reiterated their devotion to Great Britain and its—and their—monarch. They were seeking indeed, the rights of Englishmen and surely, on its face, this did not mean independence from England.

Yet, independence was the logical result of the historical development of colonial America and its seeds were sown with the colonies' founding. This logic is not a matter of hindsight but was perceived and discussed by contemporaries, from the colonies, from England, and from the Continent.

The actual shift, however, within 15 months, from a movement swearing loyalty and allegiance to the British Crown to one pledged to sever such allegiance, itself needs tracing. It sprang from four intertwined forces: The desire of the Left in the revolutionary coalition; the obduracy of the British rulers; the cumulative effects of the actual fighting and the requirements pressing for immediate solutions which the warfare imposed; and the international situation.

I

As to the first: It is a fact that there was a widespread public opinion—how widespread the evidence does not make clear—in the colonies during the '60's and '70's, favoring independence from England. The idea was treasonous and so not openly proclaimed, yet the contemporaneous atmosphere clearly shows the presence of the idea, its growth, and the fears it evoked from the Crown and its servants. The problem of measuring opinion is complicated by reaction's tendency to smear dissent as treason. Thus, the King's officials were quick—no doubt, too quick—to terminate debates as to the merits or demerits of this or that feature of the imperial system with the accusation that their opponents sought to overturn and not to improve the system.

Still, the question of independence certainly was being discussed in pre-Revolutionary America. It was with the un-propertied or meagerly propertied segments of the colonial population that the idea had most favor; from the wealthy it evoked most horror. As the actual fighting commenced, it was the Left which increasingly distinguished itself from the Center and Right by the vehemence with which it announced colonial grievances, and the vigor with which it pressed for colonial action. It is the Left which had least illusions concerning the beneficence of the King and which first saw that independence was the only alternative to complete subjugation.

The policy of the American Left was fostered and vindicated by the program of the British Right, controlling the British state. This program, especially after the *Gaspee* incident, was increasingly one of total suppression, aiming at something approximating a complete elimination of colonial self-government and its replacement by a consolidated, militarized, anti-democratic satrapy. As this became ever more clear, the practicality of "moderation," of a "safe and sane," conservative effort to return to the pre-1763 days, became increasingly dubious.

The whole momentum of resistance, and particularly its organization and implementation, by and following the First Continental Congress, led towards separation. And on the day the Second Congress assembled, Lexington and Concord were three weeks old, and Ethan Allen took Ticonderoga—followed two days later, May 12, with Seth Warner's capture of Crown Point.

By this time, the delegates to the Second Congress, though in no case authorized to declare for independence, were given instructions of greater elasticity than was true in 1774. But whatever their instructions, they gathered in the midst of a revolutionary situation. They acted accordingly and the result, given the intransigence of the Crown—had to be independence.

Thus, the first resolution of the new Congress, June 3, 1775, reads:

> That a committee be appointed for the purpose of borrowing six thousand pounds for the use of America; for the repayment of which with interest, the Congress will make full and ample provision, and that the said committee apply the said sum of money to the purchase of gunpowder for the use of the Continental Army.

Here, in a single paragraph, is the Congress establishing the rudiments of a Treasury Department (for a non-existent government) by incurring a debt and promising to pay off principal and interest; and of a War Department by providing for supplies to reach a Continental Army, itself in the process of creation.

Further, when the Second Congress met it was faced with a letter from Massachusetts pointing out that the King had revoked its charter and that, in fact, government had ceased to exist. What, asked the letter, did the Congress advise? So, on June 9, the Congress resolved that the Massachusetts provincial convention hold its own popular election of an Assembly, and that this Assembly choose a Council and that this Assembly and Council function as the Massachusetts government—until His Majesty saw the light! Here was the Second Congress assuming supra-colonial governmental powers in fact, while in law it had no existence and even in its own eyes had but a purely advisory capacity.

Having by resolution on June 3 referred to a Continental Army, the Congress, on June 14, brought it into being by ordering Virginia, Maryland and Pennsylvania to raise ten companies of riflemen each and ordering them to march north and join the thousands of New Englanders besieging the King's troops in

Boston. The next day the office of General of this army was created (again a fiscal problem; his salary was to be $6,000 annually—luckily, however, the wealthy Virginian refused payment for his services). Colonel Washington was chosen "to command all the continental forces . . . for the defence of American liberty." Before the troops or the commander could get to Massachusetts, the first major engagement—on Breed's Hill though called the Battle of Bunker Hill—was fought June 19, 1775.

II

The necessities of conducting a war produced other beginnings of government even before the Declaration of Independence; these beginnings are of consequence in tracing the roots of that Declaration, as they are in understanding the form of the actual government subsequently established.

Thus, in November, 1775, the Congress established a Committee of (Secret) Correspondence which with a very modest budget had the task of winning friends abroad for the revolutionary effort. This Committee of international sedition became, in 1777, the Committee for Foreign Affairs and is the actual ancestor of the present Department of State. Again, even earlier —in September, 1775—the Congress established a Committee for Purchases, which in 1777 became the Committee of Commerce, ancestor of the present Department of Commerce. Similarly, appropriate committees to handle maritime and financial matters had been appointed in 1775 to form the institutional origins of the Treasury and Navy Departments.

Meanwhile, the King and his Ministers were scorning American petitions and, by refusing to believe their protestations of loyalty, were destroying its last remnants. As early as September, 1774, the King wrote his Prime Minister, "the die is now cast, the colonies must either submit or triumph." A few weeks later he insisted that New England was "in a state of rebellion" and added: "Blows must decide whether they are to be subject to this country or independent." Those were the alternatives as the King saw them; "either master them or totally leave them," as he wrote in a letter to General Gage, in October, 1774. This British policy played a major part in determining the colonists' choice.

In November, 1774, a majority in Parliament let the King know that it approved his view of the matter, and in an Address to the Throne, urged him to take all necessary steps "to enforce [in the colonies] due obedience to the laws and authority of the supreme legislature." By the spring of 1775, Parliament enacted additional legislation further curbing colonial trade, and forbidding New Englanders from fishing on the Newfoundland Banks —devastating blows to thousands of families.

By August, 1775, the King officially declared the American colonies to be in a state of rebellion and promised to hang their leaders; in December, 1775, Parliament announced the colonies to be outside British protection, forbade all trade with them and authorized the seizure and confiscation of American ships at sea.

Obviously all this provoked colonial replies in kind. In March, 1776, Congress provided for the outfitting of privateers and the issuance of letters of marque; the next month Congress repealed all British Acts of Trade so far as they affected America in any way—two acts of economic independence presaging the political pronouncement soon to follow.

By the summer of 1775, Franklin had drawn up a plan for "Articles of Confederation and Perpetual Union." Jefferson favored it, but stated that approval of independence—implicit in the plan—was not yet sufficiently widespread and so urged that it be put aside, temporarily, in order not to endanger the unity of the revolutionary coalition.

The actual fighting enhanced the trend toward independence, for it helped develop the American nationality on the anvil of common suffering in a civil war. Moreover, the actual creation of a Continental Army tended to undercut sectional and local provincialisms and to replace it by a national feeling. The fighting, too, exacerbated the bitterness toward Great Britain as the brutalities of war, and especially civil war, came home to the population. Thus, such events as the British burning of Falmouth (now Portland, Maine) in October, 1775, and of Norfolk in January, 1776, and the hiring of German mercenaries for battle against the colonists, made the idea of separation appear agreeable and necessary to increasing thousands.

Responding to, and feeding, the development of a desire for independence was the appearance of a literature urging this step. Historic in this regard was the publication, in January, 1776, of Thomas Paine's magnificent pamphlet, *Common Sense*. Its appearance was itself indicative of the shift in mass opinion towards independence and its phenomenal sale is conclusive evidence of that shift. Within three months, in a land of less than 3,000,000, and with a high percentage of illiteracy (quite apart from the 600,000 slaves), over 120,000 copies of *Common Sense* were sold. It is likely that by the spring of 1776 there was no American white adult who had not read or heard read the stirring and unequivocal words of Paine.

It will be remembered that the rebellious colonists had originally attacked Parliament's right to lay internal taxes upon them; they had then moved to attacking its right to tax them at all and finally to questioning Parliament's right to legislate for the colonists in any particular. There was left only the tie to the monarch and the still powerful idea of his divine right to rule.

It is against the person and the symbol of the King, therefore, that Paine turned his most bitter attack. See the founder of the modern line of English kings, William the Conqueror, he wrote, and what does one actually behold?

> A French bastard landing with an armed banditti, and establishing himself King of England against the consent of the natives, is, in plain terms, a very paltry, rascally original—it certainly hath no divinity in it.

Paine then developed the advisability, practicality and necessity of a clean break from Great Britain. He concluded by unfolding the dream—so important to American history—of a new country being founded in the new world, fresh, untouched by the decadence and the miseries of Europe and opening up the vista of a veritable Elysium on earth:

> O ye that love mankind! Ye that dare oppose not only tyranny, but the tyrant, stand forth! Every spot of the old world

is overrun with oppression. Freedom hath been hunted round the globe. Asia and Africa have long expelled her. Europe regards her like a stranger, and England hath given her warning to depart. O! receive the fugitive, and prepare in time an asylum for mankind.

The actual shift in the Second Continental Congress to independence, made despite the fears of many of the wealthy that with it would come anarchy, was the result of pressure brought upon its delegates from the individual rebelling colonies. This was done either by instructions coming from the colonial revolutionary conventions or, in Pennsylvania and New Jersey, as the result of overturning the local governments.

Typical of the former action was that taken by the Virginia convention, on May 15, 1776, with the unanimous concurrence of its 112 delegates. These delegates declared that:

> Forasmuch as all the endeavours of the united colonies by the most decent representations and petitions to the King and Parliament of Great Britain to restore peace and security to America under the British government and a reunion with that people upon just and liberal terms, instead of a redress of grievances, have produced from an imperious and vindictive administration increased insult, oppression, and a vigorous attempt to effect our total destruction.

therefore it was unanimously resolved:

> That the delegates appointed to represent this colony in general congress be instructed to propose to that respectable body to declare the united colonies free and independent states . . . and that they give the assent of this colony to such declaration, and to whatever measures may be thought proper and necessary by the Congress for forming foreign alliances, and a confederation of the colonies, at such time, and in the manner, as to them shall seem best.

In Pennsylvania and New Jersey the colonies declared for independence as part of the actual change in local government and the coming into power of the Left. In New Jersey, in June, 1776, the Assembly finally ousted the Royal Governor, William Franklin (Benjamin's son), and then sent a new delegation to the Continental Congress with instructions to vote for independence.

In Pennsylvania, the Left wing, as part of its long battle to democratize the local government by granting the West adequate representation and giving the suffrage to the artisans, mechanics and unpropertied freemen of Philadelphia, succeeded early in 1776 in voiding the old Charter and establishing a more democratic governmental form. The result of this Left victory in Pennsylvania was that its delegates in the Continental Congress, who in November, 1775, had been specifically instructed to "dissent from and utterly reject any propositions . . . that may cause or lead to a separation" from England, were early in 1776 instructed to work for independence.

III

Reinforcing all the factors making for independence was the significant question of foreign support. England, in a war ending in 1763, had established its hegemony over Europe and had emerged as the dominant colonial power. This result of more than a century's warfare and maneuvering in the jungles of diplomacy had produced, of course, many vengeful enemies of the British state, among whom the foremost were France, Spain, and Holland.

The rebellion of the thirteen colonies offered magnificent opportunities for England's enemies; but these enemies—and especially France—would not be interested in helping rebels who sought not to sever their British connections but only to improve the imperial relationship. Hence, the position of the European powers, while ideologically closest to the American Right, politically furthered the Left. Hence, too, the American Left had a trump card in the fact that it was only their program—independence—which carried with it the certainty of foreign assistance, itself a pre-requisite to victory in the war with England.

On both sides there was great hesitation, some of the "democratical Republicans" wondering if they could accept help from a Bourbon tyrant; the tyrant worried lest his assistance let loose a force more deadly than British power. In each case, however, the necessities and the logic of the time and the movement pushed for a Franco-American alliance, and these forces, in turn, supported the drive towards American independence.

Thus it came about that, on June 7, 1776, Richard Henry Lee of Virginia offered a resolution in the Continental Congress that the colonies "are, and of right ought to be, free and independent States." Four days later a committee of five (Thomas Jefferson of Virginia, John Adams of Massachusetts, Benjamin Franklin of Pennsylvania, Robert Livingston of New York, and Roger Sherman of Connecticut) was appointed by the Congress to draft a Declaration of Independence. On July 2, the Congress voted for independence (12 for, none against, New York abstaining).

On that same day, the drafting committee returned with its Declaration, largely the work of young Jefferson, and for two days debated it. With some changes, each of which sorely troubled the sensitive author, the Declaration was approved by the Congress on July 4 (again New York abstained) and signed by John Hancock, president, and Charles Thomson, secretary.

The Declaration was publicly proclaimed on July 8, endorsed by the New York provincial congress the next day and engrossed on parchment, for signing, on July 19. By early August most of the 55 "signers" had affixed their names, though not all did so until November, 1776. The names of the signers, however, (with the exception of Hancock and Thomson) were not made public until January 18, 1777—for it was no light thing the 55 did, since the King of Great Britain ardently desired to make each forfeit his life for his signature.[1]

Chapter VII

The Declaration of Independence

IN JUNE 1776 a 33-year-old Virginian, working in a room rented from a bricklayer, wrote—in the words of Moses Coit Taylor—a "passionate chant of human freedom" whose influence has been as momentous as that of any other single human creation.

He made no claim to originality; on the contrary he strove to present the "common sense of the matter"; to convey, as he said, the "American mind"; to put into a brief declaration the essential facts driving the colonists to separation, and the theory of government which, to those colonists, was so universally held as to appear "self-evident."

The members of the Congress for whom it was drafted recognized it as a masterly work; their changes were few and purely verbal, with two exceptions. Jefferson's original version contained a long denunciation of the people of Great Britain because they had not opposed their own government with sufficient vigor and had not pressed forward their support of the colonists' battle so as to force an alteration in policy. This change would appear to have been wise, for pro-American sympathy in Great Britain had been and was to continue to be very widespread (the facts will be brought forward in subsequent pages). As it is, the Declaration does contain a rather bitter, and excessive, condemnation of "our British brethren" who, it incorrectly declares, "have been deaf to the voice of justice and of consanguinity."

The second major Congressional revision of Jefferson's document[1] resulted in the excision of a long passage—more than 150 words—dealing with slavery and the slave trade. This passage appeared as the final, climactic, item in the listing of abominations brought upon the colonies by George III, justifying resistance to his forcible efforts to retain them. In this passage Jefferson excoriated the King for vetoing repeated colonial efforts to curtail or to ban the African slave trade and denounced not only the trade but the system of production which it served. Due to the heated objections of the delegates from slaveholding Georgia and South Carolina and the somewhat less intense objections from several delegates from Massachustts, Connecticut, and Rhode Island, where slave-trading had been an important business, this entire passage was excised. In the Declaration not a word is found of the slave trade, and slavery appears obliquely and very briefly in an attack on the King for having "excited domestic insurrections amongst us." [2]

Most of the Declaration, as adopted, consists of an enumeration of the "repeated injuries and usurpations, all having in direct object the establishment of an absolute Tyranny over these states," the details of which have been presented in earlier pages. Its philosophic, and immortal, pronouncements consist of less than 300 words.

The Americans in their manifesto of revolution begin by declaring that "a decent respect to the opinion of mankind requires that they should declare the causes which impel" them to their momentous step. This itself is new and reflects the essence of the Declaration's political philosophy—the sovereignty of the people. Believing in this sovereignty and staking their lives on an attempt to establish it, they naturally are impelled to explain their cause and their motivation to the peoples of the world. If the people's will is to be supreme, then their good will is omnipotent.

Then comes the enunciation of that cause. It consists of three basic ideas: (1) human beings—essentially equal in attributes, needs, obligations and desires—possess basic rights to life, liberty and the pursuit of happiness; (2) to obtain these rights men

create governments; (3) governments destructive of these rights
are tyrannical; such governments may be, and indeed, should be,
altered or abolished by the people who then have the right and
the duty to create the kind of government which "to them shall
seem most likely to effect their safety and Happiness."

These ideas were of international origin. Directly, in terms of
the 18th century Americans who approved them, they were de-
rived from the humanist and libertarian arguments of ancient
Greece and Rome. They were derived from the whole magnificent
Age of Reason with its titans who struggled against dogma and
authoritarianism—Bacon, Grotius, Vesalius, Copernicus, Spinoza.
More immediately the sources were the writings of the Irish
revolutionist, Charles Lucas, the Italian economist, Beccaria, the
Swiss philosopher, Vattel, and his compatriot, Burlamaqui, the
German jurist, Pufendorf, from the Frenchmen, Montesquieu,
Voltaire, Diderot, from the Englishmen, Milton, Sidney, Har-
rington, Priestley, and Locke, particularly, and from the Americans, Roger Williams, Jonathan Mayhew and John Wise.

All of these were products, as they were voices, of the central
fact in human history—the struggle against oppression, and the
dynamic, ever-advancing nature of that struggle. The international sources of the Declaration in no way, of course, contradict
its national essence. It remains American, or better, therefore,
it is American.

I

The political theory of the Declaration is intensely democratic
and profoundly revolutionary. When Copernicus discarded the
medieval concept of the qualitative inferiority of the earth's
movements as compared with those of heavenly bodies, he helped
revolutionize astronomy. So Jefferson's pronouncement signalized
the revolutionizing of political science by discarding the medieval
concept of the qualitative inferiority of earthly life as compared
with heavenly bliss.

Life on earth, Jefferson held, was not supposed to be a vale of
tears and suffering. The meaning of life was not unending pain
to be endured meekly in order to get into heaven; and man's

travail was not his cross to be borne because of original sin—because man was naturally evil. Moreover, governments were not the secular arm of the Lord, as priests were not his ecclesiastical arm.

No; this entire elaborate machine for the justification and perpetuation of the hierarchical, non-dynamic, burdensome feudal order is denied. Men are good, not evil; men are capable of governing themselves well; governments are man-made; the purpose of life is its ennoblement here on earth. The "freedom and happiness of man," Jefferson wrote to Kosciusko in 1810, must be the objects of political organization and, indeed, "the end of all science, of all human endeavor."

Hierarchy is, then, rejected and with it aristocracy and monarchy and the divine right of ruler or rulers. Equality of man replaces it and therefore sovereignty lies with these equals, and it is their will which is divine, if anything is; at any rate, it is their will which must be decisive where government seeks their welfare. And this is dynamic, not static. The (then new) idea of progress permeates the whole argument, for with man good, with government well provided, surely then, as Jefferson later said, his "mind is perfectible to a degree of which we cannot form any conception," and they speak falsely who insist "that it is not probable that anything better will be discovered than what was known to our fathers."

If to the above is added its logical corollary—that government must rest on "the consent of the governed," as the Declaration says—then the right of revolution is indubitable. It is a right not to be lightly exercised, as the Declaration also declares, but, nevertheless, an inalienable right, which exists so long as government exists. It was later asserted that the right of revolution ceases where a democratic republic exists, for the people cannot rebel against themselves. This misses the point: the people must consent to being governed; if enough of them do not and if the grievances are sufficiently serious, the right of revolution is theirs. The Declaration of Independence admits of no exceptions to the right of revolution; it only warns against hastiness and adventurism.

Where governments oppress, where they stifle and are engines of exploitation, where they do not serve to further happiness (and clearly the majority of the people living under such governments are the authority as to whether or not they so act), they have then become tyrannical and acquiescence in tyranny is treason to man.

Certain rights are fundamental, in the Declaration's view. These are the people's "unalienable rights," expressed in that magnificent phrase, crashing through the corridors of history—"arousing men to burst the chains," as Jefferson himself wrote in his last letter—"Life, Liberty and the Pursuit of Happiness."

It is the idea of man's right to the pursuit of happiness which is the heart of the document's revolutionary enunciation and one which, by its magnificent, timeless generalization makes the document meaningful and stirring for all time.

That Jefferson chose this expression rather than the more usual Whig—Lockeian one of "life, liberty and property" was deliberate and reflects the advanced position of Jefferson personally and of the revolutionary coalition which adopted it. True it is, as Ralph Barton Perry stated in his *Puritanism and Democracy* (1944) that: "Property as an inalienable right is not to be identified with any particular institution of property, such as the private ownership of capital, or the unlimited accumulation of wealth, or the right of inheritance, or the law of contract."

Also, in order not to exaggerate the significance of Jefferson's change of the Lockeian phrase, it is important to note that Locke viewed property in a sense much broader than mere material possession. Typically, in his *Two Treatises on Government,* Locke wrote that "every man has a property in his own person" [3] and also referred to "that property which men have in their persons as well as goods." Howard Mumford Jones, in his study of *The Pursuit of Happiness* (1953), aptly summarizes Locke's idea: "Property is what belongs to a man as a man, not merely his physical possessions but also that extension of intangible values—life, freedom, one's stake in society."

It is also to be noted that when Jefferson stated he had tried to say nothing novel in the Declaration, but rather to offer in summary fashion the generally accepted view of things to most Americans, he did not mean to exclude the idea of the pursuit of happiness. Indeed this idea, expressed in identical language, recurs in Locke himself and appears in the writings of such influential contemporaries of Jefferson as Oliver Goldsmith, Joseph Priestley and Adam Smith.

Nevertheless, Jefferson's choice of words to omit and words to include is indicative of the intensely democratic content of the American Revolution, especially at its high point. Jefferson did conceive of liberty, as had the Levellers in the 17th century, in the sense of freedom of speech and press and person, and of the pursuit of happiness, as more elemental, more profound than property rights.

Relevant, too, is it that Jefferson—while, of course, in no way conceiving of, let alone favoring, Socialism, but, on the contrary, assuming private ownership of means of production—was very sensitive to the concentration of property-holding and felt it to be the central threat to democratic rights. He saw "enormous inequality" of property ownership, especially in land, as the cause of "so much misery to the bulk of mankind" that he insisted, in 1785, that "legislators cannot invent too many devices for subdividing property."

Basic to the Declaration also, of course, is its affirmation of a nation's right to self-determination. This clearly is the meaning of the first sentence in the Declaration, affirming the right of "one people to dissolve the political bands which have connected them with another, and to assume among the powers of the earth, the separate and equal station to which the Laws of Nature and of Nature's God entitle them." This right is also derived from popular sovereignty, but it is simultaneously expressive of another central force in modern history—the sense of nationality.

The revolutionary content of the Declaration refutes Louis Hartz's insistence that in their Revolution, "the Americans refused to join in the great Enlightenment enterprise of shattering the Christian concept of sin, replacing it with an unlimited humanism, and then emerging with an earthly paradise as glittering as the heavenly one that had been destroyed."

On the contrary, the Declaration of Independence is the greatest political expression of "the great Enlightenment," is expressive of an "unlimited humanism," and does reflect the idea of discarding pie in the sky for milk and honey here on earth. On the committee drafting it was Benjamin Franklin, personifying, with Voltaire, the Enlightenment, and convinced that "It is impossible to imagine the height to which may be carried, in a thousand years, the power of man over matter." Franklin was sure of progress, of man's developing mastery, not only over nature but over himself and so expressed regrets that he had been "born so soon."

John Adams, also of the drafting committee, saw man's capabilities as unlimited, and especially in his younger years, was certain of his steady progress. Man, he wrote, "by the exercise of his reason" could and would accomplish "the most astonishing designs." He would make mountains of valleys and valleys of mountains, he would "rend the rocks and level the proudest trees," he would solve the mysteries of the heavens and of the infinitely small, so that even that which "escapes the observation of our naked sight" would still be comprehended and mastered.

Jefferson himself, typical of the American revolutionary feeling, saw that effort as the light and inspiration of all mankind. His sense of a universal humanism and of the creation of a social order throughout the world fully worthy of human beings runs through his life and works, as it pervades the bold and confident language of his Declaration. Characteristic is his letter to John Dickinson, March 6, 1801:

> A just and solid republican government maintained here will be a standing monument and example for the aim and imitation of the people of other countries; and I join with you in the hope and belief that they will see from our example that a free government is of all others the most energetic; that the enquiry which has been excited among the mass of mankind by our revolution and its consequences, will ameliorate the condition of man over a great portion of the globe. What a satisfaction have we in the contemplation of the benevolent effects of our efforts, compared with those of the leaders of the other side, who have discountenanced all advances in science as dangerous innovations, have endeavored to render philosophy and republicanism terms of reproach, to persuade us that man cannot be governed but by the rod &c. I shall have the happiness of dying in the contrary hope.

It is necessary to notice, also, the widespread idea, as repeated by Boorstin in his already cited *Genius of American Politics,* that the colonists "were fighting not so much to establish new rights as to preserve old ones" and that actually it was "Parliament that had been revolutionary, by exercising a power for which there was no warrant in English constitutional precedent."

But such an exercise of power can also be counter-revolutionary, rather than revolutionary. Which it is, depends upon who exercises it and for what purposes. It is true that the colonists had insisted that they were seeking "the rights of Englishmen," but insisting upon this in the face of rulers who declare that colonists do not have such rights is revolutionary, though the rights themselves may not be new. Moreover, insisting upon the exercise of old rights under new conditions may also be revolutionary. It is exactly because the colonists discovered that under the new conditions they would not be granted the rights of Englishmen—and would be forbidden them by force and violence—that they came to see that to have the rights of Englishmen they had to cease being Englishmen. Contemporaries made this quite explicit. Thus, as early as September 6, 1769, one finds this sentence in a leading article in the *Georgia Gazette:* "If we are no longer to be allowed the rights of Britons, we MUST be Americans." They had to become what in fact they were—Americans; for this purpose they adopted their Declaration of Independence, indeed a revolutionary act.

II

The limitations of the Declaration of Independence are the limitations of the century and the class which produce it. The Declaration presents the State in an idealist fashion; it sees man in an abstract manner, not men and women in a class society, with the state as a reflection and a bulwark of the dominant class.

The revolutionary bourgeoisie sees the state, which it is capturing and remolding, as an object in itself, standing above classes, or as some sort of an arbiter between conflicting classes within society. While its insistence that men create the state for their own purposes is a leap beyond the feudal concept, it is perhaps an even greater distance short of the historical-materialist class concept of the state.

This supra-class view limits, too, the Declaration's theory of equality, for while that theory is revolutionary *vis-á-vis* feudal hierarchical notions, it is largely illusory in terms of the material base of bourgeois society, in terms of property and class relationship, in terms of effective power—considerations of vital importance for a full understanding of equality.

The relationship between property ownership and inequality was, of course, axiomatic to the Revolutionary Fathers. Said Alexander Hamilton, for example (in the 79th number of *The Federalist*): "In the general course of human nature, *a power over a man's subsistence amounts to a power over his will*" (italics in original). But they generally saw the State in abstracted political terms and so expressed a theory of equality, which while of the highest consequence in the whole democratic struggle of mankind, was itself largely confined to the political and even there, in practice, was highly partial.

As a result, property limitations on the political power of adult white males are not per se condemned in the Declaration and existed in the rebellious colonies while their delegates signed the document. Other limitations, as religious tests for the enjoyment of political power, were viewed by many as not incongruous or inconsistent.

As the disabilities become even more complete, the incongruity becomes less apparent to the Declaration's signers. Thus, the full, if temporary, disability of the several hundred thousand indentured servants was quite compatible, to the signers, with the Declaration.

Especially striking is the fact that while the Declaration spoke of equality, liberty, and the pursuit of happiness, 600,000 American slaves—slaves for life, who transmitted their status to all offspring, through the maternal line—were held to labor under the lash. It is indeed one of the most painful and yet most revealing facts in American history that the author of the Declaration of Independence was himself a slave-owner.

This central failing of the Declaration, and of the American Revolution, reflects the organic connection between the rise of capitalism and the ideology and practice of racism, as elaborated in *The Colonial Era*. It is certainly racism which helps account for the revolutionists going into battle with the slogan, "Liberty or Death" on their banners, and over half a million slaves on their fields.

That which Frederick Engels wrote, in *Anti-Duehring*, of the American Constitution is pertinent also to the Declaration: "It is significant of the specifically bourgeois character of these human rights that the American Constitution, the first to recognize the rights of man, in the same breath confirmed the slavery of the colored races in America."

Also reflective of the limitations of the Declaration is the fact that when it said, "All men are created equal," it did not mean all men and women; had this been offered for ratification the document would not have been signed. This limitation did not go unremarked at the time, for both in England and in the colonies there were rudimentary stirrings of what, in three generations, was to become a major social movement.

Thus it is that John Adams' wife, Abigail, wrote him: "I cannot say that I think you are very generous to the ladies; for, whilst you are proclaiming peace and good-will to men, emancipating all nations, you insist upon retaining an absolute power over wives." Somewhat later, in 1778, this splendid woman declared: "I regret the trifling, narrow, contracted education of the females of my own country." Rare were the men in America who agreed, but there were some. Among others, James Wilson and William White, both of Pennsylvania, criticized the subordination of women and denied their mental inferiority by 1768.

Women were frequently outstanding in support of the Revolution and this, too, made more pointed Mrs. Adams' comments. Thus, in the colonies, Mercy Otis Warren—sister of James Otis and wife of General James Warren, slain at Bunker Hill—began publishing material in support of the American cause by 1773, and consistently threw her support to the Left wing of the revolutionary movement. In England, one of the staunchest supporters of the Revolutionists—beginning in the 1760's—was Catherine Sawbridge Macaulay, author of an eight-volume *History of England*. She wrote pamphlets and articles in defense of the American struggle during the Revolution, too, and corresponded or conferred with Benjamin Franklin, Ezra Stiles, George Washington, James Otis, Josiah Quincy and other leading rebels.

Even earlier, in fact, in the work of Mary Astell and Daniel Defoe in England, there were protests against the social and political subordination of women, and during the Revolution itself Yale men were debating: "Whether Women ought to be admitted into the Magistracy and Government of Empires and Republics."

Thus, the ignoring of women in the Declaration, drawing comment from Abigail Adams, must be pointed to as a limitation, not only in the clear view of hindsight, but also in the view of some of the more advanced contemporaries.

But, of course, it is not the limitations of the Declaration of Independence which define its historic impact. Those limitations, of time and place and class, are omissions; the actual words of the document, having universality and humanity, remain fresh and inspiring.

Elie Halévy aptly wrote that for the radicals of its day the Declaration represented "to a large extent the cause of the whole of humanity"; "it seemed to foreshadow the fulfillment of the Bibilical prophecies, the coming reign of reason and virtue in which the Gospel of Peace should be better understood and should be glorified."

For generations, as Merle Curti has pointed out, the Declaration was abhorred as seditious by the earth's rulers; its distribution or possession in many places was a capital crime. Professors in Italy, France, Denmark, Austria, and Prussia, well into the 19th century, were fired, and even imprisoned, for insisting on teaching their students its challenging ideas.

Butt of cynics, yet scourge of tyrants, the birth certificate of the American Republic stands today as Lincoln said in 1859—when a slave-holding class jeered at it as pernicious and false—"a rebuke and a stumbling block to the very harbingers of reappearing tyranny and oppression."

Chapter VIII

The Military Conduct of the Revolution

WITH THE WAR won and the fighting at an end, Washington wrote to his extremely capable comrade-in-arms, General Nathanael Greene:

> If historiographers should be hardy enough to fill the pages of history with the advantages that have been gained with unequal numbers, on the part of America, in the course of this contest; and attempt to relate the distressing circumstances under which they have been obtained, it is more than probable that posterity will bestow on their labors the epithet and marks of fiction; for it will not be believed, that such a force as Great Britain has employed for eight years in this country could be baffled in their plan of subjugating it, by numbers infinitely less, composed of men oftentimes half starved, always in rags, without pay, and experiencing every species of distress, which human nature is capable of undergoing.

Washington recurred to the same idea in his last orders to the Revolutionary troops, issued November, 1783: "The unparalleled perseverance of the armies of the United States through almost every possible suffering and discouragement for the space of eight long years was little short of a standing miracle."

These public and private references to nearly insuperable difficulties were not boasting—something quite foreign to Washington's character—and were not the conventional exaggerations of a "veteran."

I

At first glance it appeared sheer madness for the thirteen colonies to challenge Great Britain to a test of arms. In Great Britain at that time lived nine million people; in the colonies less than three millions, with 20 percent of that total made up of slaves. Great Britain had the world's greatest navy; the colonists had none. Great Britain had a tried and tested and numerous regular army; the colonies had ill-trained militiamen. Great Britain was a mature, stable, well-knit governmental unit; the colonies were thirteen hastily formed, separate, turmoil-filled sovereignties. Great Britain was the center of the greatest empire in the world, and colonies to the north and south of the rebels—Canada, the Floridas, the West Indies—were loyal to the Crown and could serve as bases for attack. Great Britain had a stable currency and unlimited credit; the colonies had neither. Great Britain had the greatest merchant fleet and the most powerful industry in the world. British troops were universally held to be invincible; their bayonet charges, irresistible. Great Britain had never been beaten in war and had recently established her world-wide hegemony by defeating Spain and Holland and France. She was then at peace with all countries, so that, apparently, the rebellious Americans would get her undivided attention.

These hard facts lay behind the confidence with which England's rulers undertook to suppress the rebels. When to them was added the further fact that these rebels were rabble and colonial rabble at that, and that, allegedly, they were but a minority of the population, imperial confidence turned to arrogance—a dangerous attitude to take into battle. Thus, the Earl of Sandwich, perhaps the most corrupt First Lord of the Admiralty in the history of the British Navy, speaking in the House of Lords in March, 1775 (before Lexington), for a policy of forcible repression, declared:

> Suppose the colonies do abound in men, what does that signify? They are raw, undisciplined, cowardly men. I wish instead of forty or fifty thousand of these brave fellows, they would produce in the field at least two hundred thousand; the more the better; the easier would be the conquest. . . . Be-

lieve me, my Lords, the very sound of cannon would carry them off . . . as fast as their feet could carry them.

Colonel Rall, of the Hessians, felt it would be child's play to subdue the "country clowns"—one of whom killed him at the Battle of Trenton. General Grant spoke with contempt of the "skulking peasants" who had dared offer resistance to His Majesty. Major Pitcairn was sure that "if he drew his sword but half out of the scabbard, the whole banditti of Massachusetts Bay would flee before him"—a bandit, Peter Salem, a Negro, put a bullet between his eyes at Bunker Hill. Lord Rawdon, in 1775, hoped "we shall soon have done with these scoundrels for one only dirties one's fingers by meddling with them."

The contempt for the colonists had an almost racist ferocity; some of its rationalization was akin to the widely-held European view that the American environment produced stunted flora and fauna. General James Wolfe, the British hero of the French and Indian War, who died in 1759, expressed this opinion: "The Americans are in general the dirtiest, the most contemptible, cowardly dogs you can conceive. There is no depending on them in action. They fall down dead in their own dirt and desert by battalions, officers and all." The idea of inferiority was institutionalized in the military—a colonial colonel ranked with, but was junior to, a British captain.

With each passing year of scoundrelly resistance, British rulers assured everyone that next year was the year of victory. For all the world like Chiang Kai-shek announcing the impending collapse of the Communist "banditti" (just before taking off for Taiwan), so Lord Germain, in 1781 (just before Cornwallis surrendered at Yorktown), announced, "so vast is our superiority everywhere, that no resistance on their part is to be apprehended, that can materially obstruct the progress of the King's Army in the speedy suppression of the Rebellion."

Noteworthy, too, was the fact that British officers, having read or been told that the rebellion was the work of a mere handful of mischievous fanatics, expected to find in the colonies widespread support and assistance in suppressing the "disturbance." In England, itself, major campaigns were worked out in terms of such support, but efforts to implement them, in America, petered out when the support was not forthcoming.

British officers, on the ground, however, if not later American historians, acknowledged the near-universal hostility of the colonial population as fatal to efforts at subjugation. General Gage reported to Lord Dartmouth late in 1774 that "a ferment throughout the continent united the whole in one common cause." General Burgoyne, in the midst of the 1777 New York campaign that ended so disastrously for him, wrote Lord Germain: "The great bulk of the country is undoubtedly with Congress in principle and zeal"; another officer, in 1778, wrote: "Every soul in the Jersies is a rebel." Lord Cornwallis, in his Carolina campaign of 1780, found that instead of expected reinforcements from the allegedly numerous Tories, as he conquered areas he had to detach some of his own regular troops to hold these down before advancing to new battles, and that, at times, executions were necessary. But, said a British contemporary, "by these measures he greatly inflamed the animosity of the provincials." Another officer, in Charleston after its capture in 1780, observed that the men "being prisoners" maintained a sullen silence, "but the women make full amends for their silence; they amuse themselves by teaching their children the principals of rebellion, and seem to take care that the rising generation should be as troublesome as themselves."

There are repeated notes of the use of terror by the British forces, but this seems to have boomeranged, as it did in the Carolina campaign of 1780, by increasing colonial hostility. The burning of towns recurred, as of Charlestown and Bedford, Massachusetts; Kingston, New York; Bristol, Rhode Island; Georgetown, South Carolina; New London, Groton, Fairfield and Norwalk, Connecticut; Springfield and Connecticut Farms in New Jersey. There were also cases involving the slaughter of men who had already surrendered, as by the Hessians in the Battle of Long Island, and by British troops under the traitor, Arnold, at Fort Grinnell. Occasionally, especially early in the conflict when the British refused to concede (formally) a prisoner-of-war status to captured Americans, some American officers—as Captain Josiah Huddy and Colonel Isaac Haynes—

were hanged. Retaliation in kind by the Americans and their threat to continue to extract an "eye for an eye" helped put a halt to this ghastly business.

At first, the attitude of the Crown—once it was apparent that Britain faced major resistance—was to wage a war of deliberate cruelty in order to bring the rebels to their knees. In 1776, a general officer expressed the policy this way: "I think we should (whenever we get further into the country), give free liberty to the soldiers to ravage it at will, that these infatuated wretches may feel what a calamity war is." The application of this policy that year and early in 1777, especially in New Jersey, provoked a cry of disgust from a Captain Ferguson of the British Army against "the ravages everywhere wantonly committed, without regard to sex or age, friend or traitor." These, he went on, resulted not in overawing the population, but rather in completing "the alienation of every thinking mind from the royal cause."

Most horrible was the treatment of American prisoners of war. Here the notorious corruption of 18th century British officialdom combined with typical aristocratic contempt and hatred for rebellious provincials to produce an inferno for the victims. Characteristic was the fact that the post of commissary of prisoners was awarded by the British commander, Sir William Howe, to Joshua Loring—husband of Howe's mistress. (Incidentally, paying with one's wife for special financial favors seems to have been characteristic upper-class conduct—thus, Burgoyne's mistress while he was in America was the wife of one of his commissary officers.) Hundreds of prisoners starved to death because of a shortage of rations, the funds for which went into Loring's pockets. Conditions aboard the prison ships were especially awful, comparable only to those aboard the slave-traders. Each morning the first order given the ship-board inmates was: "Prisoners, turn out your dead!"

About 1,200 Americans, including Ethan Allen, were held as prisoners, for varying periods, in England. Conditions there were bad, but not as thoroughly abominable as in America. Efforts were made to persuade the prisoners held in England to take loyalty oaths to the King, but not one did so.

II

The general military nature of the war consisted of a British effort at strangulation through blockade and the seizure of ports plus conquest by dividing up the rebeldom, North and South and East and West, and subduing it section by section. In grand strategy there were two phases to the British effort; that in the North in the first half of the war, and in the South in the second half.

The basic nature of the American defense was to take advantage of terrain and distance and to try to force the British to attack frontally, prepared and elevated positions. Further, the Americans tried so to maneuver the fighting as to pull the British as far as possible from the coast, since every mile the British marched west brought them that much further away from their only secure base of supply—their fleet.

In the course of the war the British held, for varying periods, every port of any consequence in the colonies—Boston, Newport, New York, Philadelphia, Baltimore, Norfolk, Wilmington, Beaufort, Charleston, Savannah. Almost all of these were taken with relative ease and with little resistance—a notable exception being Charleston, whose fall in May, 1780 was accompanied by the surrender of about 5,500 American troops. In nearly every major campaign[1] the British would attempt, with main ports in their rear, to engage significant bodies of American troops in classical, European-like, definitive struggles, so that the campaign might be climaxed by a decisive battle and the conflict terminated. But the Americans, especially when personally led by Generals Washington or Greene, maintained an open, fluid, almost frontier-like, tactic. They sought surprise and ambush; they disengaged quickly; they marched rapidly; they violated 18th century rules by fighting at night and attacking despite rain or fog or snow. They depended heavily, too, on marksmanship, at a time when, in Europe, armies pointed their guns in the general direction of the foe, fired, and then charged, doing greatest damage with bayonet and butt, not with bullet.

The American command appreciated that the revolutionary army was something new—a citizens' army, which in a generation in France was to conquer nearly all Europe. This had disadvantages in terms of discipline, but the disadvantages were more than overcome by the advantages. Chief among the latter was morale—most of the men for most of the time were fighting because they wanted to fight; they were fighting at home for their homes; they were fighting against alien enemies, from England and Germany, who sought to enslave them.

There was not the disregard of leadership in the American forces that some of the more extreme or untutored equalitarians at first desired; but neither was there the rigid, unquestioning, brutal and dehumanizing discipline of the European armies of that day which some of the officers at first favored. The soldier in the American revolutionary regiments was not the same kind of soldier as those filling the ranks of the Georges and Fredericks of Europe. Hence they needed their own manual of arms and drill, their own military law (with punishments notably less severe than in the British army); hence, these American troops would bear more, fight harder, march further, and show more individual initiative than their opponents.

"No European army would suffer the tenth part of what the Americans suffer," said Lafayette. "It takes citizens to support hunger, nakedness, toil and the total want of pay, which constitutes the condition of our soldiers, the hardiest and most patient that are to be found in the world."

George Bancroft, the historian, wrote that when Washington reached the rebel troops before Boston, in 1775, to assume his command, "the camp contained a people in arms, rather than an army." Israel Putnam, the fifth ranking General in the Continental Army, rode at the head of his Massachusetts men in shirt sleeves, a tattered civilian hat on his head. So varied were the clothes of his troops, that Washington urged all to adopt the hunting shirt, so that there would be some appearance of uniformity.

As the war progressed, the discipline and maturity and uniformity of veterans appeared, but up to the end the American Army was really "a people in arms."

This army that was a people and not an army never knew when it was beaten. It defied all the rules and would suddenly spring back with a stunning victory, when, by the book, it should have given up. Thus, in the winter campaign of 1776, the Americans had lost five battles in twelve weeks, suffered 5,000 casualties and had seen their second-ranking officer, General Charles Lee, captured by the British. This was followed by the Trenton victory.

Thus, in 1780-81, the Americans had lost the main cities of the South, an army of near 6,000 had surrendered to the British, Arnold had betrayed the cause, mutinies rocked the lines of Connecticut, Pennsylvania and New Jersey troops. In April, 1781, George Washington was writing in strictest confidence to Henry Laurens, "we are at the end of our tether," while on May 1, 1781, he confided to his military journal:

> Instead of magazines filled with provisions, we have a scanty pittance . . . instead of having our arsenals filled with military stores, they are poorly provided . . . instead of having a regular system of transportation upon credit, or funds in the quartermaster's hands to pay the contingent expenses of it, we have neither . . . instead of having the regiments completed to the new establishment scarce any state in the Union has, at this hour, an eighth part of its quota . . . instead of having everything in readiness to take the field, we have nothing, instead of having the prospect of a glorious offensive before us, we have a bewildered and gloomy defensive one.

At tether's end in the spring; Yorktown in the fall.

Part of Washington's greatness lay in the fact that, commanding this new kind of army, he appreciated its qualities and realized its necessities. He insisted that it was necessary, as he wrote, November 10, 1775, "to impress upon the mind of every man, from the first to the lowest, the importance of the cause, and what it is they are contending for." British officers spoke of the Americans' "implacable ardor and revenge, which happily are a good deal unknown in the prosecution of war in general."

The guerrilla-like conduct of the war showed itself in the first place in the decisively significant contributions of such out-and-out guerrilla fighters as Andrew Pickens, Thomas Sumter, Francis Marion, James Williams, William Davies, and Elijah Clarke. These men had been Indian fighters and they applied the tactics thus learned to the anti-British effort. They led small groups—Marion's force never exceeded 100—of extremely hardy men (Negro and white) in brief but damaging assaults on the British. Blacksmiths equipped them, farmers fed them. Their victories ranged from defeating a dragoon company to annihilating an entire British regiment, as Sumter did (with an orphan boy of 13 named Andrew Jackson in his band) at the battle of Hanging Rock in South Carolina, August, 1780.

By the summer of 1780, the British had "conquered" Georgia and South Carolina. What fighting continued was of the strictly guerrilla-kind, *i.e.*, conducted by armed civilians who fed themselves and were not paid. From July 12 to August 27, 1780, guerrillas in these areas conducted 15 major attacks on British forces, inflicting over 1,100 casualties and themselves losing, in killed and wounded, nearly 650 men.[2]

In addition, any major British campaign saw the appearance of militia units, out of the surrounding countryside, for the purpose of defeating that particular campaign; that done, the militiamen would return to their civilian tasks. This was true, for example, in the Burgoyne campaign. As Burgoyne moved into New York State and as his covering wings probed from Lake Erie to the Hudson and from the Hudson into New England, his main body and especially his covering forces were subjected to continual harrassment, not only by the regular troops under Gates, but by highly irregular bodies of men, fighting under Stark and Herkimer, and other local leaders. Burgoyne, himself, wrote to Lord Germain, August 20, 1777:

> The great bulk of the country is undoubtedly with Congress in principle and zeal; and their measures are executed with a secrecy and dispatch that are not to be equalled. Wherever the king's forces point, militia to the amount of 3 or 4 thousand assemble in 24 hours; they bring with them their subsistence, etc., and the alarm over, they return to their farms.

Lord Germain, explaining early British failures, noted that "the manner of opposing an enemy that avoids facing you in the open field is totally different from what young officers learn from the common discipline of the army." The "chief qualification" of the rebels, said a British officer in 1778, "is agility in running from fence to fence and thence keeping up an irregular, but galling fire on troops who advance with the same pace as at their exercises."

"American" became synonymous with "sneak" to many of the British rulers. All (including women) could handle firearms, and in every American home there was a gun. Thus, universally armed, and ardent in their cause, "never," said an English officer

> had the British army so ungenerous an enemy to oppose; they send their riflemen five or six at a time who conceal themselves behind trees, etc., till an opportunity presents itself of taking a shot at our advance sentries, which done they immediately retreat. What an unfair method of carrying on a war!

III

The conduct of naval warfare by the Americans was also guerrilla-like. Though, in 1775, Congress provided for something approximating a Navy, under the command of Esek Hopkins, it never really functioned in coordinated, squadron fashion. Any idea of challenging British naval supremacy as such was, of course, absurd.

Rather, the naval vessels took part in surprise, hit-and-run raids for supplies, as upon Prince Edward Island, and Nassau in the Bahamas, and, individually, tried to damage the merchant marine of England. Naval vessels commissioned by the Continental Congress and by the individual states, and American privateers-men, served the Revolutionary effort in two ways: (a) they did bring in important quantities of supplies, especially by trading with the West Indies and running the British blockade; and, (b) they did succeed in destroying thousands of tons of British shipping; privateers accounted for 753 English merchant ships in the first 20 months of fighting.

There were some strictly naval engagements and in them the fledgling American force did well. This was especially true of the remarkable seamanship of John Paul Jones, with his spectacular raids upon the coast of Ireland and even several points in England itself.

The organization, industry, training and skill necessary to an effective naval force require not only great resources, which the Revolutionary country had, but also maturity, which it lacked. At the same time, so long as British naval domination was complete and hardly challenged, so long could Britain dominate the (then) major American cities and so make success in the rebellion impossible. This could terminate either through war-weariness on the part of Britain or through some challenge to her naval supremacy. A combination of the two—plus continued and effective American resistance on land—produced Yorktown and British acknowledgment of defeat.

It was the supreme consequence of naval power to the war which made the French contribution so decisive. In subsequent pages we shall examine briefly the diplomatic history of the Revolution. But here, in considering its purely military features, it is necessary to note the French role. France's efforts were consequential in embarrassing England in terms of the European balance of power. They were important in providing money, credit and supplies to the rebels; in encouraging the enlistment of trained officers (many of whom were not of French nationality) in the Continental Army; and in sending troops to fight on American soil (at Yorktown, there were 7,800 French and 8,845 American troops—French casualties were more than twice the American).

But it was the 36 ships of the line under Admiral DeGrasse that made Cornwallis surrender. These ships had beaten off a delaying action by Admiral Graves, off Chesapeake Bay, early in September, and then ferried American and French troops into position below and above Cornwallis, saving the infantry many a weary mile. Having done that, DeGrasse's vessels took up siege positions before Yorktown, completely blocking the sea entrance between Cape Charles on the north and Cape Henry on the south.

Virginia militia and French marines surrounded the British forces under Tarleton just north of Gloucester point, and across the York River, at Yorktown itself, Cornwallis was locked in by the French fleet to his north and east and by American and French troops to his south and west, with Washington, himself, in supreme command.

Cornwallis, outnumbered two-to-one on land, hemmed in by 36 French ships, (General Clinton in New York had no more than 27 vessels) and subjected to continual infantry assaults and artillery barrages—the British suffered 482 casualties—decided to surrender his full force of 8,000. The surrender occurred on October 19, 1781.

Lord Cornwallis, pleading illness, had a subordinate deliver his sword. When the latter handed the Earl's sword to the rebel commander, Washington refused it and directed that it be given to *his* subordinate, the New Englander, General Lincoln, who a year before had surrendered Charleston to the British. The British troops, arrayed in fresh, sparkling scarlet uniforms, marched out, to stack their arms, between rows of nattily-attired, blue-uniformed French soldiers, and still unkempt, shabbily-dressed, variously uniformed American Continental and militia troops. The British ostentatiously avoided the faces of the rebels, looking only upon the French, to whom—as to one legal and regal power to another—surrender, while terribly painful was, at any rate, thinkable. Yet the music from the British band hinted that this surrender was something new, was not the time-honored ceremony of one monarch's hirelings having bested another, but was rather the triumph of revolutionary republicans. The band was playing "The World Turned Upside Down."

Chapter IX

Tories and Traitors

R ICHARD C. HASKETT, in an illuminating essay on "Prosecuting the Revolution," (*American Historical Review,* April, 1954), pointed out that the suppression of its internal foes was a prerequisite to the Revolution's accomplishment. Hence,

> the success of the Revolution was impossible without a revolutionary government which could enforce its will. The fight of patriot against loyalist was a struggle for survival: Washington's army might maintain a precarious existence in the face of British troops, but if the civilian government crumbled away behind it, there would be nothing left.

How significant was the internal counter-revolutionary threat, and how was it dealt with?

First, of course, there very definitely was a civil war aspect to the Revolution. The split in family relations most dramatically illustrates this phase. Thus, Benjamin Franklin's son, William, was the Royal Governor of New Jersey; John Hancock's brother-in-law was Judge Jonathan Sewell, a Tory refugee; General Henry Knox's son-in-law was Thomas Flucker, a banished Tory whose estate was confiscated; General John Stark's brother was a British colonel; Gouverneur Morris' brother was an English army officer, and his brother-in-law was a Tory refugee.

This civil-war aspect of the Revolution, though not so consequential in this instance as in some other revolutions—in part because the Tories were, relatively, so few—nevertheless was marked by extreme bitterness. Typical was the wish of one

Connecticut Tory to "kill more damned rebels than the best Britain." The patriots were normally referred to by the Tories as "Beasts of the People," "Sons of Darkness," "The Vulgars," as "ungovernable, riotous, high-handed bandits and murderers" and other choice epithets of upper-class temper. On the other hand, rebels were not exactly restrained in expressing their opinions of the Tories. John Adams, not the most explosive of the patriots, thought, in 1774: "A Tory here is the most despicable animal in the creation: Spiders, toads, snakes are their only proper emblem."

Basically, the Tories were made up of the wealthier elements in colonial society. This does not mean that none amongst the poor persisted in a more or less ardent loyalty to the Crown; a minute percentage did. It does not mean that all of the wealthier components in colonial society were Loyalists—a majority of them were not. But it does mean that most of those who were Tories were well-to-do, or the direct servants of the well-to-do. This included most of the British mercantile factors, especially in Virginia and North Carolina; it included most of the Anglican clergy and most of the Crown officialdom in the colonies. A number of the wealthiest slave-owning planters of the eastern seaboard, especially in South Carolina and Georgia, and a number of the richest merchants, especially in New York and Philadelphia, preferred, often with great vacillation, to remain loyal to the established Crown rather than to offer fealty to a new-fangled Congress. Certain among the most considerable landowners, especially in Maryland and up-State New York where feudalistic forms were most pronounced, also chose the Crown.

In no State were the Loyalists a majority, but in Delaware, Maryland, Georgia and North Carolina they were sufficiently important to present a serious problem; in certain localities, as Philadelphia, they were numerous. Contemporary figures, of any precision, are quite few. There are some: A British Army return at the end of 1778 stated there were not quite 7,500 Loyalists enrolled therein; in 1781 the Army rolls listed less than 5,500 Loyalists; at the close of hostilities, when the British withdrew in 1783, a total of about 7,000 Loyalists left with them. A British government commission to hear claims for compensation from Loyalists, terminated its services in 1790 having authorized the payment of almost three and a half million pounds to 4,118 individual applicants. Ezra Stiles, the President of Yale from 1778 to 1795, stated in his diary, in 1783, that the number of Tories "in all the States during the whole eight years of war" did not exceed "fifteen or twenty thousand souls."

Other general figures are quite frankly guesses. The most frequent one holds that from 1775 through 1783 a total of about 100,000 Tories—men, women, and children—left the rebellious colonies for either Canada or Great Britain; that is to say, about 4% of the white population. Of course, additional Loyalists did not flee the country, but how many they were is not known.

The two areas with the heaviest concentration of population during this period—New England and Virginia[1]—were those least troubled by Toryism. A careful student of revolutionary Connecticut, Oscar Zeichner, concluded that not more than six per cent of that State's population was Tory. Isaac S. Harrell, in *Loyalism in Virginia* (1926), stated that Toryism there was never widespread, its adherents "at no time exceeding a few thousand," and Jefferson, in his contemporaneous *Notes on Virginia,* referred to "the unanimity of its inhabitants" in favor of the Revolution.

I

How was the question of Toryism dealt with by the Revolutionary fathers? Up to Lexington, the main resort of the patriots was persuasion and exhortation, liberally spiced with extra-legal pressures ranging from boycott to physical assault. After Lexington, persuasion gave way to compulsion, which took five main forms. These were: (1) deprivation of all civil and some social rights; (2) confiscation of property; (3) exile; (4) confinement; (5) execution.

In all the States, Tories were expelled from whatever public offices they may have been holding, and were barred from being elected to any. They generally were forbidden to serve as ministers, teachers, lawyers, and doctors, either by law or by social practice. They were disfranchised, by law, in five States, and by

practice throughout the Revolutionary area. Richard P. Mc-
Cormick, in an excellent study of New Jersey, stated the attitude
on this question that prevailed throughout the thirteen States:
"only those who were willing to support the Revolutionary cause
should be permitted to enjoy full political freedom." Certain of
the disabilities continued in several of the States, for some years
after the peace treaty of 1783.

Prominent or notorious Tories were banished, by law, from
the territory of nine States; in fact, unless the Tory was very
discreet or located in some area held by the British, exile was his
most common lot. Confiscation of Tory property was done in the
beginning by tax laws doubling or trebling their assessments.
Later, confiscation was accomplished directly; courts or attorneys
general, acting with statutory sanction enacted in all the States,
simply appropriated Tory property. Property so confiscated was
subject to sale for the benefit of the Revolutionary governments
—an important source of revenue. For example, New York obtained nearly four million dollars and Maryland over two million
dollars in this way. It was also, of course, an important source of
graft and, needless to say, the bourgeoisie missed no opportunities to enrich themselves in the midst of this war, as in any war.
Thus, William Paterson, the Attorney General of New Jersey,
and his friend, Frederick Frelinghuysen, profited handsomely
through this process.

During the course of the Revolution several thousand Tories,
including clergymen, were subjected to house arrest (*i.e.,* confined to a severely restricted local area), or imprisoned. Those
jailed were denied trial by jury, or bail, or habeas corpus, or the
right of appeal. Usually incarceration was to last for the duration of the conflict. Sometimes the imprisonment carried with it
forced labor for the benefit of the Revolution, as the use of Tory
prisoners in the Simsbury mines in Connecticut. There were
several cases of banishment *en masse;* not uncommon was the
jailing of the relatives of Tories otherwise beyond the reach of
the patriots, with the jailed ones being held as hostages for the
neutral behavior of their absent relatives.

The execution of civilian Tories, as Tories, was rare, but it
did occur. Thus, two were hanged in Philadelphia in 1778 and

several were executed in North Carolina, some even after the Treaty of 1783 had been signed. Irregular, terroristic executions of particularly active Tories, especially by State militia and guerrilla units, were more common. So were executions of armed Tories, especially in reprisal for the hangings of patriots.

How numerous were the injustices and crimes committed in the name of and during the prosecution of the Revolution, it is impossible to say. It is a singular fact that the whole question of the civil rights of the Tories seems to be missing from the writings of the Revolutionary Fathers. One letter, and only one, so far as this writer knows, is a partial exception. In June, 1780, Pennsylvania vested in its President (*i.e.*, Governor) very great powers. Madison, then in Congress, wrote to Jefferson: "I understand they have invested the Executive with a dictatorial authority from which nothing but the *lives* of their citizens are exempted. I hope the good resulting from it will be such as to compensate for the risk of the precedent."

The original basis for the anti-Tory campaign came from the revolutionary seizure of power by local and province-wide conventions and committees. The first nation-wide provision on this question is contained in a recommendation issued by the Continental Congress, in October, 1775, that provincial Committees of Safety "take into custody every person who, going at large, might in their opinion endanger the safety of the colony or the liberties of America." In November, 1777, Congress recommended to the States that they confiscate the property of all Tories—of those who, in its words, had forfeited "the right of protection."

Typical of the revolutionary instrumentalities was New Jersey's Council of Safety. This appeared in March, 1777, consisted of twelve men (including the Attorney General), chosen by the legislature, and was empowered to jail anybody suspected of opposing the Revolution. Professor Haskett has described the functioning of this Council, which, under a similar or identical name, operated in more or less the same manner in every State:

> the patriots of the council traveled over the state encouraging local officials and taking the administration of the law into their own hands whenever necessary. The attorney general and his

council colleagues would descend upon a county, hear a procession of witnesses, order the sheriff or even the militia to seize suspected Tories, and send them off to jail in whatever part of the state seemed safest. Then the council would move on to another county and repeat the process. The work was hasty but comprehensive: at Morristown in July of 1777 council members ordered the arrest of 48 people in the course of one day's work. Normal judicial safeguards were ignored in the emergency of the moment.

One does not have, then, in the American Revolution that absence of "fury and madness" that Louis Hartz reports in *The Liberal Tradition in America* (1955). There was ruthlessness in the American Revolution, but happily, this feature was somewhat muted. The limited nature of the revolutionary program, *in terms of the home population and its economy,* and the overwhelming support given the Revolution, served to allay the civil war aspects of the struggle. Yet, for its time and place, these aspects were notable enough, and to the thousands who felt its force, very real.

II

Traitors, as well as Tories, sought to defeat the Revolution. Here we refer only to those who, while apparently adherents of the Revolutionary cause, in fact actively assisted the British; we do not have in mind those who, with changes in the fortunes of war, altered their allegiance under duress or as matters of more or less convenience.

The facts show that treason was never a really serious danger to the Revolution—not even in the case of Benedict Arnold. Just after Arnold's treason became known to Washington, he wrote to the French General Rochambeau: "Traitors are the growth of every country, and in a revolution of the present nature it is more to be wondered at that the catalogue is so small than that there have been found a few."

This, however, is not because the British did not try to terrify or buy many into betrayal. While holding Ethan Allen prisoner, they offered him a colonelcy in the army and a large grant of land after the rebellion's defeat; later, commissioners sent from

London came prepared to pay George Washington, Henry Laurens, president of the Continental Congress, and Joseph Reed, Adjutant General of the Army, anything they might demand in money and titles if they would return their allegiance to George III.

These efforts failed and the overwhelming majority of the Revolutionary leadership and rank and file remained true, despite grave set-backs, because their movement held the devotion of the American people as a whole. The movement was bulwarked by measures of security and by the repression of the Tories; but the Revolution was accomplished because of that mass devotion and support.

The main features of what treason there was may be briefly described.

The first engagement of the Revolution was the result of a traitor's work. Gage, in sending troops to Concord and Lexington, did so in order to confiscate hidden powder and ammunition and to capture two anxiously sought political refugees, Samuel Adams and John Hancock. The locations of the military stores and of the revolutionary leaders were sent to the British by Dr. Benjamin Church. This informer was on the payroll of the British; his tip to General Gage was by way of earning his silver.

In the Revolutionary movement of Massachusetts, Church stood below only the Adamses and Hancock, with whom he was a warm friend. He was a member of the Provincial Congress and the Committee of Safety; with the outbreak of fighting he became the Army's first Surgeon General. All the while, he was the hired agent of the British.

When the evidence of his treason became known, late in 1775, one of the revolutionary leaders, Samuel Ward, expressed the normal incredulity of all faced—before and since—with a similar phenomenon:

> Dr. Church, who could have thought or even suspected it, a man who seemed to be all animation in the cause of his country, highly caressed, employed in several very honorable and lucrative departments, and in full possession of the confidence of his country, what a complication of madness and wickedness

must a soul be filled with to be capable of such perfidy! What punishment can equal such horrid crimes?

Church, caught in Connecticut, was jailed for a brief period, then returned to Massachusetts and paroled on his promise not to leave that state. He kept his pledge, in inimitable fashion, by sailing for the West Indies, but the ship was lost and with it went Church.

Another informer for General Gage early in the war was Benjamin Thompson, later Count Rumford, the celebrated scientist. Suspected by his New Hampshire neighbors, he was arrested, tried and acquitted, but he was guilty and had been supplying military information to the British. Nevertheless, he wrote his father-in-law: "I never did nor (let my treatment be what it will) ever will do any action that may have the most distant tendency to injure the true interests of this my native land." Later, he went over to the British openly, and before the war's end was secretary to Lord George Germain.

In the Spring of 1776 a plot to assassinate General Washington was uncovered. The Royal Governor, Tryon, had supplied a large sum of money to David Mathews, Mayor of New York City. With this money the services of perhaps a dozen traitors were procured, including that of Thomas Hickey, a member of Washington's personal guard. Several of those involved being civilians, and the plot being exposed prior to the Declaration of Independence, there was some doubt on the part of both Congress and Washington as to how to proceed in terms of punishment. In the end, several were jailed and Thomas Hickey was hanged on June 28, 1776.

Late in 1776 the adjutant of the 5th Pennsylvania Regiment, William Demont, betrayed his position and deserted to the British. He brought with him detailed plans of Fort Washington, held by his regiment. This helped the British in their successful attack upon the Fort. It fell November 6, 1776, one of the greatest blows of the entire war—American casualties and prisoner-loss totalled 3,000, and the material loss, particularly of artillery, was also heavy. The disaster set off Washington's retreat through New Jersey and—as Paine wrote, in the middle of December, in *The Crisis*—"the times that try men's souls."

Other prominent individuals became traitors; in some cases their treason remained unknown throughout their lives. Among others were Metcalf Bowler, Rhode Island Chief Justice and simultaneously an informer for Sir Henry Clinton; Captain Joseph Hynson, a Maryland shipmaster, diligent in carrying secret diplomatic messages back and forth from Europe to America and careful to sell exact copies to the British. Col. William Rankin of the Pennsylvania militia was a traitor; so was Lt. Col. Herman Zedwitz of the First New York Regiment—he, however, was caught and imprisoned. The British had their agents in state legislatures, as William Heron of Connecticut, and in important Continental offices, as Edward Fox of Maryland, employed in the treasury service.

The British were especially anxious to keep informed of American diplomatic efforts. At their service was not only the favored courier of Benjamin Franklin (the aforementioned Captain Hynson) but they also succeeded in having traitors serve as confidential secretaries of two of the three American commissioners in France—Edward Bancroft for Franklin and William Thornton for Arthur Lee. They also succeeded in driving the third commissioner, Silas Deane, away from the Revolutionary cause and, in the 1780's, on to the King's payroll.

Of these characters the most interesting was Edward Bancroft. A native of Massachusetts, long resident in England, close friend of Franklin's in Paris, and his confidential secretary, he was in the employ of Great Britain for years. Arousing the suspicion of Arthur Lee, he arranged to be arrested by the British and then "talked his way out" to confirm his ardor for the Revolution. The fact is that his treason was not made known until documents proving it were published, in 1891, by the American scholar, Paul Leicester Ford.

There is something less than certainty, to this day, as to the degree of duplicity shown by Silas Deane and Congress in 1842 decided that the charges against him were false. These charges, preferred by Arthur Lee, dealt with financial peculation and at the time were enough to result in his removal from his diplomatic post. Thereafter, he lived in England, in Royal employ, until his death in 1789.

It is of some interest that Deane and Arnold were close friends, prior to their active treason, and that both were important leaders of a generally conservative wing of the Revolutionary coalition.

The treason of Benedict Arnold has made of his name an epithet. He bore the name of his great-grandfather who, in the 17th century, had thrice been Governor of Rhode Island. Himself a New Haven merchant, he was active in the early Revolutionary movement and, showing a combination of great physical courage with tactical imagination, advanced rapidly.

Yet, from the beginning, his military career was marked by repeated charges of dishonesty and irregularity and even doubts as to his patriotism. Arnold's correspondence is filled with assurances that, to cite a typical example, dated March 11, 1776, "though I sensibly feel the ingratitude of my countrymen, every personal injury shall be buried in my zeal for the safety and happiness of my country, in whose cause I have repeatedly fought and bled and am ready at all times to resign my life."

Having been twice wounded, Arnold, in 1778, was assigned to the non-combatant post of commandant of Philadelphia. Here he entertained very lavishly, married the daughter of a rich Loyalist, and fell under the suspicion—again for financial irregularity—of the civil government. Charges having been brought against him, he was court-martialed in June, 1779, the trial dragging on for months.

Though in the trial Arnold passionately defended his honesty and devotion to the cause—and got off with a light reprimand— he had, already in May, 1779, entered into treasonable negotiations with Clinton.

Eager to receive a military command whose betrayal would be attractive to the British, and the price for which could also be attractive, Arnold, through the active (and innocent) intercession of General Philip Schuyler, received from Washington command of the key to the Hudson, West Point. He offered it to the British for £10,000.

The accidental exposure of the whole plot, through the arrest of the British courier, Major Andre, led to Arnold's flight, in September, 1780, to Clinton. Despite Clinton's personal appeals, Washington had Andre hanged, but he never could get his hands on Arnold. That gentleman was appointed a Brigadier-General in the British Army, given £6,315, plus yearly pensions of £500 for his wife, £100 for each of his children and, some years later, over 13,000 acres of land in Canada.

After informing on several American agents in British-held New York City, Arnold conducted two particularly vicious raids in Virginia and in Connecticut, went to England in December, 1781, and was scorned by all but the King. He never again received a command of British troops, lived in Canada for some years as a merchant, returned to London and died, bankrupt and despised, in 1801.

III

The most serious internal military threat that Washington faced came from mutiny, rather than treason. In a sense, of course, mutiny may be considered as a kind of mass treason, but the fact is that the mutinies which three or four times afflicted units within the Revolutionary army were in no sense pro-British in sentiment. Rather, they were outbreaks by devoted Americans made desperate by inadequate food and clothing and certain bureaucratic injustices, particularly revolving around the duration of enlistments.

The most serious of the mutinies was that involving some 1,300 men in the veteran and excellent Pennsylvania Line. Under command of their sergeants, the men demanded their pay (months in arrears), better food and clothing and release, if their papers showed that they had served their time. One officer, attempting to break up the outbreak, was killed. Even General Wayne, respected by his men, could not control them and they set off from Morristown to Trenton, where Congress was then sitting.

Clinton, misreading the affair, sent two agents to the mutineers offering them full back pay if they swore allegiance to the King, and the right to fight or not as they wished. But the men did not wish to give up the Revolutionary effort; they were seeking justice the better to conduct it. Hence, both agents were turned over to Wayne, who promptly had them executed. When the

General offered to reward the sergeants who turned them in, they rejected it.

After a week's parley with Congressional leaders and the granting of most of their demands, the mutiny ended. Encouraged by this success, the less numerous Jersey line mutinied on January 2. Washington now responded with vigor, sending a large body of New England troops to stamp out this uprising. The mutineers were forced to surrender, without fighting, and a leader of each of three regiments was ordered shot, and to be shot by twelve other leaders. One of the three was spared, but the other two were summarily executed without trial, and the mutiny ended.

More sinister was the action of certain Continental Army officers, though this came after the fighting had ceased, and so, while it threatened the purposes of the Revolution, it did not threaten military disaster.

The intent was to replace the civilian-dominated Republic with either a military dictatorship or a more or less absolute monarchy. Either form required the active support of the natural choice for the supreme position, George Washington. The prestige of this man, especially after it became clear that Cornwallis' surrender marked the actual triumph of the Revolution, was colossal; contemporaries, indeed, likened him not only to Moses but to Christ. His power, as Commander-in-Chief of the victorious Revolutionary Army, was not very much less than his prestige and had he yielded to the temptations offered him, it is difficult to see what could have effectively opposed him, at least, in any immediate sense.

Washington's behavior in this crisis is one of the most admirable chapters in the life of this great man. It is at the same time a reflection of the genius of the American people—at least this early in their history—who had great distrust of the military arm and the military mind, and had especially objected to Britain's efforts, prior to Lexington, to impose the supremacy of the military over the civilian.

Washington at all times conducted himself as the servant of Congress (even when that body, in the winter of 1776, gave him dictatorial powers for six months), and though this was frequently exasperating, he never once overstepped these bounds;

from the evidence, he seems never to have ,even contemplated doing so.

This, however, was not true of all associated with power during the Revolution. Beginning in 1780 there appeared the clear suggestion of the alleged need, in the name of the Revolution, of one-man domination. By the spring of 1782 this had reached the point where a Colonel of the Pennsylvania line, Lewis Nicola, suggested in his own name and on behalf of other officers—how numerous is not known—that Washington overthrow the Republic and assume the position of a King.

On May 22, 1782 Washington replied to the Colonel, as follows:

> With a mixture of great surprise and astonishment, I have read with attention the sentiments you have submitted to my perusal. Be assured, Sir, no occurrence in the course of the war has given me more painful sensations, than your information of there being such ideas existing in the army, as you have .expressed, and I must view with abhorrence and reprehend with severity. For the present the communication of them will rest in my own bosom, unless some further agitation of the matter shall make a disclosure necessary.
>
> I am much at a loss to conceive what part of my conduct could have given encouragement to an address, which to me seems big with the greatest mischief, that can befall my Country. If I am not deceived in the knowledge of myself, you could not have found a person to whom your schemes are more disagreeable. . . . Let me conjure you, then, if you have any regard for your country, concern for yourself or posterity, or respect for me, to banish these thoughts from your mind, and never communicate, as from yourself or anyone else, a sentiment of like nature.

It is indicative of the marked generosity with which illegal reactionary schemes and counter-revolutionary activities—not challenging property relationships—generally have been treated in American history, that Colonel Nicola's treasonous communication brought him no more discomfort than the rebuke in Washington's reply.

Though Washington's rejection of this particular proposal marks a signal victory for the Republican idea, it is not true to declare, as did John Richard Alden, in his study of *The Ameri-*

can Revolution, that "the Nicola incident actually signifies the death of the monarchical idea in the United States and the total triumph of representative government." On the contrary, the monarchical idea was to recur in future years and the threat to representative government has not only continued on to our own day, but reappeared immediately after the Nicola affair.

Then, the aim was the supercession of the existing civil government, the creation of a highly centralized federal government maintained with a numerous standing army to be commanded by an officer with supreme overall authority—and the first choice for that office was again Washington.

This movement fed on the demonstrable incompetence and lack of sufficient power of the existing Congress, functioning under the Articles of Confederation. It fed, too, on the bankruptcy of that Congress so that it literally did not have the funds to pay the expenses of the courier who brought news of Yorktown, and it could not pay the rent for the building housing its Treasury department! It fed on the apparent incapacity of the Congress to meet pledges of half-pay for life to officers enlisting for the duration and to meet payments due its civilian creditors.

What ensued was a merger of some of the leading public creditors with the disaffected officers in an effort to overpower and in fact overthrow the authority of Congress and replace it with the authority of a "strong man." This is the meaning of the threat voiced in 1783 by William Bingham, a partner of Robert Morris in the Bank of North America and one of the country's earliest "war millionaires," that if justice were not done the creditors a "violent convulsion must take place."

Hamilton, writing to Washington, February 7, 1783, tried to enlist him in the effort to combine the two demands: "This is the object of all men of sense; in this the influence of the army, properly directed, may cooperate." The same day Gouverneur Morris wrote General Knox that Congress would "see you [that is, the Army] starve rather than pay a six-penny tax"; he suggested, therefore, that the Army impress Congress with its wishes.

Relevant is the fact that this same Morris had written to General Nathanael Greene, in December, 1782: "I have no hope that our union can subsist except in the form of an absolute monarchy and this does not seem to consist with the taste and temper of the people. The necessary consequence, if I am right, is that a separation must take place and consequently wars."

In March, 1783, while a committee of officers was presenting claims to Congress, a Colonel Walter Stewart, an emissary for Robert Morris, appeared at the Army's headquarters in New-burgh, New York. There followed, on March 10, the first of two documents, since come to be known as the Newburgh Addresses. This, issued anonymously, was the work of a Major John Arm-strong, aide-de-camp of General Gates and son of a General of the Pennsylvania Line; it vigorously denounced the vacillations of Congress, urged boldness on the part of the officers and suggested that they "suspect the man who would advise to more moderation and longer forbearance." It closed by calling a meeting, for March 11, of all officers for the purpose of planning how best to force Congress to do their will and warned Congress "that, in any political event, the army has the alternative."

Washington, reading the document, immediately issued orders forbidding the meeting on March 11 and setting another for March 15, at which time a report might be forthcoming from the officer's committee visiting Congress. This was met by the second of the Newburgh Addresses, acquiescing in Washington's order and implying that since he himself had called for a later meeting, he "sanctified" the officers' claims.

At the March 15 meeting, chaired by Gates, Washington made an unexpected appearance and spoke briefly. He drew out a paper on which he had prepared his remarks, and then put on his reading glasses. This surprised many of the officers and Wash-ington explained: "Gentlemen, you will permit me to put on my spectacles, for I have not only grown gray, but almost blind, in the service of my country."

Washington complimented the author of the Addresses for the vigor of his prose and the cleverness with which his phrases were turned. He appealed to the officers to bear witness if the Army had a more constant and devoted friend than himself and a warmer advocate of its cause. But how did the anonymous author propose to advance that cause? He offered two alternatives—if war continues, abandon the front and withdraw to the West;

if peace comes, do not lay up your arms "until you have obtained full and ample justice." So: "either deserting our country in the extremest hour of distress, or turning our arms against it, which is the apparent object, unless Congress can be compelled into instant compliance." "My God!" exclaimed Washington, "is the author of such proposals a friend of the army or of the country? Rather, is he not an insidious foe? Some emissary, perhaps from New York [where the British still were] plotting the ruin of both by sowing the seeds of discord and separation between the civil and military powers of the continent?" He reminded the officers of the burdens and problems of Congress; he appealed to their patriotism; he reiterated his sympathy with the reality of their grievances; he entreated them to rely on the justice of Congress and to do nothing which would besmirch the record of the American Revolutionary Army.

Having spoken perhaps 20 minutes, he pointedly withdrew, so that his presence might not intimidate them, and as though in testimony of his faith in their rectitude. The assembled officers were tremendously moved—Gen. Schuyler said "the whole assembly were in tears." A committee, headed by General Knox, was appointed to submit draft resolutions expressing the sense of the meeting. Two were brought in: One reported "unshaken confidence in the justice of Congress"; another expressed "abhorrence and disdain" of the "infamous proposals" in the Newburgh Addresses. The resolutions were adopted unanimously, even the putschists voting for their own condemnation!

Satisfactory solutions, which in effect did meet most of the demands of the officer and civilian creditors, were forthcoming from Congress and the army was successfully disbanded at the close of 1783. How very serious this matter was is indicated in what Hamilton wrote Washington on March 25, 1783. He declared his own complete sympathy with the creditor-claimants and reported that some officers still wanted to use force against Congress. He, himself, opposed this, but not on principle; he felt it had no chance of ultimate success because the country would not support it. The soldiers would not follow the officers, said Hamilton, and, "There would be no chance of success without having recourse to means that would reverse our revolution."

Because of certain failure, Hamilton opposed an effort at a coup: "I cannot myself enter into the views of coercion which some gentlemen entertain, for I confess could force avail, I should almost wish to see it employed."

Washington answered Hamilton, April 4, and admitted the existence of real grievances, the weakness of the central government and the need for reform in that regard, and the inefficiency, perhaps corruption, of many of the politicians. But, he emphasized that he viewed "with astonishment and horror" any suggestion of a forcible undoing of civilian power. The army, said its commander-in-chief, "is a dangerous instrument to play with," but with public sentiment being what it was, "the idea of redress by force, is too chimerical to have had a place in the imagination of any serious mind in this army."

The uproar aroused throughout the country, and the prohibitive laws and official resolutions of condemnation, aimed against the hereditary Society of Cincinnati, whose membership was confined to officers, showed how accurate both Hamilton and Washington were in their estimate of public opinion. Indeed, so intense was this opposition that at the Society's first convention, in 1784, its nature was at once changed—the hereditary feature was abolished, its funds were thereafter to be in the keeping of the various state legislatures, and it promised not to intervene, as a body, in politics.

IV

On April 11, 1783, Congress issued a proclamation formally announcing the end of the War of the Revolution; four days later it ratified the provisional Treaty of Paris. In the ensuing months the revolutionary units disbanded, and on November 3, 1783, Congress formally discharged all troops which had enlisted for the duration.

In December, 1783, the last British soldier was evacuated from the east coast (but not from several western frontier posts, of which more will be said in another place). Washington then made his way to Annapolis, where Congress was in session. On the way, he stopped at the treasury office in Philadelphia and left an itemized account of the official expenses incurred through the years of his generalship (they amounted to $64,315). Before Congress, he spoke with his usual brevity, concluding: "Having now finished the work assigned me, I retire from the great theater of action, and bidding an affectionate farewell to this august body, under whose orders I have so long acted, I here offer my commission and take my leave of all the employments of public life."

Congress' reply was delivered by its newly-elected President, Thomas Mifflin of Pennsylvania, formerly the Army's quartermaster-general and one who, in the past, had not been sparing in his criticisms of Washington. Mifflin's words were nobly eloquent and wonderfully true; undoubtedly he expressed the well-nigh unanimous sentiments of the American people when he said:

> The United States, in Congress assembled, receive, with emotions too affecting for utterance, the solemn resignation of the authority under which you have led their troops with success through a perilous and doubtful war. Called upon by your country to defend its invaded rights, you accepted the sacred charge before it had formed alliances, and while it was without friends or a government to support you. You have conducted the great military contest with wisdom and fortitude, invariably regarding the rights of the civil power through all disasters and changes.
>
> You have, by the love and confidence of your fellow-citizens, enabled them to display their martial genius, and transmit their fame to posterity.
>
> You have persevered till these United States, aided by a magnanimous king and nation, have been enabled, under a just providence, to close the war in freedom, safety, and independence, on which happy event we sincerely join you in congratulations.
>
> Having defended the standard of liberty in this new world; having taught a lesson useful to those who inflict and to those who feel oppression, you retire from the great theater of action with the blessings of your fellow-citizens; but the glory of your virtues will not terminate with your military command —it will continue to animate remotest ages.

Chapter X

England and the
Revolution

J O H N   A D A M S declared that a comprehensive history of the American Revolution would have to be a
"history of mankind during that epoch." Certain it is that an
understanding of British history during that epoch is necessary if
one is to understand the American victory.

During the reign of George III, until his defeat in the American Revolution, the government of England as reflected in Parliament was dominated by the Crown and the landed nobility. The
rising mercantile and especially industrial bourgeoisie, supported
by an increasingly articulate mass opinion, was challenging this
domination, but the domination is a fact.

I

In the England of George III, 29 out of 30 adult English men
did not vote; about 6,000 voters, throughout Great Britain, were
able to elect a majority of the Parliament. As Leslie Stephen
wrote, in his *History of English Thought in the 18th Century:*
"The House of Commons was at this time the object of popular
distrust instead of the organ of the popular will." Furthermore,
though it has become customary to deride the Revolutionists'
depiction of George III as a monarch misusing his enormous
power in order to establish a more fully personal tyranny, the

evidence suggests that it is the derision, not the depiction, which is in error.

Edward Channing, in the third volume of his *History of the United States* noted that the King had "purchased the balance of power in the House of Commons with the nation's money, and thus converted government responsible to the great families of England into government responsible to himself." At another point, Channing declared: "It is certain that the King by the use of national funds and the gift of places and pensions was able to keep a sufficient band of followers in the House of Commons from 1767 to 1781 to enforce his personal rule."

This conclusion is re-affirmed in the work of John Richard Alden, who finds that "especially after 1767," through corruption and bribery, "George III was able during several critical years to influence and eventually to dominate both Cabinet and Parliament." The King became, said the English historian, Reginald Coupland, "not only his own Prime Minister, not only the leader of his own political party, but also its chief whip, its organizer of victory at the polls."

Throughout the '60's and '70's, the King held in his pocket at least 200 Parliamentary seats, with members then in office for seven years. Unlike certain of his predecessors, George III did not seek to defy Parliament; rather, in unity with the landed elite, he succeeded in capturing Parliament.

Frank E. Manuel summarizes the most recent British historical studies on this point by declaring that they "show that about half of a typical mid-century House of Commons consisted of crown dependencies—ministers and civil servants, holders of civilian sinecures, court officials, army and navy officers, government contractors, and secret service pensioners. Of the other half, most were hand-picked representatives of the local gentry of the counties."

Certain historians—notably Sir Lewis Namier, and the late Eric Robson—have insisted that the King was actually upholding Parliamentary government and the powers of Parliament in refusing to accede to the colonial demands for greater self-government. Mr. Robson, for instance, declared: "The conflict with the American colonies was engaged in and conducted by George III

and his ministers to uphold the supremacy of Parliament at Westminster. It was this, rather than the rights of the Crown, which
was at stake."

This misses the point that the King, through the Court Party,
was the master of Parliament. The supremacy of Parliament in
the English governmental system having been established through
two revolutions, the King was seeking to reestablish monarchical
domination, in fact, by securing effective control over Parliament.
This he had done by the end of the 1760's, so that he saw the
American colonial revolt as one threatening not only the world
position of his Empire but also the internal political position of
parliamentary domination which he had secured.

II

Conversely, the opposition to the King, led by the newer English
bourgeoisie, which looked upon his activity as subversive of Parliament's independence and power, tended to view favorably the
American resistance and to consider the leaders of that resistance
as their political allies. Radical and reform movements appear
simultaneously in both England and America (and Ireland);
they have similar ideologies and programs; their leaders are in
frequent communication with each other; their literature invigor-
ates and guides both; and their organizational forms are highly
similar. It is frequently difficult to decide which has priority in
any particular argument or program or organizational form; it is
perfectly manifest that each gained strength from the other.

"Two poles of attraction began to appear," wrote A. L. Morton, the English Marxist historian, of this period,[1] "the imperial-
ism of the Court, Government and financiers, drawing to itself all
the privileged classes, and a new radicalism, at first aristocratic
and slightly cynical but later proletarian and genuinely revolutionary, drawing a mixed following of the dispossessed, the un-
privileged, and, in each generation, a host of those who saw in
the profession of radicalism a means of entering the ranks of the
privileged." Of "the first developments of English radicalism,"
Mr. Morton continued, "it had the closest connections" with the
American Revolution. Specifically, it is clear that if one omits the

strong opposition to the policy of George III that existed inside England, he cannot understand the American victory and the defeat of the King's policy.

Informed English contemporaries believed that important to the King's policy of suppressing the Americans was his desire to create thereby an effective military instrument for the overpowering of England and an inexhaustible source of revenue to make himself—supported by the landed aristocracy and the older trading bourgeoisie—master of a full treasury quite independent of the will of Parliament. There is good evidence, too, though not conclusive, that the King was not averse to forcing a war upon the Americans in order to make opposition to him at home appear treasonous and, through war-time fever, to make his grip over Parliament completely secure.

It is the link between the English and American radical movements which explains why it was a speech made in Parliament by Colonel Isaac Barré, in February, 1765 that christens the Americans, "Sons of Liberty." It explains why the South Carolina House of Commons, in 1770, remitted £1500 to the London Society for the Defense of the Bill of Rights, to help pay the debts of John Wilkes, persecuted leader of the English radical opposition. It explains the election of John Adams, in 1773, to membership in that same London Society. It explains the raising of funds by the Constitutional Society in England, to help the widows and orphans of the Americans slain at Lexington and Concord, with a leader of this Society, John Horne Tooke, sentenced to jail for seditious libel.

The tie between the American and English radical movements is exemplified not only in the person of Thomas Paine, as is well known, but also by the career of John Wilkes, leader of the latter. His correspondence with Americans of a political nature, goes back at least to 1758, and in the 1760's and 1770's he was in frequent contact with American radicals, especially those active in the Boston Sons of Liberty. Indicative is the letter to him, signed by a "Committee of the Sons of Liberty" of Boston (including John Adams, Joseph Warren and Benjamin Church) dated June 6, 1768, a few months after Wilkes' return to England from exile in France. One paragraph will sufficiently indicate its character.

That the British constitution still exists is our glory: feeble and infirm as it is, we will not despair of it— To a Wilkes much is already due for his strenuous efforts to preserve it. Those generous and inflexible principles which have rendered you so greatly eminent, support our claim to your esteem and assistance. To vindicate Americans is not to desert yourself.

It was the American effort, and the English effort, which together form the theme of mass-distributed pamphlets published in England, like Catherine Sawbridge Macaulay's *Address to the People of England, Scotland, and Ireland, on the Present Important Crises of Affairs,* and John Cartwright's, *American Independence, the Interest and Glory of Britain,* both issued in 1775.

Williams' *History of Modern Wales* (1950) makes the point that "it was the American War which developed a political awareness," and that "the first publication in Welsh of a purely political nature appeared in 1776 and was a translation by David Jones of Trefiw, of a pamphlet on the nature of the dispute in America."

Two leading Welsh dissenters who took militantly pro-American stands were Richard Price and David Williams. The work of Price will be discussed later; Williams, a friend of Franklin, published in 1782, *Letters on Personal Liberty,* which, defending the American Revolutionists, also went on to urge that Britain adopt universal male suffrage, annual parliaments, the payment of Members, complete publication of Parliamentary debates, and full freedom of the press.

Another outstanding Welsh defender of the American cause was Great Britain's most distinguished Orientalist, Sir William Jones. He also produced a pro-American pamphlet in 1782, *The Principles of Government in a Dialogue between a Scholar and a Peasant.* The publisher of this work, Jones' brother-in-law, William Davies Shipley, dean of St. Asaph, was prosecuted for seditious libel and defended by the great Sir Thomas Erskine. This trial dragged on for years and was finally won. In it Erskine established, in English jurisprudence, that which had been gained in the Zenger case—the right of the jury and not the court to determine whether or not a particular publication was libelous.

It was the Aldermen and the Lord Mayor of London—John

Wilkes, firm friend of the American cause and leader in the effort to democratize the English Parliament—who petitioned the King in 1775 to dismiss the Ministers oppressing the colonies. The government of London, said this petition, "declare our abhorrence of the measures which have been pursued, and are now pursuing, to the oppression of our fellow-subjects in America." These measures seek "to establish arbitrary power over all America." They have been passed into law "by the same fatal corruption which has enabled them [the Ministers] to wound the peace and violate the Constitution of this country." Such oppression in America concerns us in England not only because it stems from corruption at home, but also because "the liberties of the whole [Empire are] inevitably connected with those of every part." Hence, the petitioners cannot observe "without the greatest concern and alarm, the Constitution fundamentally violated in any part of your Majesty's Dominions." The petition continues with an enumeration of colonial grievances that could not have been more vehement had it been written by Samuel Adams, and it draws to a close with a scorching denunciation of Crown policy:

> Your petitioners are persuaded that these measures originate in the secret advice of men who are enemies, to your Majesty's title, and to the liberties of your people. That your Majesty's Ministers carry them into execution by the same fatal corruption which has enabled them to wound the peace and violate the Constitution of this country; thus they poison the fountain of public security, and render that body, which should be the guardian of liberty, a formidable instrument of arbitrary power.

This was the petition of the Lord Mayor and the Aldermen of the city of London, wherein lived one million of England's total of seven million people.

III

In February, 1776, there was published in London a pamphlet destined to have very nearly the instantaneous success of Paine's *Common Sense,* published in Philadelphia a month earlier. It was entitled, *Observations on the Nature of Civil Liberty, and the Justice and Policy of the War with America.* Before the year ended this pamphlet made its author, Richard Price, hitherto a divine and philosopher greatly respected by his peers but hardly a public figure, one of the most widely-known men in England and in America.

The phenomenal popularity, in Great Britain, of this pamphlet is again reflective of the profound dissatisfaction felt by most Englishmen with the war against America. Price's work was directly stimulated by political considerations—it was a defense of the Left wing of the Whig Party, then led by Lord Shelburne,[1] against that of the Right, led by Edmund Burke. On the American question—then, of course, to the fore—the Burke group embraced the Declaratory Act of 1766, which, it will be remembered, while repealing the Stamp Act, insisted upon the complete supremacy of Parliament over the colonies in every particular. The Shelburne group rejected this and replaced it with the idea of complete independence for the colonies in all internal affairs and a tie existing only in terms of preferential arrangements for intra-imperial trade. As a result, Price began by attacking the Declaratory Act and equating it with a policy of enslavement. "I defy anyone," he wrote, after quoting the Act, "to express slavery in stronger language."

Price went on to develop his concept of the "nature of civil liberty." The essence of civil liberty, he wrote, lay in the necessity of the government being "the creature of the people." The government must originate with them, must be conducted under their direction and must seek their happiness. The form of government is not of the greatest moment, wrote Price, so long as it retains the three basic features just enumerated.

In the objection to the Declaratory Act, in his definition of civil liberty and in his views as to taxes, laws and officials, Price was re-stating the fundamental position of the American Revolutionists.

Even more directly, he developed a general philosophical defense of revolution strikingly similar to that which was, six months later, to appear in the Declaration of Independence—even the language suggests Jefferson's document:

> Mankind are naturally disposed to continue in subjection to that mode of government, be it what it will, under which they

have been born and educated. Nothing rouses them to resistance but gross abuses, or some particular oppressions out of
the roads to which they have been used. And he who will examine the history of the world will find there has generally
been more reason for complaining that they have been too
patient than that they have been turbulent and rebellious.

Having defined civil liberty in terms redolent of the American
argument, and having defended revolutionary undertakings in
the broadest terms, Price went on to consider the specific rebellion that the British government was then seeking to suppress. He
did this as explicitly, not to say provocatively, as the English language allows:

> Our colonies in North America appear to be now determined
> to risk and suffer every thing, under the persuasion that Great
> Britain is attempting to rob them of that Liberty to which every
> member of society, and all civil communities, have a natural
> and unalienable right. The question, therefore, whether this is
> a reasonable persuasion, is highly interesting, and deserves the
> most careful attention of every *Englishman* who values Liberty,
> and wishes to avoid staining himself with the guilt of invading
> it.

Price's opinion was that the Americans were right in their
complaints and noble in their resistance; that efforts to repress
this resistance were oppressive and dangerous *to English liberty.*
"Had we nourished and favored America, with a view to commerce, instead of considering it as a country to be governed:
Had we, like a liberal and wise people, rejoiced to see a multitude
of free states branched forth from ourselves, all enjoying independent legislatures similar to our own . . . there is nothing so
great and happy we might not have expected."

In such a case, "The Liberty of America might have preserved
our Liberty; and under the direction of a patriot king or wise
minister, proved the *means* of restoring to us our almost lost
constitution."

That then, is the need, *for the sake of English liberty*—to establish a commonwealth of equals, to replace the concept of Empire,
with that of a unity of states "forming different *parts* of a *Kingdom.*" To try to maintain the unity of the Empire by force, and
to insist on superior and subordinate units thereof, is to destroy

civil liberty, wage unjust war and subvert the English Constitution. Price concluded: "An important revolution in the affairs of this kingdom seems to be approaching. If ruin is not to be our lot, all that has been lately done must be undone, and new measures adopted."

It is not surprising that this work was reprinted at once in Boston, New York, Philadelphia and Charleston and also published in Hartford and Boston newspapers, but it is highly instructive of the British state of affairs that it was issued in Edinburgh and Dublin, too, and in London went into 13 re-printings before the end of 1776!

It is this pamphlet which the great English radical and scientist, Joseph Priestley, forwarded to his very dear friend, Franklin. The delivery of the pamphlet with a covering letter, Priestley entrusted to Major Carleton, brother of the Governor of Quebec; that the Major executed his trust is clear since Franklin's acknowledgment exists.

In the covering letter (dated February 13, 1776), Priestley referred to Price's "most excellent pamphlet," which, he hoped, might "make some impression upon this infatuated nation." Priestley went on to record his fears that the British Administration would make reconciliation impossible, wherefore he thought "it is most probable you will be driven to the necessity of governing yourselves." In this case, he continued, "I hope you will have wisdom to guard against the rock that we have fatally split upon; and make some better provision for securing your natural rights against the incroachment of power, in whomsoever placed." Priestley concluded his communication to a leading rebel against his Monarch, by assuring him that the friends of American and British freedom remained staunch: "Our zeal in the good cause is not abated."

IV

Lafayette's participation in the American Revolution is universally known, but not so well known is his own statement as to what determined him on this course. A fellow-guest at a dinner given in Paris in 1775 by the Comte de Broglie was the Duke of

Gloucester, brother of George III. The young Lafayette was astonished to find in the Duke a friend of the American rebels; the strangeness of the man's position lent interest to his argument. Lafayette listened as the Duke "told of the treatment the American colonists had received, and spoke warmly of these patriots struggling for liberty," and forthwith resolved to join them.

Thomas William Coke, for 50 years the representative of Norfolk in Parliament, toasted George Washington, rather than King George, during the Revolution. Major Cartwright, a leading English radical, hung the Declaration of Independence in his dining room—and, in 1776, Nottingham presented him with the freedom of the city. The Patriotic Society of London sent a note to John Adams, addressed to the Continental Congress in Philadelphia (and duly published in *Lloyd's* newspaper, October 11-14, 1776):

> Your cause and ours is one and the same. The present Parliament of England, not being duly elected, has no right to make any laws, and consequently the people are not obliged to obey such as may be made by them. Be assured in us you will find every support in our power to give.

Charles James Fox, a leader of the Whig party, but not quite so far to the Left as Shelburne, wrote the following remarkable lines to a political ally, Lord Ossory, on June 24, 1776, soon after news had reached England that the Americans had been beaten in Canada:

> It will give the tools and Tories here such spirits as to make them insufferable. As to myself, you know little matters do not distress me much. I am still convinced the Americans will finally succeed, whether by victories or defeats; and if they do not . . . it will check all future enterprise to such a degree as to give the completest triumph to Toryism that it ever had. . . . Whatever happens for God's sake let us all resolve to stick by them [the Americans] as handsomely . . . in their adversity as we have done in their glory, and still maintain the Whig cause, however discredited by defeats, to be the only true principle for this country.

The idea of the identity between the Whig cause in England and the patriot cause in America could hardly be stated more clearly than in the above letter.

As the war progressed, bold statements by leading political figures opposed to its continuance were being made not only in private letters but in public addresses. Lord Chatham (the elder Pitt) himself, in one of his last speeches before his death, though opposed to granting independence to the Americans, nevertheless declared in the House of Lords in November, 1777—"In a just and necessary war, to maintain the rights and honor of my country, I would strip the shirt off my back to support it. But in such a war as this, unjust in its principle, impracticable in its means, and ruinous in its consequences, I would not contribute a single effort, or a single shilling."

By this time other powerful figures went as far or further than Pitt in their opposition to the war—Walpole, Lord Rockingham, the Duke of Richmond, General Conway, Sir George Savile, and many more. Even Edward Gibbon—with Samuel Johnson, one of the few Tory intellectuals, and as a member of Parliament from 1774 to 1783, bitterly opposed to the Americans—admitted by December, 1777, that in England there was "a universal desire for peace."

Horace Walpole, in March, 1778, affirmed his belief that the King deliberately provoked rebellion in the colonies so that they might be conquered by arms and subjected to complete tyranny. And, he went on, when America was subjugated, "the moment of the victorious Army's return [to England] would be that of the destruction of our liberty." For, he asked: "Would that Army, had it returned victorious, have hesitated to make the King as absolute as they had made him in America? Would they not let loose against the friends of liberty as mere rebels?" It is interesting that Frederick the Great of Prussia had expressed, in September, 1775, substantially the same views.

Fox, speaking in Parliament, on November 25, 1779, charged that the Court party, with its insistence on the American War, was driving England to destruction and its people to despair. He warned: "When a nation was reduced to such a state of wretchedness . . . the people would inevitably take up arms and the first characters in the Kingdom would be seen in their ranks."

This brought a delicate editorial warning from the Tory *Morning Post* of London, two days later: "Mr. Fox, in his parliamentary invocation to rebellion seems to strive as hard for a halter as any gentleman ever did in his desperate circumstances." Several other Members of Parliament—David Hartley for Hull, Henry Cruger, for Bristol, for example—spoke with equal sharpness in opposition to the Crown's War. By June, 1779, Sir William Meredith moved, in the House of Commons, an address in favor of ending the war in America. The motion was rejected, with Lord North's spine being stiffened by a personal note from the King, insisting that the American contest was "the most serious in which any country was ever engaged." American victory, wrote the King, June 11, 1779, would mean the beginning of the end of our colonial empire, "and this Island, reduced to itself, would be a poor Island indeed."

By 1780 the majority in Parliament expressed themselves as troubled by the undue increase of the influence of the Crown. In April, John Dunning (Lord Ashburton) introduced the famous resolution "that the influence of the Crown has increased, is increasing, and ought to be diminished"; it was adopted in Commons by a vote of 233-215. By 1781 even the landowners, vexed by rising taxes and convinced the Americans were never to be conquered, were bringing pressure on the North Ministry to terminate the conflict. With the dawn of 1782, Yorktown was history, France, Spain and Holland were at war with England, and five other powers had joined together in the anti-British "Armed Neutrality." Minorca and Gibraltar were beseiged, West Florida and the Bahamas had fallen to Spain, Tobago and several British posts in West Africa had been taken by the French, and rising popular discontent, primed by mounting unemployment, made power at home precarious. Hence, in February, 1782, the House by a large majority, adopted a motion renouncing all further efforts to subjugate the American colonies. Now British recognition of American independence awaited only the conclusion of diplomatic efforts.

V

The Whig-Tory split over the American Revolution, and the British Whig-American patriot alliance, manifested themselves in the British officer-corps, as well as in Parliament. It is probable that the influence of Whiggism in restraining the military ardor of the Howe brothers, in command of land and sea operations early in the American War, has been exaggerated. At any rate, as to the Howes, large doubts remain, but as to others, there is no doubt at all concerning their decided opposition to the War.

The late Eric Robson, who made a special study of the military aspects of the Revolution, as viewed from the British side, found that poor morale among officers and men was of great consequence in explaining the British defeat. He supplied convincing evidence that a large number of the British officers who fought in that war did so with, as one said, "uncertainty respecting the justice of their country's cause."

This uncertainty tended to increase with length of service in America, as the officers saw for themselves that the official picture of the rebellion as the work of a pernicious minority was quite false. Typical was the reaction of a young Scot officer, Sir James Murray: "As to the matter of right, if the Americans are convinced that it is more for the good of that country to be independent of Great Britain and at the same time are able to accomplish it, they are most indisputably in the right to make the attempt."

Perhaps of even greater moment was the large number of British officers who simply refused to participate in the war at all, and who, on refusing, publicly asserted their reasons. A few examples are in order.

Admiral Augustus Keppel flatly refused, on political grounds, to command ships in war upon America; court-martialed, he was defended by Thomas Erskine and won an acquittal. Lord Effingham, perhaps as well known in the Army service as Keppel was in the naval, took exactly the same stand. Lord Chatham refused to allow his son, the future Prime Minister, to fight against the Americans, and once again the political reasons for this decision were made public.

A final instance, among many possible examples, is that of Granville Sharp, grandson of the Archbishop of York, and son of the Archdeacon of Northumberland. By the time of Lexington, Sharp had earned some distinction as a scholar and considerable

fame as an Abolitionist, having been the main figure in getting
the Somersett case before Lord Chief Justice Mansfield, resulting,
in 1772, in the outlawry of slavery within England.

Sharp earned his living in the employ of the Ordnance Office;
by 1774 he had been promoted to assistant of the Secretary of
that Office. In this position, he directly processed the orders for
munitions with which to suppress the American rebels. In July,
1775, Sharp expressed his distaste for such employment to the
Secretary and was given leave for two months, by which time,
apparently, it was felt the American subversives would have been
overcome.

At the end of the leave, Sharp asked for its extension since, as
he said: "I cannot return to my ordnance duty whilst a bloody
war is carried on, unjustly as I conceive, against my fellow-subjects." Leave was extended a second time, and a third, but thereafter Ordnance required that he return or be dismissed.

The position was Sharp's sole means of livelihood, but he resigned. It is significant of public sentiment that he was applauded
for his act, and provided financial support by his two brothers,
William, the King's surgeon, and James, a successful iron-manu-
facturer.

VI

The political and intellectual turmoil that characterized the upper
circles of English society during the 18th century—reflected in
the Parliamentary struggles, debates among the literati, and disaffection among the officer corps—was the surface bubbling of a
more profound phenomenon. Herbert Butterfield speaks of the
"long, slow, and deep" movement of this era. He refers to it as
"a tide," which, "throughout the century is bringing wider classes
of Englishmen to intellectual awareness and a realization of the
part they might play in politics." He sees "the advance in education, the spread of literature, and the growth of towns" as "chang-
ing the character of the world itself." Basic was the fact that:
"Greater masses of people were being brought by various means
to a consciousness of their importance, a sense of their public

rights, a habit of local self-help and an interest in the destiny of their nation."

The stability of the British Crown itself was at question, because of *internal* challenge, at the very moment that the integrity of the British Empire was being attacked on the American mainland. George III was seeking to suppress American rebellion, the better to keep his control over Parliament; the success of that rebellion would cost him that control. At the same time those who would contest that control, in England, had to change the character of Parliament. That change would destroy this particular King's strangle-hold and would assure that no future Monarch achieved the same power again.

By no means all the opposition to the King, both in America and in England, wanted it to go so far as it did; but once set in motion the process could not be halted short of independence on the one hand, and supremacy by a reformed Parliament on the other. And, as we have indicated, the two movements were intertwined and were themselves part of a world-wide movement—the achievement of hegemony by the bourgeoisie and the growth of democracy.

The efforts of Pitt and Townshend, during the Seven Years' War (1757-63), to create a national militia in England met with tremendous resistance, and armed outbreaks in the rural area required the employment of Regular troops for their suppression. With the end of that war and mass demobilization, unemployment and hunger appeared. The political expression of mass discontent was the John Wilkes movement. Three times elected to Parliament and each time unseated, exiled and, in 1764, outlawed by the King, he was the popular idol of the English population. He was, too, precious to the Americans.

By 1767 England was on the verge of civil war—sailors mutinied, seamen, hatters, weavers were on strike. Benjamin Franklin, from London, wrote on May 14, 1768 (four days after soldiers had killed six strikers and wounded many) that there were:

> mobs patrolling the streets at noonday, some knocking all down that will not roar for Wilkes and liberty; courts of justice afraid to give judgement against him; coal-heavers and porters pulling

down the houses of coal merchants that refuse to give them more wages; sawyers destroying sawmills; sailors unrigging all the outward-bound ships and suffering none to sail till the merchants agree to raise their pay; watermen destroying private boats and threatening bridges.

It was not only American papers that were filled with reports of Liberty clubs and insubordinate political demands. Here, as a typical instance, is the *Leeds Intelligencer,* December 14, 1773, reporting that in Yorkshire

> Farmers' Clubs in several towns of the East Riding of the county have formed themselves into an association under the title of the Liberty Club . . . the fundamental law of the society is to unite in future elections in support of such candidates as will engage to promote short parliaments, and the abolition of tithes.

"Tis a time of most licentious and plentiful abuse of all persons of eminence among us, whether in or out of power," wrote the Earl of Malmesbury in October, 1765. "Where this humour may stop, God only knows," he went on, and: "The American example will certainly operate strongly with our common people."

During the war itself, as Parliamentary opposition to the King grew, mass unrest mounted. This unrest impeded the full mobilization of English strength against the Americans. Much of the unrest took organized forms reflecting American influence; and the program of these mass movements often included, explicitly, support of the American cause.

The internal disaffection revealed itself in the difficulties of recruiting that Lord North was forced to admit by 1776. Efforts to supplement recruiting—such as attempts to enlist Irish Roman Catholics and to place foreigners individually in British regiments—were unsuccessful. This was of prime importance in explaining the British King's strong, though futile, efforts to purchase cannon-fodder from Catherine of Russia, and his buying several thousand "Hessians" from various petty German principalities.

The disaffection showed itself in the '70's, as in the '60's, in long and bloody strikes, notably the textile machine-wrecking struggles near Manchester in September and October, 1779.

Thousands, armed with scythes and crude guns, were involved and the military was used to suppress the outbreak, with several killed and scores wounded.

In Parliament, beginning at the latest in 1772, proposals were introduced seeking fundamental reforms—annual elections; widening the suffrage; paying members; the exclusion of pensioners and placemen. With these invariably went defenses of the popular struggles in America and Ireland.

This struggle for Parliamentary reform reached its climax in 1779 in the so-called Yorkshire Agreement—"the first presentation of this issue on a genuinely national scale," as Butterfield declares.

In June, 1780, occurred the insurrection known as the Gordon Riots. Here the masses expressed their unwillingness to endure intolerable burdens in a misguided (possibly provoked) anti-Catholic outbreak. Scores of thousands rebelled against all constituted authority in several cities of England, but the main uprising was in London. For days, the insurrectionists could not be suppressed, though the King had invoked martial law. Only with great difficulty and much bloodshed was the outbreak curbed, and for weeks thereafter the gallows claimed dozens of victims, including women and children.

These events had the greatest influence in forcing the overthrow of the North ministry—with the House finally voting, February 27, 1782, for an end to the war against America, and with Lord North resigning a month later.

Professor Coupland has written truly: "The fact that the collapse of George III's system of government was due to the 'disgraces and reverses' of the American War is one of the most certain facts in history." Richard Price began his work, *Observations on the Importance of the American Revolution and the Means of Making it a Benefit to the World,* published in London, in 1785, (reprinted the same year in Trenton, New Jersey) with these words: "Britons themselves will be the greatest gainers [by the Revolution] if wise enough to improve properly the check that has been given to the despotism of their ministers and to catch the flame of virtuous liberty which has saved their American brethren."

With some temporary reverses, related to England's role during the French Revolution and the Napoleonic era, the impetus towards governmental reform in England associated with the roots of the American Revolution and greatly stimulated by the Revolution's victory, did go forward to notable, if still incomplete, achievements.

A feature of historical writing that appears to contradict what has been developed in the preceding pages must be noted. The consensus among those historians who have expressed an opinion as to the sympathy of the majority of the people of England is, with rare exceptions—notably that of John Richard Alden—that this majority was hostile to the American cause and favored the war's prosecution by the King. However, specific studies of the British press—highly distorted mirrors of mass opinion, it is true—as those by Hinkhouse and Clark, support the idea of the widespread unpopularity of the American War in England. And most certainly, the history of English politics during the years of the Revolution makes clear that there was considerable doubt as to the wisdom and justice of that war. Also, it seems certain that at the latest by 1780 the war was strongly disliked by the overwhelming majority of the English population. This lack of support was of great importance in explaining the American victory.

The unity between the English and American opponents of George III is demonstrated not only in the service the former performed in the latter's victory; it is shown too in the fact that the American radical victory assured English radical victory. Professor A. L. Burt put this very well. The Americans, he wrote, "by wresting liberty from Britain . . . also confer [red] it upon her." The failure of the King's policy in America, he continued, "broke his power in Britain." The American war, "shattered George III's system of personal direction and control, and it freed parliament." The King, wrote Burt, "continued to reign [but] he could no longer rule, nor could any of his successors." Now when North fell and Rockingham became the Prime Minister, he did so only with the regal understanding that certain important parliamentary reforms would be introduced to insure independence from and supremacy over the Crown.[2] This prior agreement in itself constituted an unprecedented restriction upon the King's veto power; it heralded also, as Richard Pares has observed, that henceforth "change of Ministry became inseparable from reversal of policy," *i.e.,* a foreshadowing of the 19th century's two-party system.

Chapter XI

The British Empire and the Revolution

BRITAIN'S OPPRESSION OF Ireland preceded and exceeded that visited upon her American colonies. The revolutionary movements in both areas were closely interwined and each profoundly affected the other. Thus it is that the work of William Molyneux, first published in 1698, *The Case of Ireland's Being Bound by Acts of Parliament in England*, was reprinted in both England and America, in 1776, as part of the tripartite—Irish, American, English—effort to reform England at home and revolutionize her imperial features.

Again, Granville Sharp in 1775 published a study called *Declaration of the Rights of the People to a Share in Legislation* which was directed against the disfranchisement of the Irish, and which, through the activities of his Pennsylvania comrade-in-arms against the slave trade, Anthony Benezet, became widely known in America. In America, of course, Sharp's arguments were applied to the local scene and became part of the freedom movement. This relationship unquestionably strengthened Sharp's resolve, which we have already noticed, not to assist the King's efforts to suppress the American rebellion.

I

We have also noted Lord Effingham's refusal of a military command against the Americans; it is instructive that, in the summer

160

of 1775, the city of Dublin officially voted Effingham its thanks for his steadfastness in the cause of liberty. Further indication of joint support of revolutionary efforts, with rather ironic overtones, came in the assistance which both Irishmen and Americans gave to Pasquale Paoli, Corsican patriot, and leader of the rebellion against French rule in 1768. In 1769 he was exiled to England and while there became a part of the English-Irish-American radical movement.

American resistance to the Stamp Act of 1765 found active sympathy and support in Ireland, while its repeal, in 1766, in the Declaratory Act brought pointed reminder to the Irish that its provisions affirming the supremacy of the English Parliament over America, were a word-for-word copy of the Declaratory Act of 1719 affirming the same thing but having Ireland as its object.

Thereafter as the revolutionary situation ripened in America, it developed in Ireland, too; regular correspondence developed between the leaders of each. It was typical, for example, that one of the first people to whom the Boston Town Meeting sent word of the Boston Massacre in 1770, was Charles Lucas in Dublin, a leader of the Irish radicals.

Benjamin Franklin, apostle of the American Cause, came to Ireland in 1771. He visited the hamstrung Irish Parliament twice, admitted each time to the floor as a mark of respect and regard, and actively informed himself of the details of Irish politics, while in turn making friends for America. Carl Van Doren, in his biography of Franklin, remarked that "the Americans looked to Ireland for support in their conflict with the English Parliament." He continued:

> The Irish were watching America. They too had long endured the repressive regulation of their trade by England. They too claimed the right to make their own laws and lay their own taxes. If the Americans held out, Ireland would be encouraged and benefited. If the Americans lost, Ireland would lose with them.

Meanwhile, during the early 1770's the first major wave of Irish immigration came to America; from 1770 to 1775 about 50,000 Irish arrived. This served to make quite palpable the tie between American and Irish unrest under English domination.

The Irish masses were overwhelmingly pro-American. "All Ireland was America mad," wrote Horace Walpole in 1776.

In Ireland itself conditions were intolerable. Though 90 percent of the population was Roman Catholic, no one of that faith was allowed to vote or to hold office; they were forbidden schools of their own. Poyning's Law, dating back to 1495, had put all legislative power into the possession of the English Parliament, and this situation prevailed unchanged for almost 300 years. Ireland was forced to maintain an army of 12,000 men—increased to 15,000 by the Augmentation Act of 1769—and yet no Catholic was permitted to hold an Army commission. The land was possessed by a handful of owners, many of them absentee Englishmen, rents were ruinous, trade was regulated by and for England, and Catholics were forbidden to purchase land. Meanwhile pensions and patents were granted English residents that totalled enormous sums and further ground down the peasantry. From 1763 to 1765 Irish pensions were increased £150,000; their total far exceeded the whole sum England obtained through taxing the thirteen American colonies.

Terrorism and rebellion were rife. Veritable civil war, led by the "Whiteboys," prevailed in Catholic Ireland from 1761 to 1771, and the repression by the English was fierce; in 1763 the "Oakboys'" uprising and in 1771, the "Steelboys'" rebellion, occurred in the Protestant North. A literature of protest appeared. Among the earlier and certainly the best known of these were the writings of the great satirist, Jonathan Swift, whose *Proposal for the Universal Use of Irish Manufactures* (1720), *Drapier Letters* (1724), and *Modest Proposal for Preventing the Children of Poor People from being a Burden to their Parents or their Country* (1729)—by fattening them up and then using them as food—were all blasts at English tyranny over Ireland, and simultaneously, had a considerable impact on American opinion.

By the time of George III's accession (1760), the Protestant middle class and landowners in Ireland began insistently to demand certain basic rights exercised by propertied Englishmen—the right to habeas corpus, security of tenure for judges, Irish parliamentary control over the army, a Parliament of regularly limited duration (seven years was most often suggested) rather than one which continued throughout one monarch's reign (the Parliament in existence before George III had sat without elections for 33 years).

Of these demands only the last was granted prior to the American Revolution; the Octennial Act was passed in 1768 limiting the life of the Irish Parliament to eight years. It is with the election first held under this act, in 1776, that Henry Grattan entered the Parliament; so consequential a member was he to be that for the next 15 years the Irish governing body was known as Grattan's Parliament.

This Parliament, as the late Professor Falkiner wrote, "was in no real sense of the word a representative institution"; rather it was "filled with the nominees of absentee noblemen." The members—landlords, placemen and Protestants—constituted a legislative assembly that was quite "aristocratic in its sympathies."

Nevertheless, though this body represented only the Protestant minority of an overwhelmingly Catholic country and only the well-to-do minority of a terribly impoverished land, it was the representative of a colonially-enthralled bourgeoisie. As such it resented the efforts of the English king to enhance his power— which George III tried in Ireland, as in America and in England —and it sought a greater degree of power for itself. It raised as a body, therefore, two main demands: (1) free trade rather than English mercantilist regulation;[1] (2) full power of the Irish Parliament to legislate freely in all matters pertaining to Ireland. To these basic demands, Grattan himself and some of his closest followers added a desire for some Catholic relief, but this was not true of the majority of the Parliament.

The independence-seeking Irish Protestant bourgeoisie completely and openly identified their cause with that of the Americans and they frankly sought to use the war's debilitating and embarrassing impact upon England to further their own efforts. The decisive impetus to their efforts came with the American-French Alliance and the consequent fear of a French invasion of Ireland. This danger, given the war against America, could be met only by raising an army in Ireland. Exactly that was done with the coming into being of The Volunteers beginning in Belfast early in 1778. By 1779, there were 42,000 men in arms throughout Ireland, by 1780 perhaps as many as 80,000; this was a national volunteer army, not a militia, and hence not under government control. Its members were all Protestant, the officers well-to-do, the rank and file merchants, tradesmen, professionals —"the armed property of the nation," as Grattan put it.

As the months passed and French invasion did not transpire, the Volunteers did not disband, but turned their armed might openly in support of Grattan's demands. This was re-inforced by the Irish adapting the American non-importation tactic. By 1780 Irish trade restrictions were lifted and while in that same year Grattan's resolution for the complete sovereignty of the Irish Parliament was rejected, and was again in 1781, it won unanimous approval in the Irish Parliament in 1782 and grudging and somewhat partial acquiescence from England. To show further the American influence, this act was called by Grattan, Ireland's Declaration of Independence.

The Volunteers no doubt could have pressed on to achieve full and complete independence for Ireland, but this would have endangered their own supremacy at home since it would have emboldened the Catholic majority. The Volunteer leaders, having obtained free trade and their own Parliament's (relative) supremacy, sought no further innovations; such efforts thereafter were to come in the 1798 uprising led by Wolfe Tone.

Wolfe Tone characterized the Revolution of 1782 in this manner:

> The Revolution of 1782 was a Revolution which enabled Irishmen to sell at a much higher price their honor, their integrity, and the interests of their country; it was a Revolution which, while at one stroke it doubled the value of every borough-munger in the kingdom left three-fourths of our countrymen the slaves it found them, and the government of Ireland in the base and wicked, and contemptible hands of those who had spent their lives in degrading and plundering her. . . . The power remained in the hands of our enemies.

Such an evaluation represents the partial truth of a devoted and bitter contemporary revolutionist. The Revolution of 1782 certainly was limited, but it quite as certainly marked a sufficient breakaway from English domination over Ireland to merit the description "Revolution"; and to make clear its organic connection with the whole history of the Irish national revolution. The tie between the American Revolution and this Irish Revolution is direct and plain.

II

As we have already observed, French possession of Canada was widely understood to be a deterrent to aspirations for American independence. Similarly, contemporaries expressed the opinion, after the Treaty of 1763, that British ownership of Canada would encourage separatist tendencies.

The rulers of Great Britain were not unaware of this danger. George III's policy of absorbing the power of Parliament at home was coordinated with his policy of strengthening the imperial control of the thirteen colonies; and his policy *vis-á-vis* Canada was to use that northern colony as a club for the retention of the thirteen. Subversion in the south was to be curbed by reaction in the north.

Though the Treaty of 1763 annexing Canada had promised representative assemblies and traditional English rights (such as already existed in Nova Scotia, for example), the promise was never implemented prior to the American Revolution. On the contrary, the promise was repudiated by the Quebec Act of 1774 where such an assembly and such rights were explicitly denied. The failure to implement the promise, and its repudiation after a dozen years, were in accordance with the warning of the Governor of Quebec, Sir Guy Carleton, in a letter to Shelburne, January 20, 1768: "The British form of government, transplanted into this Continent, never will produce the same fruits as at home. . . . A popular assembly, which preserves its full vigor, and in a Country where all men appear nearly upon a level, must give a strong bias to republican principles." The results, continued Carleton, were "uncontrollable notions" and the "independent spirit of a Democracy."

Carleton intended to base the stability of his rule on the support of the great landowners and of the Catholic hierarchy; he sought, as Professor McInnis has written, "on this oligarchical foundation to establish a firm system of aristocratic rule."

At the same time, the royal purpose of making Canada not only a center of reaction, but a military bastion from which to help suppress disorder to the south, is clear. The projection of this purpose is plain in the correspondence of Carleton, whose ideas, the King declared, had his "full concurrence." Writing to General Gage, February 15, 1767, the Quebec Governor declared:

> The more I consider the state of affairs on this Continent, more and stronger reasons present themselves, and I am the more convinced, it is not only expedient, but indispensably necessary for the interest of Great Britain and His Majesty's service, not only to keep these in good repair, but to erect a proper Place of Arms near the town of New York, and a Citadel in or near the town of Quebec. . . . They will facilitate the transport of ten or fifteen thousand men in the beginning of a war, from the one to the other, as the circumstances require.

Such a "Place of Arms" and "Citadel" could "properly curb and overawe" discontents; moreover New York and Quebec, so prepared and interlocked could serve, if needed, to "separate the Northern from the Southern colonies" and would "afford an easy and advantageous opportunity for transporting His [Majesty's] Forces into any part of this Continent, and may prevent the greatest of all inconveniences, delay and loss of time in the beginning of a war."

Having thus anticipated, to a large degree, that which ten years later, matured into the plan for the Burgoyne Campaign, Carleton, on November 20, 1768, anticipated the entry a decade later of France into British intra-imperial conflicts, and suggested a key role for Canada.

> Should France begin a war in hopes the British colonies will push matters to extremities, and she adopts the project of supporting them in their independent notions, Canada, probably, will then become the principal scene, where the fate of America may be determined. . . . Your Lordship must immediately perceive the many disadvantages Great Britain would labour under in a war of this nature; and on the other hand, how greatly Canada might for ever support the British interests on this Continent, for it is not united in any common principle, interest or wish with the other Provinces, in opposition to the Supreme-seat of Government.

The Crown's motive and tactic in connection with Canada—to retain the thirteen colonies and to check subversion with reaction —are vividly illustrated in the Quebec Act of 1774, whose provisions we have previously described. That Act, by tripling the area of Quebec at the expense of the northwestern zone of the thirteen colonies, preserving semi-feudal land tenure, denying representative government, and extending the area dominated by an established Roman Catholic Church, had the effect of surrounding castrated colonies with a desert of reactionary institutions.

This act did serve to bind the seigneurial aristocracy and the Church hierarchy to the Crown, and it did tend to placate the national and religious fears of the 70,000 French-Canadian peasants. But in confirming those peasants to a life of feudalistic deprivation—from which since 1763 the had sought relief—it did not win their ardor, and in challenging the American colonists geographically, affronting them ideologically and threatening them economically, it earned their passionate disapproval.

William Knox, undersecretary to the Secretary for American Colonies, in arguing for the Quebec Act and justifying its unprecedented measures relative to the Catholic Church, insisted that the French Canadians would be "a security against the insurgents of the other parts of America for in a case of emergency a force can easily be raised from thence." Burke, on the other hand, speaking for the Opposition, warned that the 1774 Act was "meant to be both an instrument of tyranny to the Canadians, and an example to others of what they have to expect; at some time or other it will come home to England." "Canada," Burke continued, "will become a dangerous instrument in the hands of those who wish to destroy English liberty in every part of our possessions." With this Act, said Barré, "The Americans will look on the Canadians as their task-masters, and, in the end, their executioners."

American oppositionists reacted as did their English comrades. Thus, Alexander Hamilton saw "two great purposes" in the Quebec Act: "First, the subjugation of the colonies and afterwards that of Great Britain itself."

The Crown policy did win the active support of the large land-owners and the Catholic hierarchy during the Revolutionary crisis, but it did not gain the favor of the peasants who, of course, formed the vast majority of the population, nor of the English merchants, a class of some consequence in the towns of Quebec and Montreal. The merchants in these cities, inhibited by imperial regulations, and socially and politically disadvantaged by the semi-feudal regime, joined New Englanders in setting up Committees of Correspondence and, when the Port Act closed Boston, sent relief supplies, even as did New York and Philadelphia.

In February, 1775, the Boston Committee of Safety wrote to the Montreal Committee expressing thanks for past aid, and urging a more active policy of opposition on the part of the Northerners. To this the Committee, composed of merchants, replied April 28, 1775, assuring the Bostonians that their own dearest wish was "to prosper your righteous cause, which alone will free us from those jealous fears and apprehension that rob us of our peace." Yet, they did not feel able to do more than they had done for, "you will please to bear in mind, that not only those who hold the helm of government, but also all those who make wealth or ambition the chief objects of their pursuit, are professedly your enemies." But, concluded the Montrealers, "the bulk of the people, both English and Canadians, are of quite contrary sentiments; and wish well to your cause."

This estimate of general Canadian feeling towards the American cause would appear to be accurate. Yet there was a sharp division between the English-speaking merchants and the French Canadian masses which was not narrowed by the arrogant racism and anti-Catholicism of the former. There seems to have been more than a grain of truth to the complaint of the first Governor of Quebec, made in 1764, concerning "a set of free British merchants, as they are pleased to style themselves," who, eager for "great gain," considered "themselves superior in rank and fortune to the soldier and the Canadian, deeming the first voluntary and the second born slaves." This chauvinism tended to throw the peasantry back towards officialdom which, at any rate, pursued a policy of respect for their religion and their national origin.

Thus, while the merchants tended to a keen dissatisfaction with the political and economic limitations of Canadian quasi-feudalism, and while the peasants who bore the brunt of the burdens of that system were anxious to throw them off, what Professor Gillis well calls "the condescending arrogance of the traders" helped prevent the achieving, for some time, of unity.

Fundamental, also, to the limited support given the American cause by the Canadian merchant class was its numerical insignificance. According to Governor Murray there were, in 1764, about 200 Protestant householders in the towns of Montreal and Quebec taken together; at the same time, while the French-Canadians also were few, they did number some 70,000, throughout the Province.

Furthermore, while British conquest of Canada had resulted in severe blows to French merchants and fur-traders, it was clear to their English class-brothers in Quebec that if they actively associated themselves with the southern rebels and, especially, if they joined with them in their economic reprisals aimed at England, they would lose their favored position in exploiting the riches of Canada. Thus it is that while John Brown, the agent sent by Massachusetts in 1774 to Canada for the purpose of estimating the situation and winning support, did report early the next year a very considerable sympathy among Canadian merchants for the rebels, he also reported that they would not fully join the movement and would not send delegates to the Continental Congress. "The difficulty," he reported, early in 1775, to the Boston Committee of Correspondence, "consists in this; should the English join in the non-Importation agreement, the French would immediately monopolize the Indian trade."

The fact is, too, that the merchants of the St. Lawrence were developing their own economy, largely based on the fur trade, and very much more dependent upon London, than upon the Atlantic seaboard. Hence, as Professor Creighton has written, "Union with the Americans would at once submerge the identity of Quebec in a general American federation and cut the vitally necessary economic relations with England; and these consequences were inimical to every interest of the northern commercial state."

The result of the merchants' resentments against British officialdom on the one hand and divergence of interest from the Americans on the other was a sort of cagey and precarious neutrality on
their part during the conflict itself. There were exceptions, especially insofar as a small number did rather actively side with the
Americans, and, of course, the policy of neutrality was viewed as
one of hostility by a British officialdom facing actual war and
invasion. Nevertheless, on the whole, the American rebels were
disappointed in the lack of enthusiastic support and concrete help.

The divergence of interests appeared sharply when, in 1775,
the Americans captured Montreal and immediately imposed a
trade blockade with the West, in the interests, of course, of hurt-
ing the British. This, however, provoked anguished opposition
from the merchants, and though the blockade was withdrawn in
1776 at the suggestion of the Carroll Commission[2] this came too
late and, with the British re-conquest of the city, was in any case
academic.

The colonial officialdom, the ecclesiastical hierarchy and the
seigneurs were united in desiring that the southern rebels be
crushed, the Canadian *habitants* be spared infection, and that
Quebec have the glory not only of preserving herself for His
Majesty but also of helping decisively in preserving the thirteen
colonies for him.

On the other hand, the vast majority of the French-Canadian
population was distinctly hostile to the reactionary and repressive
purposes and actions of the ruling groups. Their feeling towards
the American Revolutionists was sympathetic, but ambivalent
since the Catholic religion had been denounced with great viru-
lence, in Congress' "Address to the People of Great Britain,"
issued in October, 1774—a religion, said the Address in protesting the Quebec Act, "that has deluged our island in blood, and
dispersed impiety, bigotry, persecution, murder, and rebellion
throughout every part of the world." The suspicion and hostility
such phrases would naturally evoke among Canadian Catholics
were not likely to be effectively overcome by the soothing words
in Congress' "Address to the Inhabitants of the Province of Quebec," which, following the other by five days, hailed religious
tolerance, and cited the example of the Swiss Confederacy, where

Catholic and Protestant states were united, as proof that Quebec
would do well to join the thirteen colonies.

Mason Wade sums up the situation very well:

> The double-faced attitude of the Congress, which denounced
> Catholicism in England and praised freedom of conscience in
> Quebec, destroyed much of the effectiveness of its appeal, but
> nonetheless the new gospel of the *Bostonnais* caught the ear of
> the Quebec masses, who did not welcome a return to the old
> system of feudal dues and obligations.

Moreover, while the English merchants of Quebec feared a
submergence of their budding economy within that of the thirteen
colonies should Canada become the Fourteenth, so did the French
masses of Quebec fear the destruction of their own rather rudimentary sense of nationality by the same eventuality. It is the
opinion of the distinguished French-Canadian historian, Gustave
Lanctot, that such an awareness of distinctive nationality was
present by the 1760's. Professor Lanctot has written:

> At the time of the [English] Conquest, despite her small
> population of some 70,000, French Canada possessed all the
> essential elements, economic and cultural, of a political com-
> munity different from that of the mother country, and even
> tending to throw off useless colonial restrictions. This people
> stood almost ready to assert its right to a separate nationality
> in America, distinctively French and Roman Catholic, evolving
> towards a particular destiny.

These facts explain the rather restrained, somewhat benevo-
lently neutral attitude that the mass of French-Canadians took to
the American visitors. Altogether wrong, though regrettably common, is the opinion, to quote the chauvinist writing of one U. S.
historian, Carl Wittke, that:

> The simple-minded French-Canadian *habitant* had little un-
> derstanding of the issues involved and no desire to run after the
> American goddess of liberty who, his clergy taught him, was
> after all of rather doubtful divinity.

III

It is doubtful even if the Canadian populace had supported most
actively the American Revolutionists that it would have been

possible for Canada to be freed, at that time, from British domination. But, while historical literature has concentrated on this failure, it has tended to ignore the fact that Britain's effort to use Canada as a base from which to suppress the Revolution failed. That latter failure was due, very largely, to the benevolent neutrality of the Canadian populace and to their decided hostility against serving as taskmasters for the Crown.

The hostility was displayed despite strong measures taken by State and Church. In June, 1775, Governor Carleton declared martial law, and at about the same time the Bishop of Quebec announced that rebels and their sympathizers were to be excommunicated. Somewhat later, in response to British orders that he raise 6,000 troops in Canada, Carleton imposed compulsory military service for all men from 16 through 60.

The conscription was everywhere evaded and, in some places, forcibly resisted. The peasants declared that military service, once owing the seigneurs, had ceased with the Treaty of 1763 and they therefore held Carleton's unilateral conscription act to be illegal. They simply refused to be drafted and instead of 6,000 troops, Carleton could barely enroll a Canadian militia numbering 300— a few hundred *less* than the number of Canadians who joined the American forces. In several places—Terrebonne, Vercheres, Berthier—there were actual revolts against mobilization; in other areas, the seigneurs were driven away. Elsewhere, as Trois Rivieres, the Canadian militia, finally embodied, refused to march against the Americans. The few hundred Indians and Canadians who did set out with Burgoyne on his fateful campaign of 1777-78, deserted at their first opportunity.

While Carleton had told his London superiors in 1767 that Canada "could send into the field about eighteen thousand men," he neglected to consider that while the men might be "sent," they also might refuse to go. Certainly, that is what happened during the American Revolution, and so ten years later (May 29, 1777) Carleton wrote to Burgoyne:

> If Government laid any great stress upon assistance from the Canadians for carrying on the present war, it surely was not upon information from me. . . . These people had been governed with too loose a Rein for many years and had imbibed

too much the American spirit of Licentiousness and Independence administered by a numerous and turbulent Faction to be suddenly restored to a proper and desirable subordination.

At one time Carleton thought he could get 18,000 Canadians into the army; at another he was ordered to raise 6,000; he succeeded in enlisting 300 far from ardent fighters. Had this not been so, had instead several thousand Canadian men joined Burgoyne and fought with him, it is hard to see what the American forces would have been able to do to prevent the juncture of Clinton and Burgoyne. Thus it came about that Isaac Barré was mistaken when he prophesied that, "The Americans will look on the Canadians as their task-masters, and, in the end, their executioners." The prophecy did not come true though British imperial policy sought to realize it. To a considerable extent it was the courageous refusal of the "simple-minded French Canadian *habitant*" so to be used that defeated the policy and helped save the American Revolution.

IV

The success of the American Revolution brought a Whig government to London. That government listened with considerable sympathy to the demands of the English traders in Montreal and Quebec City for a more representative form of government. These demands, of ancient vintage, were reinforced by the petitions and memorials seeking the same reform that came from the perhaps 50,000 Loyalist exiles who settled in British North America— about 28,000 in Nova Scotia, the remainder in Canada.

There was, however, a pull in the opposite direction upon the British government. That government, Whig or Tory, sought to enhance the interests of the ruling groups in England and to protect the country's strategic interests. These considerations led the British authorities to tread lightly and move slowly in granting reforms or making changes. This restraining influence was reinforced by those in authority—and they were numerous—who held, with the Chief Justice of Quebec, William Smith (formerly Chief Justice of New York), that, "All America was abandoned to democracy." The policy of delay was strongly reinforced with

the outbreak of the French and the Irish Revolutions which induced a reactionary course in imperial policy.

Nevertheless, changes of considerable importance were produced following the American Revolution, in Canadian political
development. The tactic pursued by England was to subdivide
her North American possessions into as many administrative units
as possible and to provide reforms that nevertheless maintained
an authoritarian, anti-democratic nature in these units.

As a result, and in the face of the post-Revolutionary influx,
separate colonial administrations were set up for Cape Breton
Isle, Prince Edward Island, New Brunswick (split away from
Nova Scotia), Nova Scotia, and Upper Canada (Ontario) and
Lower Canada (Quebec). Typical of the political content of
these administrative moves was the Act of 1791 establishing
Lower (French) Canada and Upper (English) Canada. In each
case a legislative council and assembly were provided, with the
Council appointed by the Governor, and with the members of
the Assembly elected on the basis of a franchise limited very
severely by property qualifications.

Yet, these severe limitations are not to obscure the fact that
th Act of 1791 did provide a legislative form of government, thus
fulfilling the Whig pledge "to give Canada a free constitution in
the British sense of the word." Further, the suffrage was limited
by property qualifications, but not by religious tests, thus establishing the principle of Catholic enfranchisement—a step taken
in 1789 by Nova Scotia.

V

In none of the English-American colonies outside the Thirteen,
did the British find such loyalty as to be of any significant
assistance in suppressing the rebellion. The attitude of the
approximately 17,000 inhabitants of Nova Scotia in 1775 was
summarized by John B. Brebner in the title of his definitive study,
The Neutral Yankees of Nova Scotia (1937). This colony,
sparsely settled, largely without roads, with only a rudimentary
consciousness of any kind of solidarity, nearly surrounded by
water (hence dominated by British naval power), with the
economy of its chief town, Halifax, dependent upon London,

could not mount any effective protest movement against England.

On the other hand, most of its inhabitants were newcomers from New England with very strong family and political ties thereto; this made natural a warm sympathy for the rebels. Further, the colonial status had induced ill-will towards the North ministry in Nova Scotia.

The result was a certain amount of popular demonstrations against the British, including arson directed at military supplies, and a refusal to respond to an effort at conscription. So general was this refusal, in fact, that the colonial officials put the best possible face on the matter by announcing that the militia would not be asked to leave Nova Scotia, thus, in effect, yielding to the wholesale evasion. Some outbreaks and raids—led by two ministers, James Lyon and Seth Nobel, and by others, notably Jonathan Eddy and John Allan—were attempted; the inhabitants of St. John valley and of Passamaquoddy actually sent requests to the Continental Congress that they be admitted. But all these efforts, in the face of British domination of the ocean, came to nought; at the same time, however, England was unable to employ Nova Scotians effectively in the battle to suppress the Revolution.

In the British West Indies, the revolutionary record is similar. Here, however, an additional restraining influence—so far as joining the American rebels was concerned—was the great numbers of slaves: Thus, in 1774 in Jamaica slaves outnumbered the whites by 16 to 1 (192,787 slaves; 12,737 white); in Bermuda the ratio was about 1 to 1 (5,632 white; 5,023 slaves.) Yet, the economies of these islands depended very heavily upon the thirteen colonies, and their residents themselves were not indifferent to English economic and political domination.

Thus, the protest against the Stamp Act was about as vehement in the islands of Nevis and St. Kitts as it was in New York and Boston. Again, Grenada and Tobago all expressed, in one form or another, sympathy with the rebels and adherence to the principle of self-rule in internal matters. The inhabitants of the Bahamas offered no resistance when Americans under Esek Hopkins landed, "captured" New Providence and made a prisoner of the Governor; indeed, rather than resistance, the Americans received assistance in locating and hauling off the island's store of munitions.

Bermuda's residents decided that the thing "to do," wrote W. B. Kerr, "was to keep clear of the conflict; preserve their trade and for that reason to cultivate good relations with the Americans even at the risk of giving Great Britain a little offense." In pursuance of that policy, an official delegation from Bermuda to the Continental Congress arrived in 1775, to plead for her exemption from the American trade boycott. This was agreed to, with the promise that, in exchange, the powder stored on the island would be turned over to the rebels, a deal that was consummated though the Governor shouted, quite truly, "treason." All the British West Indies, in fact, maintained an active trade with the rebels throughout the conflict (directly, and also via Dutch and French islands) and their sympathies were heavily pro-'American. It was only British naval power, plus the danger of slave rebellion, which kept these islands from formally affiliating themselves with the United States.

The loyal British colonies in America, once the war ended, capitalized on their loyalty by demanding the removal of the heaviest restrictions of the mercantile system. To maintain such restrictions would amount to rewarding rebellion and punishing loyalty, clearly an impossible position. Within about 20 years after the signing of a peace treaty with the Americans, the petitions of the remaining colonials were answered with the nearly complete elimination of the ancient Trade and Navigation Acts.

The loss of the American colonies was also an important stimulus to Britain's shifting the main emphasis of her imperial system to India[3] and to Africa. And, by eliminating those colonies as dumping grounds for criminals sentenced to deportation, it was directly responsible for the colonizing in 1788 of New South Wales. This colony, to which also went some Loyalists, survived despite much adversity, and became what is today 'Australia.

The American Revolution, then, in decisively rupturing British imperial power, simultaneously evoked sympathetic responses and helped produce significant alterations throughout the vast domain controlled by that power.

Chapter XII

The Diplomacy
of the Revolution

To OBTAIN THE "rights of Englishmen,"
the Americans had to cease being Englishmen. To accomplish
this, against the will of England, would require a long and difficult struggle; to accomplish it meant to add a new member to
the society of sovereign nations. So momentous a shift in the
world's balance of power could not occur without strenuous
diplomatic activities.

The diplomacy of the American Revolution involves three
fundamental and inter-related questions: (1) the rebels' efforts
to gain recognition of their national sovereignty with an optimum
territorial and strategical position; (2) the efforts of Great
Britain to minimize the effect of American independence upon
her position and prestige—once such independence appeared
inevitable; (3) the efforts of the Continental European nations
—France and Spain, in particular—to reap the greatest possible
benefits for the present and the future from the embarrassment
of Great Britain flowing from the American uprising.

I

So far as the powers of continental Europe were concerned, and
especially the strongest amongst them, France, the prime objective in relations with the rebellious colonies and with the young

United States was to use them to redress the balance of power in Europe. With England's victory, sealed in the treaty of 1763, the balance had been completely upset and no European power was really comparable in might to Great Britain. A rebellion of the American colonies of King George resulting in their independence would help redress the imbalance, it was believed, by removing the weight of the thirteen colonies from Britain's side of the scales. Hence, the first objective of French diplomacy was to guarantee the achievement of that independence.

At the same time, if the colonies could not only become independent of England, but could become diplomatically dependent upon and economically tied to France, the scale's balance would be even further enhanced. Hence, a second prime objective of French diplomacy was to hitch America to the French wagon.

Connected with this second objective and related to some of the consequences of the first was the question of what was to be the newly-independent United States' position in the New World. The policy of France (and of Spain) was to have an independent United States, but not a particularly powerful United States—with its ideas of revolution and republicanism and self-determination—and surely not one which bestrode the Western Hemisphere, or even the Northern half of it, as an undisputed and unrestrained master. Hence, France and Spain tended to oppose United States' efforts to expand northward at the expense of Canada, or to expand westward, even to the Mississippi River, at the expense of Spanish holdings, or to obtain concessions in Newfoundland fisheries, or to move southward into the Floridas.

While having certain objectives, such as American independence, which directly coincided with American policy, and others, such as exclusion of the United States from the Newfoundland fisheries, which directly contravened American policy, France above all faced the need of preventing British-American reconciliation and developing the closest partnership between herself and the United States, with, of course, the new nation in the position of a distinctly junior member of the firm. This tended to produce vacillation in French diplomatic conduct. On the whole, however, French policy and influence distinctly favored the Americans in the arena of European power politics, for in the last resort she would yield on everything rather than see the independence of America lost and a reconciliation between the colonies and the mother country.

Spain, on the other hand, less directly challenged on the Continent by England; intensely hostile at home to the libertarian ideas of the Americans; and possessing a colossal but restless American colonial empire, much of it adjacent to and all of it influenced by the rebellious colonies, was less insistent upon American independence, generally less friendly to American efforts (even after she joined France in war against England), and was especially anxious to keep the troublesome Republic away from the Mississippi River and the Gulf of Mexico.

England, finding herself unable to retain the colonies—even after, in a conciliation mission of 1778 she offered them everything they had ever demanded, except independence—and unable to conquer them, and increasingly isolated in a growingly and actively hostile Europe, tried to make such a peace as would assuage ill-feeling in America, but not such a peace as would make the United States clearly the unchallenged master of North America. Simultaneously, she held the perspective of the more or less rapid disintegration of the new-fangled republic with the fragments returning, collectively or separately, to Mother. If this did not materialize, then perhaps the economy and the trade and later, the diplomatic weight, of the United States might be so tied to England as to make her independence more or less nominal. With these somewhat conflicting ends in view, English diplomacy, culminating in the treaties of 1783, sought to restrain the United States, but not to estrange her; simultaneously, it sought to separate the Republic from France, so that England's loss might not redound to the double advantage of France.

The diplomacy of the United States revolved around the basic aim of independence. Tied to this was the aim of securing the most favorable territorial and economic arrangements possible and of achieving such a position in the New World as to assure her domination thereof simply as the result of natural growth. It was, therefore, a diplomacy which resisted reconciliation, sought universal recognition, desired liberal trading agreements

with all Powers, wanted the Mississippi Valley, would have de-
lighted to have Canada, and became increasingly suspicious of
Spain, in particular, and of France, also, to a lesser extent.

Before the impact of the American Revolution is finished, one
witnesses a world war, a fundamental revision in international
law as applied to maritime commerce, a shift in the emphasis
and direction of British colonial policy, the hammering out of
the basic approach of American foreign policy towards Europe
for over a century. The American thunder-clap is important in
precipitating the revolutionary avalanches that sweep away so
much of the old in France and in all Europe, in the West Indies
and in all Latin-America during the generation that follows the
Peace Treaty of 1783.

II

Easily the most significant parliamentary motion ever made in
American history was that moved by Richard Henry Lee and
seconded by John Adams, in the Continental Congress on June
7, 1776. The motion carried with it three points: (1) that
"these United Colonies are, and of right ought to be, free and
independent states"; (2) a logical conclusion from the first, that
"it is expedient forthwith to take the most effectual measures for
forming foreign Alliances"; and (3), necessary if the first point
is to be made effectual and if the second point is not to see thirteen separate entities seeking "Alliances," that "a plan of confederation be prepared and transmitted to the respective Colonies
for their consideration and approbation."

Concerning the first of these points, we have already had
something to say; of the third we shall write another time. Before
us is the second proposal, the development of a diplomacy that
would help secure American independence.

Jefferson was the man, of course, charged with drafting the
statement justifying independence; John Dickinson of Pennsylvania had the main responsibility for preparing suitable plans for
confederation; John Adams had the task of outlining the suggested provisions of treaties of alliance to be formed, especially,
it was already quite clear, with France. Adams presented his

"plan for treaties" to the Congress in July, 1776; after debate and minor amendments, his proposal was approved September 17. It contained two main provisions, in addition to the assumption of full sovereignty by the new nation: (1) there was to be a renunciation of any aim by a foreign power to conquer any parts of North America; (2) adoption of the doctrine of "free ships, free goods," *i.e.*, the full protection of the trading privileges of neutrals with all nations, including those at war, in all commodities except those of a direct military nature, as weapons and ammunition.

Nine days after approving this objective, the Congress selected Silas Deane of Connecticut, Benjamin Franklin and Thomas Jefferson to serve as a team of commissioners and negotiators in Europe. Jefferson, beset by the serious illness of his wife, refused the assignment; he was replaced by Arthur Lee, also of Virginia, and then already in Europe. By December 28, 1776, Franklin, the senior member of the mission and then the best-known of all 'Americans, was being received in informal audience by Vergennes, the French Foreign Minister.

Prior to these formal arrangements, however, the groundwork had been laid of America's revolutionary foreign policy; and of European, especially French, foreign policy as regards the rebels and Great Britain. First it is to be noticed that the idea and the policy of revolution was used by all the Great Powers against each other. This, of course, is not to suggest concurrence with the police theory of revolution as something produced by hostile foreign agents; counter-revolution may come from such a source, but not revolution. However, it is true that revolution involves questions of sovereignty and power and international relations; therefore foreign powers will be interested, at least, in revolutionary currents passing through the body of other foreign powers and from time to time will seek to encourage such activities.

The British, for example, certainly by the 1740's, were distinctly interested in the possibilities of revolution in the Spanish colonies and, a little later, in Dutch and French possessions. Typical evidence of this was the letter written in June, 1741, by Admiral Edward Vernon to the English Admiralty urging "the necessity of Great Britain undertaking the emancipation of the

Spanish establishments in America in order to open their markets to the merchants of London." Again, the Corsican armed resistance to French appropriation in the 1760's was widely supported in England with money being raised there for the rebels and with the Government openly sympathetic towards them.

The mutual protection of subversive elements—Rousseau in exile in England and Wilkes in France, in the 1760's—was a common occurrence and had purposes more of a diplomatic and strategic nature than humanitarian.

In the mid-1760's, as American discontent mounted, the idea of supporting such discontent and guiding it in the direction of independence reached the highest levels of the French government. In 1765 Choiseul, Foreign Minister of France, already was weighing the wisdom of such a policy in terms of undoing the British victory in the Peace of 1763.

Despite the fears of some Americans that French help in their quarrel with England would result in America becoming a dependency of France, and the fears of some Frenchmen that support to America would stimulate revolution at home and lead to a costly and dangerous war with England, the fact is that as soon as real resistance to Great Britain appeared, American contact was made with France and encouragingly received.

At least as early as December, 1774, the French chargé in London reported to his superiors in Paris that American agents had approached him and had raised the questions of an alliance between France and America and of assistance from the former to the latter. One month after George III, in August, 1775, formally proclaimed the American colonies to be in rebellion, the French Foreign Minister, Vergennes, dispatched a secret agent, Bonvouloir, to America charged with assuring the rebels of two things; France favored American independence; and France did not desire to re-annex Canada.

In November, 1775, Congress established a Committee of Secret Correspondence "for the sole purpose of corresponding with our friends in Great Britain, Ireland, and other parts of the world," which marked the beginning of an organized effort at conducting foreign affairs.[1]

By December, 1775, Parliament announced a general boycott of the rebellious colonies, seeking thus to interdict all trade with them and bring the Americans to their knees. Foreign assistance and alliances became of paramount consequence, and, that same month, members of the Committee of Secret Correspondence conferred with France's secret agent—in the dead of night, arriving at a common destination separately and via different routes.

Preliminaries thus having been completed, in March, 1776, Congress sent Silas Deane as its agent to Paris (under the rather transparent disguise of a "commercial gentleman"—unhappily an ironically apt designation for Mr. Deane). In April, Congress replied to Parliament's interdiction of American trade by announcing the abolition of all the Trade Acts, throwing her ports open to the ships of all the world, except Great Britain. This was followed in May, 1776, with Deane's first success, which required little urging on his part; the King of France decided on a policy of assisting the rebels and directed that munitions to the value of one million livres be sent to America—indirectly, through a dummy corporation set up by Beaumarchais, author of "The Barber of Seville," and ardent friend of the American cause.

That brings us to the event already mentioned, namely, Richard Henry Lee's historic three-part motion in Congress on June 7, 1776, the second point of which resolved that it was "expedient forthwith to take the most effectual measures for forming foreign alliances."

As we have also seen, Congress approved Adams' draft of a plan for alliances that followed Lee's motion, and appointed diplomatic commissioners. By December, 1776, one of these, Benjamin Franklin, was already in Paris meeting informally with the French Minister for Foreign Affairs.

By then it became a matter of the opportune moment for France to announce her active support of the American cause. That moment came when the news of Burgoyne's surrender (October 17, 1777) reached Paris on December 3, 1777. At once the American Commissioners pressed their case upon the French Foreign Office; on December 14, Vergennes assured the

Americans that he favored recognition and open assistance to their cause. All that remained was for Vergennes to gain the full approval of the King.

Decisive in Vergennes' argument to the King, in addition to the fundamental tenet of French foreign policy—to weaken England by assuring the colonies' independence—was that achieving some kind of binding alliance with the rising Western power would redound to the future benefit of the King's power. And, Vergennes argued, if France did not seize this opportunity of forging such an alliance, it might never have another. For, he wrote the King, January 7, 1778:

> We are informed that there is a numerous party in America which is endeavoring to fix as a basis of the political system of the new States that no engagement be contracted with the European powers.[2] Dr. Franklin himself professes this dogma. Necessity alone has prevented its being established; but so soon as that ceases to exist, the insurgents, who will have asserted their independence without our help, will think they do not need it in order to maintain their independence. Then we shall be without any bond with them, exposed to their avidity and perhaps to their resentment.

Six days later the French Foreign Ministry drafted a full-scale "memorandum" on the "Reasons for an Alliance with the American Colonies," which may be accepted as a definitive expression of that Power's viewpoint. Here it was held that the American contest obviously was of the greatest concern to France. In regard to that contest "two courses only" were open to France; either to abandon or to support the rebelling colonies.

The first course, abandonment, meant playing into the hands of Great Britain, which, this memorandum accurately declared, was in the process of developing a major effort at reconciliation aimed at uniting with a nearly independent America in "a league against the House of Bourbon." Should this succeed, America would become an enemy and would wrest from France (and Spain) her possessions in the Western Hemisphere. This would complete the work of 1763 and France would then become indeed a minor power.

If these be the probable results of the first course, "it follows," continued the Memorandum, "that the glory, the dignity and the essential interest of France demand that she stretch out her hand to those States, and that their independence should be her work." Adopting this, the second of only two alternatives, means humiliating Great Britain, "our natural enemy," and reducing her might; ensuring our American possessions and extending our own commerce and fisheries; regaining our former premier position in Europe.

It follows from an examination of these two alternatives that France must choose to assist the Americans and see to it that they establish independence. Such a choice means war; hence France should at once enter into a treaty of alliance with the Americans and mobilize for war, and she should do this even if Spain does not see her way clear, at the moment, to join in such a war. In the Memorandum's closing words: "Thus France must espouse the American cause, and use for that purpose all her power, even if Spain should refuse to join her. . . ."

By the time of the drafting of this Memorandum, French and 'American officials were busy drawing up proposals for the impending alliance. On February 6, 1778, formal treaties of alliance and of commerce were signed by France and the United States, to become effective upon ratification by Congress, a condition fulfilled on May 4, 1778.

The Treaty of Alliance between France and the United States provided that if war broke out between Great Britain and France, during the existence of the then current war between Great Britain and the United States, the two Powers having a common enemy would make "a common cause" and each would help the other in every way and with all means "as becomes good and faithful allies." The Treaty declared in its second article that: "The essential and direct end of the present defensive alliance is to maintain effectually the liberty, sovereignty, and independence absolute and unlimited of the said United States, as well in matters of government as of commerce."

France agreed that if the United States succeeded in acquiring Canada and Nova Scotia and the Bermudas, or any of them, she would recognize and guarantee such acquisition. At the same time France renounced "for ever the possession" of the Bermudas and of any part of North America which prior to the Treaty of 1763 or by the terms of that treaty was the property of Great Britain or of the thirteen colonies. Both countries guaranteed the present possessions of each other; France reiterated her guarantee of the complete independence of the United States. Each pledged not to "conclude either truce or peace with Great Britain, without the formal consent of the other first obtained," and each promised not to make peace unless the treaty terminating the war assured the independence of the United States.

The Treaty of Amity and Commerce between France and the United States contained a "most favored nation" clause, that is, each pledged the other "not to grant any particular favor to other nations in respect of commerce and navigation, which shall not immediately become common to the other Party." Further, it stipulated that as between the two signatories the principle of "free ships, free goods" should apply.

At the same moment that these treaties were concluded, a secret article was signed granting to Spain the right to accede to either one or the other or to both of them, at any future time.

On March 13, 1778, the French Ambassador in London informed the British government of France's recognition of the United States and of the existence of a commercial treaty between the two powers. A week later, Louis XVI formally received the American Commissioners. After Congressional ratification, in May, of the treaties with France (done despite the strongest British efforts at reconciliation), the outbreak of war between Great Britain and France was merely a question of when the first rounds would be fired; on June 17, 1778, British guns shelled French ships.

The formal acceptance by the United States of foreign assistance and intervention in their revolutionary struggle, especially since this was intervention on the part of the traditional foe (against whom Washington himself had borne arms but 15 years before), was not done without grave qualms on the part of the rebels. The Tories seized upon it as final proof of the complete treachery and depravity of the rebels. In England it surely was a severe blow to those who, having supported America in an internal, family affair, now saw America formally allied with France in war upon England.

Yet, it was the North ministry and the Crown policy which had forced the colonies to choose independence and, in order to make good the choice, to ally themselves with France. Before the North government had finished it was to succeed in bringing Spain and Holland into war with England and inducing practically all of the rest of Europe to join in a League of Armed Neutrality aimed, in fact, against Great Britain.

Moreover, the English government itself had preceded the Americans in bringing about foreign intervention in the Revolutionary struggle. She had approached Frederick of Prussia and Catherine of Russia and offered both very large sums of money and the latter, additionally, colonial territory, if they would turn over thousands of their soldiers to help subdue the Americans. It was only because both rulers lost no love for England, and because both feared revolutionary infection (especially from those of the troops which might return) that each refused. Influential also, in their thinking, though both confessed themselves as sympathetic with the Americans, was the fact that mass uprisings in Russia (the Pugachev Revolt) and in central Europe (particularly Bohemia) had but recently been suppressed.

Some of the rulers of petty German principalities were in greater need of money and felt themselves especially subordinate to British desires. From these, Great Britain succeeded in purchasing cannon-fodder with which to attempt to suppress American insolence.

Altogether Britain concluded treaties with various German states, in 1776, for the purchase of about 30,000 troops. Because of desertion and mutiny on the continent of Europe and illness and death en route to America, a total of about 20,000 actually fought against the rebels. This figure, however, is a very respectable one and demonstrates that foreign mercenaries constituted an important segment of the "British" armies engaged in suppressing the American Revolution.[3]

That the employment, under treaty, of German soldiers in the conflict would justify the Americans in seeking foreign assistance was pointed out by the spokesmen for the numerous minority in Parliament opposing the measure. Typical were the remarks made in Parliament by David Hartley, in 1776, when the North government presented the treaties for ratification:

> I call it a fatal measure, because when foreign powers are once introduced in this dispute, all possibility of reconciliation and return to our former connection is totally cut off. You have given a justification to the Americans by your example, if you call in the assistance of foreign powers. . . . When you have set the example, you not only justify America in applying for foreign aid; but every power whatever will think themselves at liberty to take such part as may best suit their own convenience.

III

Spain's declaration of war against England did not come until June 21, 1779, more than a year after her ally, France, had taken a similar stand. The wounds inflicted by England upon France were fresher and more severe than those upon Spain. Moreover, the Spanish empire in America was very much more extensive and more significant to the power of Spain than was true of the American holdings of France. Further, Spanish possession of the western two-thirds of the United States, beginning at the Mississippi, made that power a neighbor, with a long common boundary, of the swiftly-growing, manifestly expanding, and rambunctiously republican rebeldom.

Thus it is that Vergennes, in explaining to Montmorin, the French Ambassador at Madrid, the position of Paris in allying itself with America, and in attempting to persuade Spain to enter the war, emphasized, in a letter dated October 30, 1778: "We ask independence only for the thirteen states of America. . . . We do not desire that a new republic shall arise which shall become the exclusive mistress of this immense continent."

Spain, in turn, had already made clear the basic reasons for her extreme restraint in espousing the American cause. She would, and did, invest a modest sum in that cause,[4] hoping thus to help embarrass England, but she hesitated to go further. Grimaldi, the Spanish Foreign Minister, wrote February 4, 1777, that it was far from certain that the colonists would win—clearly a reasonable view at that time—and that in any case: "The rights of all sovereigns in their respective territories should be extremely sacred, and the example of a rebellion is too dangerous for His Majesty to sustain it openly."

Spain's essential purpose, as that of France, was to increase its own power at the expense of England's. To realize this strategy Spain adopted two main immediate aims: (1) recovering Gibraltar (taken from her, in 1713, by England); (2) driving Great Britain away from the Gulf of Mexico. She had, of course, additional aims—as the appropriation of Portugal and stimulating rebellion in Ireland—but the first two were held to be necessary.

Grimaldi, in putting forth, in 1776, Spain's program to Vergennes added as axiomatic that, "One does not make war except to preserve one's own possessions or to acquire those of others." Vergennes replied that of course "one makes wars only to make gains," but that, at the same time, objectives had to be carefully selected in terms of which were more certainly realizable than others, which would bring more gains and develop less hostility, etc. Thus, he thought, to be specific, that Spain's acquisition of Portugal "would be alarming to all rulers interested in preserving a just balance." On the other hand, an enemy's loss was one's own gain, and he urged that France and Spain "should regard it as a great gain to lower the power of England"; surely to separate the colonies in North America from England "will render that power less unquiet and less haughty."

Yet Spain's fear of revolutionary infection and of American domination of the Mississippi Valley and of the northern shore of the Gulf of Mexico was enough to keep her exceedingly wary of war upon England, late in declaring such war, and careful, in making the declaration, not to recognize the United States, let alone ally herself with the new power.

This policy was pursued despite the large concessions made by the rebels. Thus, Congress by resolution in December, 1776, had agreed that in return for Spanish assistance, America would aid Spain to recover the port of Pensacola. Three months later, the 'American Commissioners in Europe went even further than Vergennes (having less interest in the European balance of power) and proposed that Spain undertake, with American approval, the conquest of Portugal. And, early in 1779, when Spain's declaration of war was impending, the Americans even offered to waive their country's claim to the right of navigation on the Mississippi in exchange for recognition.

Meanwhile, as the Spanish court was moving towards war against England, Paris and Madrid signed the preparatory Convention of Aranjuez (April 12, 1779) which, unbeknown to the Americans, pledged the two Crowns not to make peace with England until Spain had gotten back Gibraltar. Since France and the United States, in their treaty of alliance, signed a year before, had agreed that neither would make peace without the prior knowledge and consent of the other, France in the Aranjuez agreement was unilaterally and secretly tying America to the continuation of war against England until Spain had regained Gibraltar—and simultaneously Spain persisted in her refusal even to recognize the United States!

Spain and England were at war but a few months when in 1780 representatives from each Power met for secret discussions. Spain at once made clear her desire for some kind of stalemate in America which would result in a weakened Great Britain and a hemmed-in new Republic. She urged termination of the American War on the principle of *uti possidetis, i.e.*, the belligerents holding what they, at the termination of fighting, actually did hold. Had this been implemented it would have meant that Great Britain would have retained Maine, New York City, all of Long Island, and practically every port south of Virginia; moreover, Spain did not insist on the independence of the colonies.

Needless to say, nothing would have persuaded the rebels to accept such an agreement, but that Spain seriously considered it, prepares one for her position two years later, when peace negotiations were formally under way. Here, Spanish policy, as Franklin wrote to Livingston on April 12, 1782, was "to coop us up," if possible east of the Appalachians. Spain actively sought to keep the Americans out of the Alabama country, north of West Florida, out of the entire Ohio Valley, and out of the Illinois country, while retaining for herself, of course, complete control of navigation on the Mississippi. It seems clear, also, that France supported this position.

At the same time, it is necessary to note, the suspicions of the American Commissioners, especially of John Jay and John Adams, had been thoroughly aroused. Jay, who had spent two fruitless years (1778-80) as American representative in Madrid, actually urged upon an English diplomat in 1782 that the British take West Florida by arms from the Spanish, though, the diplomat reported to his Foreign Office, Jay "earnestly begs that it may not be known that he advised it."

In considering Revolutionary diplomacy and Spain, it is necessary to bear in mind the Spanish colonial empire in America. Certainly, the American Revolution had a profound impact upon that empire; an eventuality foreseen by the Spanish rulers, and one which, to minimize or overcome, occupied much of their time.

The impact of the American Revolution upon Spanish-America was direct, in terms of an inspiring example. This was intensified by the fact that though Spain was not allied to the American rebels, she was at war with the enemy of those rebels. That war itself created grave financial and political problems for Spain which served further to intensify the Revolution's significance for South America. Furthermore, the whole shift in British commercial policy, furthered by the American Revolution, served to increase, in British eyes, the importance of Spanish-American trade; thus Spain's efforts to monopolize that trade met intensified English opposition. This opposition took as one of its forms, active English assistance to revolutionary movements in the Spanish colonial world.

IV

The Netherlands, at a low point of political and cultural prestige, were torn between factions among their ruling class who favored, on the one hand, a pro-British and, on the other, a pro-French orientation. The dominant line turned into one desiring neutrality and the protection of the rights of neutrals, which, given England's position, became in fact an anti-British "neutrality."

From this position the Dutch hoped to rebuild their merchant marine, increase their commerce and replenish their tills. Because of this the Netherlands rejected an urgent English request for the purchase of 6,000 soldiers, and did in fact push the development of a fabulously lucrative trade with the rebels, centering upon the Dutch West Indian isle of St. Eustatius.

This trade, plus Dutch participation in the League for Armed Neutrality, and the rich booty represented by Dutch holdings in Asia, led England to declare war upon the Netherlands in December, 1780.

The war was disastrous for the Dutch, with the English destroying much of their shipping (including 130 ships, captured by Admiral Rodney when he took St. Eustatius) and inflicting heavy blows upon Dutch influence in India and the East Indies.[5] But, at the same time, Dutch participation was quite helpful to the American rebels. This was true not only because of trade, but also because of important loans successfully negotiated by a resident of Holland, Charles W. F. Dumas, and by John Adams. In 1782, the Netherlands became the second nation to recognize the United States and to enter into a treaty of amity and commerce with the new republic.

The powers of Europe, other than those actually at war with England, also presented a generally hostile attitude towards Great Britain. This took organized form in the League for Armed Neutrality, begun in 1780 at the initiative, very largely, of France, the Netherlands, and Russia. The position represented by this League was the position urged, as early as 1776, by the rebel American Congress. It was also explicitly agreed to, as we have already noted, in the 1778 alliance between France and the United States.

The point is that for centuries Great Britain had insisted, and had enforced her insistence, that enemy goods aboard neutral ships were subject to seizure and confiscation by the navies of the belligerent powers. What this meant specifically in the case of the American Revolution was that American goods (or later, French, Dutch, and Spanish) aboard the vessel of a neutral power was legal prize if taken on the high seas by the British; the neutrality of the vessel did not protect its cargo. Obviously, this policy was made to order for the interests of a dominating maritime power, that is, for Great Britain.

From the beginning, the rebel colonies tried to overthrow this conception of marine law. Vergennes was exceedingly anxious also, of course, to deal an additional blow by not only helping to free England's colonies, but also by undermining a legal bulwark of England's sea mastery.

As the fighting of the American Revolution enveloped France and Spain, the British interpretation of international maritime law became more and more onerous and costly to the neutral European powers. With the active diplomatic encouragement of Vergennes and Franklin, the first actual move was made by Catherine of Russia. This monarch ordered an intensive study of the subject early in 1780, and then instructed T. F. Opinus, a distinguished Russian scientist, to draw up a plan overcoming England's special advantage.

This plan became the League for Armed Neutrality and was first presented by Catherine, in March, 1780, to Denmark and Sweden for their agreement. The plan carefully defined contraband goods in terms of goods actually and directly of a weapon-like or war-making character. It then went on to declare that all other cargo carried in neutral ships ("free ships") though belonging to an enemy power was not to be subject to seizure by a belligerent (*i.e.*, was to be "free goods"). Further, it denounced the English practice of "paper blockade," whereby Great Britain would simply declare the ports of her enemy, in wartime, to be blockaded, while in fact they might not be at all physically invested. To be effective, declared this document, a blockade must be actually and physically in existence, so that entry would be dangerous.

The plan called for the agreement of its signatories to enforce its provisions with arms, that is, to resist violations of it by the British Navy. Hence, the somewhat paradoxical designation, "Armed Neutrality." Before the war against the colonies was formally ended by the Treaty of Paris, this League had been joined by Russia, Denmark, Sweden, Holland, Prussia, the Emperor of the Holy Roman Empire, the Kingdom of the Two Sicilies and Portugal.

There is some doubt as to the extent of the contribution this League made to the winning of American independence. There is no doubt at all that it did serve to complete the diplomatic isolation of Great Britain from Europe and thus stimulated her to give up the American effort.

It is clear also that it is the American Revolution, and the League for Armed Neutrality that grew out of it, which led to the enunciation of a principle since recognized as international maritime law.

V

There is another feature of the diplomacy of the American Revolution that demands attention. This is the unprecedented role that European (including English) public opinion played in influencing its course.

Jacques Necker, finance minister of Louis XVI, described this new force as "that invisible power which without treasure, without guards, and without arms, imposes its laws on the city, on the court, and even in the palaces of kings."

Insistence upon the right, duty and justice of man to govern himself, and the possibility thereby of creating a better life for humanity on earth, was of the essence of the Enlightenment. To the contemporaries of the Enlightenment, the American Revolution seemed its very embodiment; hence its cause was held to be sacred.

For this was Franklin beloved. He was The American—the one who, as Turgot said, had taken lightning from the heavens and scepters from tyrants, each equally releasing the potentialities of humankind. It was Franklin who wrote, in a letter dated Paris, May 1, 1777: "All Europe is on our side of the question; as far as applause and good wishes can carry them. . . . 'tis a common observation here, that our cause is *the cause of all Mankind,* and that we are fighting for their liberty in defending our own." Franklin, as the Child of his Age, thoroughly agreed: " 'Tis a glorious task assign'd us by Providence; which has, I trust, given us spirit and virtue equal to it, and will at last crown it with success."

The young Lafayette wrote his wife from the New World, in June, 1777: "The happiness of America is linked to the happiness of all humanity; she will become the sure asylum of virtue, honesty, tolerance, equality and a peaceful liberty." A year later, the mature Turgot, one of Louis' ministers least enthusiastic about his master's American policy, nevertheless said of the Americans: "This people is the hope of the human race."

The zeal of the people of France for the American cause is universally acknowledged, but historians have tended to deny that such sympathies were widespread elsewhere in Europe. Thus, Samuel Flagg Bemis writes: "Outside of France there was little general sympathetic interest for the cause of the American Revolution, and this little was of a passive, academic kind." Despite the acknowledged expertness of Bemis in diplomacy history, the evidence indicates that in this instance he is not correct.

Indeed, in his own work, Professor Bemis noted the "sympathetic enthusiasm among liberals" in Denmark, Norway, Sweden, and the German states. The Foreign Minister of Denmark, in October, 1776, put the matter more strongly: "The public here is greatly taken by the [American] rebels, not because of any knowledge of their cause, but because the independence mania has really infected everybody, and because this poison spreads imperceptibly from the works of philosophers even into the village schools."

Professor Bemis asserts that the American Revolution "evoked no popular interest or sympathy at all" in the Netherlands, but in this he clearly "exaggerates." [5] While it is true that the 18th century is a period of decline for the Dutch Republic, with no sign of a Voltaire or Rousseau or Montesquieu, and while it is true that Franklin himself wrote that "Holland . . . does not seem to *feel* for us, or to have the least inclination to help us," it is also true that Charles W. F. Dumas and Joan Derk van der Capellen did find some response in Holland for their efforts to develop pro-American feeling. Moreover, Franklin was premature in believing the Dutch had no inclination to help, because as leaders in the Armed Neutrality movement, as providers of credit second only to France, in their trade, in active belligerency against England, and in early recognition of the United States—in all these respects, Dutch help was momentous for the new Republic.

Literature sympathetic to the American cause found a relatively wide audience in the Netherlands; notable was the fact that Richard Price's 1776 pamphlet was issued in Rotterdam, in French, and in Leyden, in two editions, translated into Dutch by van der Capellen.

The impact of the Revolution among the European intelligentsia was profound. It had, for example, great influence upon the Russian, Alexander Radishchev. Again, at the conclusion of *Faust,* Goethe's hero gains salvation "in wresting from the sea a free country for a free people," by which he unquestionably meant the new American republic. Paul C. Weber, in his study of *America in Imaginative German Literature* (1926), wrote:

> The poets of Storm and Stress, such as Klinger and Lenz, were influenced by the revolt of the colonies. Schiller, Herder, Wieland, Voss, Leopold von Stolberg, Schubart, Klopstock, Gleim and others exalted in the glory of Franklin and Washington, denounced the disgraceful soldier-traffic of German princes, and strongly supported the liberal aspirations of the Americans.

Perhaps the most dramatic manifestation of the Revolution's impact upon European contemporaries was the large-scale volunteering for service against the British. Much of this was the result of conventional professional military conduct of that time; much of it sprang out of state policy directed against England. But some of it, surely, derived from a feeling of sympathy for the liberating essence of the American effort. Among the best known of these volunteers were Lafayette, Duportail, Armand, Rochambeau from France; Kalb and Steuben from Germany; Kosciusko and Pulaski from Poland; Bille and Hauch from Denmark; von Fersen and von Stedingk from Sweden, and Kovats from Hungary.

Necker's "invisible power" was overwhelmingly on the side of the Americans. This was of the greatest consequence in the winning of independence, both on the battlefield and around the table of diplomacy. Franklin's "cause of all mankind" could be betrayed or thwarted or opposed only at the gravest peril. It was as though the great principles of the Age of Reason had come to life in the Republic of the New World; to combat her was to oppose them.

Condorcet, great French philosopher, published anonymously in Amsterdam in 1786 a study of the *Influence of the American Revolution on Europe*. First in this influence he placed the fact that it was not enough that the ideas of Enlightenment penetrate "the hearts of virtuous men." More was needed: "It is necessary that the poor and ignorant man be able to read them in the example of a great people." This was what the American Revolution had done, wrote Condorcet:

> America has given us this example. The act which declared its independence is a simple and sublime exposition of these rights so sacred and so long forgotten. . . . The spectacle of a great people where the rights of man are respected is useful to all others, despite differences of climate, of customs, and of constitutions.

By the year 1781, it was becoming clear to all in England but the wilfully blind (unfortunately the latter included the insane George III) that the Americans had accomplished, what six years before seemed so unlikely—they had fought their way to independence. England now was at war with France, Spain and Holland; the Armed Neutrality further isolated her; and an American Revolutionary Army still held the field, intact and unconquered.

In May, 1781, Pensacola fell to the Spanish, and while three months later Rodney took St. Eustatius, this was followed by the surrender at Yorktown in October, 1781; in November, the French captured San Martin and re-took St. Eustatius.

The next year opened with a series of defeats. In January, the French took Demarrara and Monserrat; in February, they seized San Cristobol and Nevis, while Minorca became Spain's prize. George III, in his mad stubbornness, stood very nearly alone now in his desire that the war against America go on. Without a division, the House of Commons adopted the resolution moved by General Conway, March 4, 1782, that peace should be concluded with America, and that any one who advised or attempted the further prosecution of that war was an enemy of Great Britain.

VI

With this, the government of Lord North collapsed, to be succeeded, March 22, by a Whig government. At its head was the same Rockingham responsible, 17 years earlier, for the repeal of the Stamp Act. In April, 1782, a more nearly independent Parliament was granted Ireland, Holland announced its recognition of the United States, and Shelburne—in charge of colonial affairs—sent an agent, the pro-American Whig merchant, Richard Oswald, to hold conversations in Paris with Benjamin Franklin.

At the same time that Oswald was being sent to Paris, the British Admiral Rodney was administering a severe defeat to a major French fleet off the West Indies. This victory, won on April 12, 1782, became known to London on May 18, and helped stiffen the spines of British diplomats. The retrieving of salvation at the brink of disaster, indicated in Rodney's triumph, was further advanced with the announcement, October 13, 1782, that the months-long Spanish seige of Gibraltar had been pierced and that the fortress was relieved.

Yet the matter at hand—an acknowledgment of American independence and the achieving of terms of settlement with the new State—was pressing. That this required the immediate attention of British diplomacy was brought home sharply to London with the announcement, in October, 1782, that the Netherlands had signed a treaty of amity and commerce with the United States.

On November 30, 1782, preliminary articles of peace were signed in Paris by the American and British negotiators. It was agreed that these were to remain preliminary until peace was agreed upon by France and Great Britain—accomplished January 20, 1783, at which time hostilities between the United States and Great Britain officially ceased. Then, following negotiations between Spain and England, and Holland and England,[6] definitive articles of peace were concluded and formally signed, as the Treaty of Paris, by plenipotentiaries of the United States and Great Britain on September 3, 1783.

Article I of this most momentous Treaty makes explicit the

British King's recognition that the United States—the thirteen states from New Hampshire to Georgia are named—is "free, sovereign and independent." The second article specifies the boundaries of the United States, given approximately as they are today in the North, then as far west as the Mississippi, thence down and across as far south as the southern border of Georgia.

The extensiveness of these boundaries was granted by the British despite Spanish urging (and French agreement) that the United States be confined as close to the Appalachians as possible. The British had no desire, however, to accommodate either Spain or France; and they were anxious to build up, for the future, American good-will. Moreover, there was some feeling among British leaders that giving the Americans a great deal of territory would compound their governing problems, exacerbate differences between North and South, and the tidal and mountain areas, and possibly hasten the cracking of the unity of the new nation. In addition, some felt that extending the area of the United States would assure its remaining overwhelming agricultural for, to quote Franklin, "while there is land enough in America for our people, there can never be manufactures to any amount or value." Obviously, to inhibit the growth of industry in the United States appealed to leading British statesmen.

One of the noteworthy features in the British agreement to American possession of the West, was that this entailed betrayal of Indian allies, who had fought very effectively. The fact is that much of this territory was in the actual possession of neither the United States nor Great Britain, but rather of the Indians who had come out on top in the prolonged military conflict during the Revolutionary years. Randolph Downes, who examined this question with the greatest care, wrote:

> The student of frontier affairs should be clearly aware of that great paradox of 1783, the acquisition by a nation whose armies had been continually beaten, of lands whose Indian inhabitants had successfully defended them against that nation. . . .
> Almost at the lowest level of effectiveness of its Indian policy, the United States was presented with victory in the shape of new boundaries that included the very lands that the Indians

had just successfully defended. The vanquished had become the victors.

Making good this "victory" was to dominate American military history during the first decades of the Republic's history.

Article III, insisted upon especially by John Adams, granted the United States right to participate in the very lucrative fishing industry connected with Newfoundland, Labrador and Nova Scotia.

The British granted these fishing rights to the Americans despite the fact that the French, secretly, had urged them not to favor their ally in this manner. France wanted to gain at American expense; Great Britain, faced with the necessity of making the grant, divided it among the French and Americans, hoping thus to split them and also, by magnanimity to the Americans, to overcome some of the hostility born of the war.

The fourth article stipulated that "creditors on either side shall meet with no lawful impediment to the recovery of the full value in sterling money, of all *bona fide* debts heretofore contracted." This was one of the two main demands of the British negotiators and had reference, mainly, to the many millions of dollars owed British merchants, especially by Southern planters, prior to the war. The debts had been repudiated and voided by State action during the Revolution; despite this Article the greatest part of them remained uncollected.

The second of the demands most insistently made by the British diplomats was met in the fifth article of the treaty. This had to do with the restitution of the property of Tories confiscated by the revolutionary State governments. Given the Federal nature of the United States government, exceedingly loose under the Confederation, the Article provided only that "It is agreed that the Congress shall earnestly recommend it to the legislatures of the respective States, to provide for the restitution" of all confiscated property. Congress did "recommend" repeatedly, but restitution was never forthcoming.

Article VI provided for the cessation of all future confiscations and prosecutions as the result of participation in or activity during the War, and the amnestying of all civilian war-prisoners.

The Seventh Article provided for the release of all military prisoners, and the withdrawal of British forces—"without causing any destruction, or carrying away any Negroes or other property of the American inhabitants"—from the United States, including "every post, place and harbour within the same"; all this to be done "with all convenient speed." [7]

The last significant article in this treaty was the eighth, in which both signatories agreed that "the navigation of the river Mississippi, from its source to the ocean, shall forever remain free and open to the subjects of Great Britain, and the citizens of the United States." Since, however, neither of the two signatories controlled the Mississippi at its southern extremity, held by Spain, the provision was not as meaningful as it appeared. Neither, however, was it meaningless, for there had been considerable pressure from Spain to get England to acquiesce in Spain's right to control navigation on the river, especially at New Orleans. When, in 1780, Spain had made clear her fears that the United States would threaten her supremacy in the Gulf of Mexico, and had therefore proposed American recognition of this supremacy, including control of the Mississippi, hinting this would bring more active Spanish aid, Franklin had rejected the proposal at once. Writing to Jay, October 2, 1780, Franklin declared: "Poor as we are, yet as I know we shall be rich, I would rather agree with them to buy at a great price the whole of their right on the Mississippi than sell a drop of its waters. A neighbour might as well ask me to sell my street door."

The eighth article of the Treaty, then, makes clear American opposition to Spanish claims of a monopoly of navigation on the Mississippi, and British support for that opposition. It does not, of course, resolve the problem of these Spanish claims; such resolution was to be a chief task in the diplomacy of the young Republic.

VII

In the diplomacy of the settlement, a brief treatment of the role of British Intelligence is necessary. William Eden, later Lord Auckland, serving as an Under-Secretary in the British Cabinet, actually was in charge of Intelligence. His right-hand man, so far as American affairs were concerned, was Paul Wentworth—originally from New Hampshire—living in London and posing as a warm friend of the American cause.

British Intelligence had considerable success, notable even for this fabled service, in gaining access to the negotiations of American diplomatic officers in Paris. Note has already been taken of the fact that Dr. Edward Bancroft, Franklin's confidential secretary, was a British agent. Mention has been made, also, of the role of Captain Hynson, courier for the American diplomatic mission, who was in the pay of the British and turned over to Eden's office the contents of the mission's messages meant only for the eyes of Congress. We have pointed out, too, that Arthur Lee's personal secretary, Major Thornton, was likewise a British spy.

Edward Carmichael, secretary to Silas Deane, was still another British agent. It is known now that six of the clerks hired by Arthur Lee in the course of his few years of service in Paris, were British agents, while Hezekiah Ford, who succeeded Thornton as Lee's secretary, and Thomas Digges, Lee's confidential agent, were also spies!

So far as the records show, the only possibly consequential result of the prodigious and expensive labors of these numerous spies and agents came from France's dispatch of Edward Bancroft, at Franklin's recommendation, to Ireland to offer guidance as to the advisability of a French invasion there. Bancroft, of course, advised against such an attempt and this does appear to have played some part in the French decision not to undertake the effort.

Although the British Foreign Office knew what the minimum and maximum demands of the Americans were, knew of internal differences among them, and probably were very well informed concerning American negotiations, agreements and jealousies relative to France, Spain and Holland, there is no available evidence demonstrating that such knowledge actually determined any feature of the final Treaty.

VIII

There is a considerable literature revolving around the question of why the British agreed to a boundary settlement which was so favorable to the Americans, especially in the Great Lakes region, included in the boundaries of Quebec after the Act of 1774. We think there were six major considerations, each reinforcing the other, which explain this result. First stands the fact that after fighting from 1775 through 1781 the British were further than ever from having subdued the Americans. Again, by the time the diplomatic groundwork for peace with the Americans was being laid, Great Britain found herself in an exceedingly isolated and disadvantageous position in the European power game. Third, by the early 1780's the majority of all classes of Englishmen were insisting that peace be made and on that basis the North Government had been forced to resign. Fourth, there was a very strong desire among the Whigs who succeeded North to salvage something from the Tory wreckage by developing a policy which would win American friendship. Fifth, there was great anxiety in the British Foreign Office that America be drawn out of the orbit of French influence and, if possible, that enmity between France and the United States be developed. And sixth, the Treaty of 1783 came as the British Government was replacing its whole original conception of colonialism from one which stressed English conquest and settlement to one which stressed English conquest and penetration and domination, but not settlement.

In the negotiations themselves, the American nation was superbly served by three distinguished men who complemented each other extremely well: Franklin, John Adams and John Jay. And they met, as the British plenipotentiary, David Hartley, a Whig member of Parliament, who had won renown as a passionate advocate of the justice of the Americans' cause. Franklin in particular never let Hartley forget the latter fact and it did not serve to stiffen England's resistance to American proposals.

IX

The question of whether or not the American negotiators deceived the French and violated the 1778 treaty in dealing separately with the British needs some consideration. It is clear that in conducting these negotiations unilaterally, the Americans were violating express provisions of the Alliance. They were, indeed, violating the express instructions of the Congress of the United States.

Congress, on June 15, 1781, agreed to new instructions for its Commissioners in Europe, which directed them to accept the proffered mediation of the Russian Czarina and the Austrian Emperor, and to place full and complete reliance on the Ministers of the French King—"to undertake nothing in the negotiations for peace or truce without their knowledge and concurrence," and to be governed finally "by their advice and opinion."

This Resolution, coming at a low point in the military fortunes of the Americans (preceding Yorktown by several months) no doubt represented the honest view of a majority of Congress. Yet it is important to bear in mind that French representatives in the United States used every possible means to influence Congressional policy. Very soon after arriving in the United States, Gerard, the French Minister, wrote to the French Foreign Minister (August 12, 1778): "Personal disinterestedness and pecuniary probity do not illustrate the birth of the American Republic. . . . The spirit of mercantile cupidity forms, perhaps, one of the distinctive characteristics of the Americans."

The researches of Arthur B. Darling and John J. Meng have been noteworthy in uncovering the details of what Professor Bailey described as "the extraordinary amount of French intrigue among the factions in Congress to influence American decisions in line with French interests." Certainly one of the greatest triumphs of this intrigue was the Resolution of June 15, 1781. Happily, however, Great Britain was not prepared to accept the Russian and Austrian offers of mediation, and the American Commissioners on the spot were far too suspicious of the intentions of France (and Spain) to permit themselves to be bound by the advice of her Ministers. A typical reaction among the Commissioners to this Congressional Resolution was that which John Adams entered into his diary, after he and his colleagues had decided to ignore it:

Congress surrendered their own sovereignty into the hands of a French minister. Blush! blush! ye guilty records! blush and perish! It is glory to have broken such infamous orders. Infamous, I say for so they will be to all posterity. How can such a stain be washed out? Can we cast a veil over it and forget it?

As for the French themselves, it is to be noted that while the American negotiations with England were begun unilaterally and the results were not conveyed to Vergennes until they were concluded, it is also a fact that the preliminary treaty contained a clause that suspended its provisions pending peace between England and France. It is also to be recalled, as already pointed out, that France had violated the 1778 Treaty in her agreement with Spain in 1779, when she pledged not to make peace with England until Gibraltar had fallen to Spain. This entered into, without American knowledge, after the United States had bound herself not to make peace with England until France did, would appear surely to have relieved the United States of such obligation.

In any case, the American Commissioners had had, as we have seen, very good reasons to suspect the amity and fraternal regard of both France and Spain by the time 1781 drew to a close. England, on the other hand, especially with the disasters that fell upon her beginning with Yorktown, jumped at the chance of negotiating with the Americans apart from the French.

Actually, Vergennes was not displeased with the American initiative. It would help relieve him from the pledge of fighting until Gibraltar was Spanish, which by the end of 1782 seemed something for the very distant future. It was, indeed, a full two weeks after Franklin broke the news of the Preliminary Treaty to Vergennes, that the Frenchman protested, and the protest, while sharp, was still formal and did not remotely resemble a break in relations. Indeed, Franklin in replying to Vergennes, December 17, 1782, italicized this sentence: *"The English, I just now learn, flatter themselves they have already divided us."* And, continued the Old Master, "I hope this little misunderstanding will therefore be kept a secret, and that they will find themselves totally mistaken." To convince himself that they were totally mistaken, Franklin, in this same letter, asked Vergennes to arrange a new French loan for the United States—and in a short time, another six million livres were placed to the credit of the new nation!

With the Treaty of Paris, the last obstacle was gone to the actual existence of an independent United States of America. Now, by 1783, four powers—France, the Netherlands, Sweden, and Great Britain—recognized that existence.

But how permanent were to be what a British novelist, Richard Graves, referred to in a book published in 1786, as "the Utopian states of America"? The upstart Republic, cursed of Kings and Lords, "the cause of all Mankind," was launched under auspicious conditions—a continent of fabulous riches before her, an ocean separating her from the jealousies and assaults of Europe. If the cause could take root anywhere and survive anywhere, it would be in America.

When the 72-year old Franklin and the 84-year old Voltaire were presented to each other before the Paris Academy of Sciences in 1778, the assembled savants stormed and cheered while Solon and Sophocles embraced and kissed and wept. The tears and cheers reflected the hopes of the Age of Enlightenment that it might yet come into its own. The United States of America was the national embodiment of that international aspiration.

Chapter XIII

The Negro in the Revolution

O F T H E T O T A L population in the rebellious colonies, approximately 20 per cent, some 600,000 people, were Negroes. The vast majority of this number, perhaps 550,000, were slaves, overwhelmingly concentrated in the area from Maryland to Georgia.

In sheer numbers, absolutely and relatively, then, it is apparent that the Negro population constituted a very significant component of the American nation at its birth time. As property, too, the slaves came to a total assessed value of something like a quarter of a billion dollars, a very considerable slice of the total national wealth and of the capital investment in the revolution-torn country.

Further, in terms of the economy, while the slaves numbered 20 per cent of the whole population, they constituted a larger proportion of the country's productive workers since slaves began work at about nine years of age, kept working so long as they could physically, and since practically all women among the slaves were workers. In terms of productivity, then, the Negro people were of the greatest consequence quite early in American history. Already, too, their presence and their particularly oppressed status were of fundamental consequence in the life and economy of the South—a region fully recognizable as such by the time of the Revolution and one taking on special features because, in large part, of the concentration therein of the "peculiar institution."

The Negro in the Revolution requires examination from several aspects. There is, first of all, the incongruity of a revolution whose banners herald "Liberty or Death" and whose borders contain over half a million slaves. The impact of this upon the minds of contemporary white Americans needs analysis; and so does its impact upon the institutions and laws of the rebellious states.

The military results of the existence of slavery require some notice: What this meant to the American effort; what it induced from the British.

The Revolution's effect upon the Negro masses demands close examination: In what way did these hundreds of thousands react to the tremendous events going on about them, revolving as they did around provocative questions of liberty or tyranny?

I

As concerns the Negro, dominant white thought in the America of the 18th century was deeply racist. Montesquieu, in *The Spirit of the Laws* (Book XV, section 5) wrote "Of the Slavery of the Negroes" and ironically summed up the content of this racism: "It is impossible for us to suppose these creatures to be men, because, allowing them to be men, a suspicion would follow that we ourselves are not Christians."

Irony aside, Negroes were widely believed to be sub-human, or, if of the human species, surely an innately inferior component thereof. If one asked, wrote a contemporary in Delaware, "Why the Negroes were born slaves . . . more than others?" The reply was clear: "And may you not as well ask why the Buzzards are obliged to eat nothing but carrion. . . ? Nature answers by saying it was necessary and therefore she has fitted them for it and made it their delight."

It is a testimony to the deep-going impact of the revolutionary struggle that it delivered telling blows against the system of Negro slavery despite the prevalence and intensity of this racist ideology. The anti-slavery feature of the Revolutionary movement was anxiously watched and, where possible, aided by the Negro people themselves.

In some of the pre-Revolutionary literature, notice is taken of the inconsistency in struggling for political and economic freedom while holding hundreds of thousands in chains. This may be found, for example, in the writings of James Otis who, in his *Rights of the British Colonies* (1764) denounced slavery, affirmed the Negro's inalienable right to freedom, and, by clear implication, even upheld the slave's right to rebel against his owner.

Some of the later writings became even more bold, as the Reverend Isaac Skillman's *Oration upon the Beauties of Liberty* (1772), which demanded the immediate abolition of slavery. In this work, its author went as far as Abolitionist literature was ever to go, for he affirmed the slave's right to rebel since that would conform "to the laws of nature."

These same years witnessed the anti-slavery work of Anthony Benezet, and of such figures as Benjamin Franklin and Benjamin Rush. As a sign of the times is to be noted the fact that some addresses delivered at the 1773 commencement in Harvard were concerned with "the legality of enslaving the Africans." Similar sentiments were expressed by Abigail Adams when she told her distinguished husband, John—upon the discovery of a slave plot in Boston, in September, 1774—that "it always appeared a most iniquitous scheme to me to fight ourselves for what we are daily robbing and plundering from those who have as good a right to freedom as we have."

The first article Thomas Paine wrote for publication was entitled "African Slavery in America." It appeared in a Philadelphia newspaper of March 8, 1775; it demanded that slavery be abolished and that the freedmen be given land, so that they would have not only personal liberty but also the means of earning a livelihood.

During the years of actual fighting, the opposition to slavery, among white people, intensified and frequently found expression in organized form and in legal enactment. Religious groups, as the Moravians, Baptists, Methodists, and particularly the Quakers made decided advances in anti-slavery opinion and action. Indeed, of the Quakers it may be said that they had generally eliminated slave-trading and slaveholding from their own ranks by about 1785. Early in the 1780's some American Quakers, perhaps inspired by the activities of English Friends, undertook to obtain anti-slavery actions from the Confederation Congress. Outstanding was David Cooper, of New Jersey, who published in 1783 *A Serious Address to the Rulers of America on the Inconsistency of their Conduct respecting Slavery,* wherein he collected "the most striking statements of Congress in favor of liberty, with parts of the Constitutions of some of the American states on the same subject, contrasted by the idea of tolerating slavery." This seems to have been preparatory to a memorial presented to Congress, in the fall of 1783, urging the outlawry of the slave-trade, and signed by 535 members of the Society of Friends in Pennsylvania and New Jersey.

By 1775 the first Society for Promoting the Abolition of Slavery was established in Philadelphia, and others soon appeared, as one in New York in 1785 and in Delaware in 1788. These groups, generally favoring a gradual emancipationist line, included, but by no means were confined to Quakers.

Representations against slavery to governmental bodies of individual colonies and states had been made during the pre-Revolutionary agitation, and increased also, during the Revolution. For example, in 1770, several petitions urging the end of slavery were received by the Connecticut legislature, which the next year forbade the slave trade. The New Jersey Assembly also received in 1773 anti-slavery petitions from groups of citizens in six counties.

In 1774 a memorial was presented to the Massachusetts Provincial Congress "purporting the propriety, that while we are attempting to free ourselves from our present embarrassments, and preserve ourselves from slavery, that we also take into consideration the state and circumstances of the Negro slaves in this province." This was read and debated, but when "the question was put, whether the matter now subside, it passed in the affirmative."

The same year Rhode Island, in considerable part because of Quaker pressure, declared that any Negro slave thereafter brought into its territory was to be free. The law's preamble states that this action was taken because:

> The inhabitants of America are generally engaged in the preservation of their own rights and liberties, among which that of personal freedom must be considered as the greatest, and as those who are desirous of enjoying all the advantages of liberty themselves should be willing to extend personal liberty to others.

It is to be observed, however, that this law did not free the slaves (of which there were about 3,500) then in Rhode Island, though later legislation permitting them to join the army did have the effect of liberating several hundred Negroes in that state.

A Massachusetts effort in 1773 to outlaw the slave trade was vetoed by Governor Hutchinson, in accordance with established Royal hostility to any interference with that lucrative business. Patriots continued to manifest hostility to the abominable traffic, however; thus, the Town Meeting of Braintree, Massachusetts, early in 1774 adopted a resolution to abstain from the slave trade and to boycott all who engaged in it. Within a year of this action, other groups in various localities in Rhode Island, Pennsylvania, Delaware and Georgia considered or adopted similar measures. Increasingly in New England, towns were taking steps to eliminate slavery within their borders.

The slave trade was outlawed by Massachusetts in 1776, while the Delaware Constitution of that year prohibited the importation of slaves from Africa, and forbade their importation from elsewhere, *for sale*. In 1777 a bill to abolish slavery was introduced into the Massachusetts General Court, but it was not passed, allegedly in order not to affront Southern slaveowners. The New York City delegation to the State Provincial Congress, headed by John Jay, urged, also in 1777, the adoption of a gradual emancipation law. This came close to adoption and might well have passed had not Jay been forced to absent himself from the chamber due to his mother's death. Twenty-two years were to pass before New York enacted such a law.

The constitution adopted by Vermont in 1777, contained a clause directly forbidding the enslavement of any individual "born in this country or brought from over sea." A law gradually abolishing slavery, written by Thomas Paine and George Bryan, was enacted by Pennsylvania in March, 1780. That year serious consideration was given to a similar bill by the Connecticut legislature, but it did not become law until 1784. Also in 1784, Rhode Island enacted a gradual emancipation law, and the New Hampshire Constitution was considered to have ended slavery in that state.

By 1780 public opinion had just about destroyed the institution of slavery in Massachusetts, and its Constitution of that year, containing a statement of man's right to equality and freedom, was considered to have legally abolished it. This was established, once and for all, in 1781 by the Supreme Judicial Court in the case of Commonwealth *vs.* Jennison. Here a white man indicted for beating a Negro defended himself by claiming the Negro to be his slave, but the Court ruled against him and he was fined. The Chief Justice, William Cushing, in rendering the decision, maintained that the State's Constitution of 1780

> sets out with declaring that all men are born free and equal—and that every subject is entitled to liberty . . . and in short is totally repugnant to the idea of being born slaves. This being the case, I think the idea of slavery is inconsistent with our own conduct and Constitution.

New Jersey was the last of the states north of the Mason-Dixon line to act in favor of abolition; her gradual emancipation law came in 1804. However, there, too, the Quakers had cleansed themselves of slavery by 1774, and agitation against the institution appeared in the Jersey press during the Revolution. Thus, an article in the *New Jersey Gazette* of November 8, 1780, declared: "A Whig abhors the very idea of slavery, let the colour or complexion of a slave be what it may. He is a friend to liberty, and a supporter of the rights of mankind universally, without any regard to partial interests or selfish views."

Petitions against slavery began to reach the New Jersey legislature in considerable numbers by 1781, and in 1786 the State enacted a law prohibiting the importation of slaves, permitting manumission under mild regulations, and forbidding the physical abuse of slaves.

In the South, too, the Revolution had a liberalizing impact on the slave system. Thus, Virginia (May, 1782) considerably eased the requirements for the manumission of slaves, though this law, under which hundreds of Negroes were granted their freedom, was repealed soon thereafter. During the same period in Delaware, Maryland and North Carolina there was a notable increase in the number of manumissions granted by masters; the evidence is conclusive that these were stimulated by the democratic and humanitarian spirit of the Revolution.

On the national scene—of course at this period the powers of the Federal government were sharply circumscribed—similar anti-slavery tendencies appeared, though rather weakly. Still, part of the agreement reached in the Continental Association of 1774 called for an end to the foreign slave trade. The Continental Congress repeated this action in April, 1776, by resolving that the importation of slaves should cease. These acts were, of course, probably more anti-British than they were anti-slavery, but clearly something of the latter feeling was present.

There was certainly latent anti-slavery sentiment in the final Declaration of Independence, particularly in the brave assertions "that all men are created equal, that they are endowed with certain inalienable Rights, that among these are Life, Liberty, and the Pursuit of Happiness." It is, moreover, relevant to note that Jefferson's original draft of the Declaration contained an explicit and strong anti-slavery statement. In his list of grievances against the British monarch, Jefferson originally had included this:

> He has waged cruel war against human nature itself, violating its most sacred rights of life and liberty in the persons of a distant people who never offended him, captivating and carrying them into slavery in another hemisphere, or to incur miserable death in their transportation thither. This piratical warfare the opprobrium of *infidel* powers, is the warfare of this *Christian* king of Great Britain determined to keep open a market where MEN should be bought and sold.

But this, at the request of delegates from South Carolina and Georgia, and some from the slave-trading New England states, was deleted from the final copy.

II

While evidence has been brought forward to demonstrate a very real advance in anti-slavery sentiment and action during the

Revolution, this is not to obscure the fact that throughout the Revolution, 20 per cent of the American population did consist of Negro slaves. Nor must it obscure the fact that, especially in the South, the enslavement of the Negro was fundamentally adhered to and that the general opinion amongst the slaveowners was severely hostile to any "meddling" with their property, human or otherwise.

In this connection it is important to note that the southern states in particular intensified during the Revolution, their machinery for slave control. Further, North Carolina, for example, passed a law in 1777 making the manumission of slaves quite difficult because, "the evil and pernicious practice of freeing slaves in this State, ought at this alarming and critical time to be guarded against by every friend and well-wisher to his country." Again, South Carolina in 1780 enacted a law granting a prime slave as part of the bounty to be given to soldiers volunteering for service in the Revolutionary cause. Indeed, this state and Georgia, made a practice of partly paying their officials' salaries, during the inflation of the Revolutionary Continental, by giving them slaves.

The Negro people did receive some benefits from the stimulation of anti-slavery sentiment that indubitably was part of the Revolutionary atmosphere. But these benefits generally came late in the period, were rarely far-reaching, and were almost always gradual. Moreover, the attitude of the Southern states, where, of course, slavery was concentrated, was not one warranting high hopes or enthusiasm on the part of the Negroes.

Where the Negro could serve his own land and simultaneously obtain or advance his own freedom, he eagerly did so, but where he discovered that his country denied him his craving for freedom, he turned elsewhere—flight, rebellion, agitation, assassination—for it was liberty he wanted, not ringing declarations.

III

With the agitation in the colonies in the 1760's against British tyranny, there appeared, at least in New England, efforts by some slaves to gain freedom through the courts. There is, for example, evidence in John Adam's diary entry for November 5, 1766, that certain Massachusetts slaves attempted to challenge the legal basis of slavery by bringing an action of trespass in the local courts against their masters. Adams, in reporting his own presence at one such unsuccessful effort, remarked that he had "heard there have been many," and records of some have survived.

There is evidence of repeated group petitions protesting their subordinate status from free Negroes as well as slaves, in New England. There are extant at least ten such collective petitions, coming from Massachusetts, Connecticut and New Hampshire, from January, 1773 to February, 1780.

Extracts from one, protesting against slavery, may serve as an example of the contents of several. This was presented to the Massachusetts legislature in January, 1777. It presents itself as "the petition of a Great Number of Blackes detained in a State of slavery in the Bowels of a free and Christian Country." These petitioners "apprehend that they have in Common with all other men a Natural and Unaliable Right to that freedom which the Grat Parent of the Unavers hath Bestowed equalley on all memkind and which they have never forfeited by any Compact or agreement whatever." Seeing your own appeals to the government of Great Britain for a redress of grievances and for greater freedom, we, said the petitioners, have several times taken our case to you, but, alas, our success in so pleading has been no greater than your own. Further: "They cannot but express their Astonishment that it have never Bin Considered that Every Principle from which America has Acted in the Cours of their unhappy Dificultes with Great Briton Pleads Stronger that a thousand Arguments in favours of your petioners."

Hence they urge the revolutionary government of Massachusetts to free all adult slaves and provide for the emancipation of slave children upon their reaching 21 years of age. Doing this, the inhabitants of Massachusetts would "no longer [be] chargeable with the inconsistency of acting Themselves the part which they condem and oppose in others."

In 1780, several Negroes of Massachusetts joined in a protest against the clause in the State Constitution adopted that year which restricted those who might vote to white [male] taxpayers. These petitioners reminded the Massachusetts lawmakers of the injustice of taxation without representation.

But the vast majority of American slaves were concentrated in the South and while emancipationist sentiment did grow there, as we have observed, it is nevertheless true that this growth represented but a fraction of the slave-holding class and that but a minute number were actually freed, as compared with the scores of thousands held in bondage.

Slaveowners knew from bitter experience that unusual excitement resulted in increased restlessness among the Negro masses, and the Revolutionary era is an excellent illustration of that fact. Slaveowners believed, as two of them from Georgia, Archibald Bullock and John Houston, told John Adams in November, 1775, that were a hostile officer to land an army within the Southern area "and proclaim freedom to all the Negroes who would join his camp, twenty thousand Negroes would join it . . . in a fortnight." For, as these same men remarked, "The Negroes have a wonderful art of communicating intelligence among themselves; it will run several hundreds of miles in a week or fortnight."

The slave area always operated under strict military, legal, and social systems of control, but during the revolutionary turmoil special safeguards were instituted.

Thus, a general policy of removing the slave population from zones close to the British armies was followed. Other special precautions were used, as when Georgia, in August, 1776, confined certain Negro pilots, and stationed a guard vessel in Savannah, "to prevent Negroes from going down to Cockspur"—an island off which were stationed enemy vessels. Similar action was taken elsewhere, as in St. Mary's County, Maryland, from whence an officer reported, in March, 1781, that he had posted guards "at the most convenient places to prevent the Negroes from going to the Enemy and Secured all Boats and Canoes." Another officer, that same month, asked Maryland's Governor for 60 more men to be kept "constantly patroling" in St. Mary's County in order to prevent the flight of slaves, "as from the late conduct of the Negroes when those ships [of the British] were in St. Marys I am well satisfied the greatest part of them that are in the County would join them."

Notwithstanding the elaborate machinery of control, tens of thousands of slaves succeeded in escaping, though, the evidence shows, many who reached the British found harsh treatment, disease, sale to slavery in the West Indies, or death. Some, however, did gain freedom eventually—in England, Canada and Nova Scotia—and many others, as fugitives, held onto freedom in the North. So bad, however, were the conditions generally found by the slaves within the British lines that this did more to discourage flight in that particular direction than all the precautions established by the Revolutionists.

References to the wholesale flight of slaves occur as soon as the fighting began. Lord Dunmore, the Royal Governor of Virginia, attempted to cripple the Revolution by offering, in a proclamation of November 7, 1775, to give freedom to the slaves of all rebels who were able to bear arms and who reached his lines. The Virginia Committee of Safety, realizing the gravity of the situation, promptly issued a counter-proclamation. This warned the slaves not to heed Dunmore's offer, and pointed out that Great Britain herself owned slaves whom it did not offer freedom, that she had been the greatest stimulator of the slave trade and had, indeed, vetoed Virginia's efforts at suppressing that trade. Moreover, said Virginia's proclamation, Dunmore's offer applied only to the adult male slaves (who would thus have to abandon their loved ones) of the patriots, not of the Tories, and he probably would betray the promise anyway and ship the Negroes to the West Indies. Added to this appeal, was Virginia's law of December, 1775, already mentioned, providing banishment or execution as the penalty for captured fugitive slaves.

Nevertheless, thousands of slaves at once attempted to flee. Edmund Pendleton, a distinguished Virginian, told Richard Henry Lee, November 27, 1775, that "slaves flock to him (Dunmore) in abundance," and two weeks later an American lady wrote her London friend: "The flame runs like wild fire through the slaves." Local Virginia county committees, in November and December, 1775, like those of Northampton and Warwick, also refer to the wholesale exodus of the slave population. The letters of Dunmore himself testify to the same phenomenon, though they confirm that many of the fugitives found disease and death rather than freedom inside the British lines.

Evidence of wholesale flight comes from other areas, too, and it is clear that efforts to gain freedom by flight continued throughout the war years.

This mass flight for freedom is surely one of the most dramatic, and pathetic, features of the American Revolution. An idea of its extent over the whole period of the Revolution may be obtained by considering some contemporary figures. Thus, for example, after the Treaty of Paris of 1783, the British ships sailed away from New York City with well over 3,000 escaped Negroes. When the British fleet evacuated Savannah, in July, 1782, it carried away some 5,000 escaped slaves, and about 6,500 Negroes sailed away in 1783, when the British withdrew from Charleston. In addition, all through the seven years of fighting, vessels filled with escaped slaves were again and again sent to Florida, the West Indies, Nova Scotia and England. Many slaves, moreover, fled to areas within the United States, and to the armies and ships of the French ally, as well as to the British.

Contemporary estimates of total losses of slaves offer further enlightenment. Thomas Jefferson declared that Virginia alone in the single year 1778 lost 30,000 slaves through flight; it is certain that many more Virginia slaves escaped both before and after that year. Responsible citizens of Georgia declared that their state lost from 75 to 85 per cent of its slaves (totalling about 15,000 in 1774), and South Carolinians asserted that of the 110,000 slaves in their state when the Revolution started, about 25,000 succeeded in escaping by the time it had ended. It is certainly a fact that though South Carolina imported slaves by the thousands in the years immediately after the Revolution, she did not again have as many slaves as she had had in 1773 until 1790. If to all this one adds the slaves who escaped from North Carolina, Maryland, Delaware and the northern states, particularly New Jersey and New York, it appears to be conservative to say that from 1775 until 1783 some 100,000 slaves (*i.e.*, about one out of every six men, women and children) *succeeded* in escaping from slavery, though very often finding death or slavery elsewhere.

It was very fortunate for the Revolutionary cause that political and economic considerations kept the British from actively waging an anti-slavery war. Had she done so she would surely have attracted many more fugitive slaves than her armies and fleets did; had she done so, too, she could have augmented the number of her fighters by several thousands. What the outcome would have been in such a case is, of course, completely conjectural. But the fact is that the reactionary government of George III was terrified by the American Revolution; it would not support so fundamentally revolutionary, in a social sense, a movement as one seeking the overthrow of the system of chattel slavery. Particularly would she not do this in face of the fact that there were about 750,000 slaves in the British West Indies, and that a number of the largest slaveowners in the southern colonies were Tories.

Of course, this worked both ways. Silas Deane wrote from Paris, December 3, 1776, to John Jay urging that the Americans try to stir up rebellions among the slaves in Jamaica. The considerations restraining the British would clearly rule out such action by the Americans.

IV

In the turbulent days just before, during and immediately after the Revolution, considerable areas in rebeldom were disturbed by the activities of maroons. This phenomenon—outlying, militantly hostile and quite destructive fugitive slaves—was a permanent feature of the American slave system, but like all other forms of protest it became most pronounced during periods of stress and excitement.

Uprisings and plots of slaves also recur throughout these years. Characteristic were the activities, late in 1767, of slaves in and around Alexandria, Virginia, which resulted in the nearly simultaneous deaths of several overseers from poisoning. The contemporary press reported "that some of the Negroes have been taken up, four of them were executed three weeks ago, after which their heads were cut off, and fixed on the chimnies of the courthouse; and it was expected that four more would soon meet the same fate." It seems probable that a few of the executed slaves be-

longed to George Mason—later author of the Virginia Declaration of Rights, and chief author of the Bill of Rights of the
American Constitution.

Another example of rebellion within revolution was a rather
modest uprising of slaves in St. Andrews Parish, Georgia, in
November, 1774, as a result of which seven white people were
killed and wounded. Two of the slaves involved in this outbreak
were burned alive as a punishment; what other measure of repression may have been take is not known. A letter written from
Charlestown, S.C., August 20, 1775, contained this line: "Yester-
day a negro was hanged and burnt for intended sedition, and
burning the Town."

The most considerable conspiracy of the period was that involving hundreds, possibly thousands, of slaves in Beaufort, Pitt
and Craven Counties, North Carolina in the summer of 1775.
Whippings, brandings, ear-croppings of dozens of slaves and the
executions of several marked the repression of this slave plot.
Throughout the years of the Revolution other instances of plots
or outbreaks occurred—in Massachusetts, New York, New Jersey,
Pennsylvania, Virginia, the Carolinas, Georgia. Generally they
produced a tightening of police measures and some impact on the
military effectiveness of the rebels' resistance to England, especially in the South. They served, too, to dramatize the awful inconsistency in waging a war of national liberation and simultaneously confining one-fifth of the population in chains.

V

Negroes, free and slave, where and when permitted to do so,
played a conspicuous part in the armed forces of the Revolution.
Much red tape had to be cut before the Negro, particularly the
slave, was allowed to contribute his services to the Revolutionary
army, but the navy—Continental and provincial—did not pursue
a Jim-Crow policy. Hence, throughout the Revolutionary years
there are repeated references to Negroes as members of the crews
of the infant nation's sea fighters.

Negroes sailed with John Paul Jones and John Barry and David
Porter, among the greatest naval commanders of the Revolution.

They were among the crews of the *Hazzard, Deane,* and *Prospect,* the *Alliance, Roebuck,* and *Confederacy,* the *Racehorse, Adventure* and *Aurora.* They served in every capacity from powder boy to pilot.

We have all seen pictures depicting the Spirit of '76 with the gallant drummer and fifer swinging along, and others depicting the poorly clad and under-provisioned army of Washington bleeding and shivering at Valley Forge. Generally, however, these pictures are lily-white; but in real life Negroes as well as whites drummed and bled and shivered.

Specifically, as examples, the drummer for Captain Benjamin Egbert's company in New York City in March, 1776, was a Negro listed as Tom. The fifer (sometimes taking a hand at the drum, too) for Captain John Ford's company of the 27th Massachusetts Regiment was Barzillai Lew, native of Groton, where he was born in 1743, and where his six-foot frame working at the trade of a cooper was a familiar sight. This Barzillai Lew drummed and fifed and fought his way through the Revolutionary War from almost the moment fighting began (he enlisted May 6, 1775), down to the day, some seven years later, when arms were stacked. That black men, as well as white, were at Valley Forge is certain, for there is record of at least one who died there that terrible winter of 1778—Phillip Field, of Dutchess County, New York, soldier in Captain Pelton's company of the 2nd New York Regiment.

Yet, as we have already stated, the existence of slavery created an embarrassing and dangerous contradiction within the Revolutionary forces. This had, as we have seen, the effect of stunting the budding emancipationist sentiment, and it had a similar effect in producing laws and regulations to hinder the enrollment of Negroes within the ranks of the Revolutionary Army. Thus, John Rutledge, a delegate from South Carolina to the Continental Congress, introduced in September, 1775, a resolution barring Negroes from use as soldiers; on October 18 this was approved by the Congress. Ten days earlier a council of general officers of the American Army already had decided unanimously against the use of free Negroes as soldiers. This was followed on November 12, 1775, by Washington's order complying with these decisions.

But soon a reversal of this trend began to take place. Both the legislative and military bodies observed with alarm the flocking of thousands of slaves to the British (particularly after Dunmore's proclamation of November 7, 1775). They realized that every element of man-power would be needed, and had already seen— at Lexington, Concord and Bunker Hill—that Negroes were able and willing to fight, and acquitted themselves well. No doubt, too, the anti-slavery agitation of Negroes and some whites played a part.

On December 30, 1775, Washington issued the following message from his Massachusetts headquarters: "As the General is informed, that numbers of Free Negroes are desirous of enlisting, he gives leave to recruiting officers to entertain them, and promises to lay the matter before the Congress, who he doubts not will approve it." The next day Washington sent Congress a letter, telling of his action. He explained that "free Negroes who have served in this Army, are very much dissatisfied at being discarded," and that therefore he had "presumed to depart from the [Congressional] Resolution [of Oct. 18, 1775], respecting them" and had "given license for their being enlisted." In a Resolution of January 16, 1776, Congress approved Washington's action, stating that "the free Negroes who have served faithfully in the army at Cambridge, may be re-enlisted, but no others."

Certain state regulations, in addition to those already mentioned, also effected the question of Negro service in the Revolutionary Army. New York, in 1776, permitted men who had been drafted to offer substitutes for themselves in the form of able-bodied men, white or Negro. This led some slaveholders to offer their slaves as soldiers, the latter's reward being freedom. Virginia, in May, 1777, passed an act for the purpose of completing its troop quota. The act contained this very interesting paragraph:

> And whereas several Negro slaves have deserted from their masters, and under pretence of being free men have enlisted as soldiers: For prevention whereof, Be it enacted, that it shall not be lawful for any recruiting officer within this Commonwealth to enlist any Negro or mulatto into this or other of the United States, until such Negro or mulatto shall produce a certificate from some justice of the peace for the county wherein he resides that he is a free man.

In February, 1778, Rhode Island, and in April, 1778, Massachusetts, finding the going getting tougher, the man-supply thinning, and the slaves as willing as ever to fight—provided they received their freedom—passed laws for the enrollment of slaves as soldiers in their state forces. As a result, several hundred Negroes gained their freedom.

An incidental phrase in a North Carolina law of 1778, passed in the vain hope of eliminating the problem of fugitive slaves, demonstrates the fact that Negroes were serving in the armed forces of that State. This act, in providing for the capture and disposal of fugitives, adds: "Nothing herein contained shall deprive of liberty any slave who having been liberated and not sold by order of any Court has inlisted in the service of this or the United States." In 1779, North Carolina explicitly provided for the enlistment of slaves, with the masters' consent, of course, and with the understanding that faithful service for the war's duration would bring liberation.

Strenuous efforts were made in 1778 and 1779 to persuade South Carolina and Georgia to permit the enrollment of Negroes as soldiers, but these never succeeded, in terms of formal enactment, though it is certain that some Negroes did serve in both states. Behind this move were people like Alexander Hamilton, Henry Laurens, James Madison, Generals Lincoln and Greene and even, though not quite wholeheartedly, Washington.

Indeed, the Continental Congress, in March 1779, adopted a resolution urging Georgia and South Carolina, for the sake of saving the cause in those areas, to permit the enlistment of 3,000 Negroes (Congress offered to pay $1,000 for each Negro who would, of course, then be free) but both states shuddered at the proposition, and even hinted that they would withdraw from the struggle before acceding to it. (It may, incidentally, be noted again, that largely because of the considerable slave population and this reactionary attitude, nearly all of Georgia and eastern South Carolina were conquered by the British.)

Maryland, in October, 1780, and again in May, 1781, passed laws permitting slaves and free Negroes to be recruited as soldiers. New York, in accordance with an act passed in March, 1781, raised two regiments of slaves, all of whom enlisted with the understanding that loyal service for the war's duration would bring emancipation.

The fact of the widespread presence of Negroes in the Revolutionary army is established by the laws and resolutions described above. In addition, there are numerous contemporary descriptions from Americans, Englishmen, Frenchmen and Hessians confirming this, beginning with 1775 and continuing throughout the war years.

References to specific Negroes who performed notably valiant deeds, and to the especially large numbers of Negroes participating in particular battles or campaigns are numerous in the contemporary literature. Casualty and pension lists sometimes distinguished Negro and white soldiers and from these one finds additional conclusive evidence of Negro soldiers participating— and being wounded or killed—in many engagements, as the battles of Brandywine (1777), the seige of Boonesborough (1778), the storming of Fort Griswold (1781), the battle of Eutaw (1781), the seige of Cornwallis (1781). Again, in the last organized military effort of the war—the futile march from Saratoga to the (intended) goal of the British forces at Oswego, New York, in February, 1783—Negro soldiers formed the bulk of the American force that was led, perhaps by treachery, off its course, with the result that dozens died or were maimed by freezing.

Negroes fought at Concord and Lexington, at Bunker Hill and Ticonderoga, at Long Island, Stony Point, Savannah, Trenton, Monmouth. They crossed the Delaware with Washington in 1776 —one, Prince Whipple, was in the General's own boat. Of the handful of soldiers who raided the British headquarters at Newport, Rhode Island, in July, 1777, and succeeded in capturing General Prescott and Major Barrington, one of the most amazing deeds of initiative and daring of the war, one was a Negro named Jack Sisson.

So conspicuous was the gallantry of the Negro soldier, Salem Poor, in the Battle of Bunker Hill, when gallantry was universal, that it was formally called to the attention of the Massachusetts legislature, December 5, 1775, by 14 officers, including three colonels. They declared that, under fire, Salem Poor had "behaved like an experienced officer, as well as an excellent soldier.

To set forth particulars of his conduct would be tedious . . . in the person of this Negro centers a brave and gallant soldier."

Negroes fought with Allen's Green Mountain Boys and were members of the guerrilla fighters led in South Carolina by Francis Marion. In some cases, entire units of Revolutionary soldiers consisted of Negro soldiers, with white commanders—as that of Massachusetts Negroes commanded by Samuel Lawrence, Connecticut Negroes under Colonel Humphreys, and Rhode Island Negroes under Colonel Olney. In at least two cases, Negro companies were Negro up to and including Negro commanders—the company of Massachusetts Negroes led by one Middleton and that of Rhode Island Negroes led by Barzillai Lew. At least one case of a Negro non-commissioned officer in a mixed unit has been found: Corporal Perley Rogers in the 2nd Massachusetts Regiment commanded by Colonel John Bailey. Negroes from every state fought in the Revolutionary Army. Indeed, in the case of several states—Maryland, New York, Connecticut, Rhode Island, Massachusetts and New Hampshire—one would have difficulty in naming many towns or cities from which Negroes did *not* enlist.

A good example is Connecticut (which contained about 6,500 Negroes in 1774) whose records were kept particularly well, and show Negro volunteers from at least 47 different localities, from Ashford to Woodstock, from Branford to Waterbury, from Canaan to Winchester. Even for Georgia there is conclusive proof that at least five Negroes from that state fought against the British, for records are extant of the manumission of all five as rewards for their service. One of these, Austin Dabney, was not only freed, but, in addition, having conducted himself—said the legislative act of emancipation—"with a bravery and fortitude which would have honored a freeman," he was awarded an annual pension of $96, and given 112 acres of land. At least one South Carolina Negro, John Eady, also distinguished himself in the Revolutionary Army and was rewarded with freedom and land.

An additional very interesting piece of evidence concerning Negroes in the Revolutionary Army appears in a Virginia law of October, 1783. The quotation is long, but worth careful reading:

Whereas it hath been represented to the General Assembly that during the course of the war many persons in this State had caused their slaves to enlist in certain regiments or corps raised within the same, having tendered such slaves to the officers appointed to recruit forces within the state, as substituted for free persons, whose lot or duty it was to serve in such regiments or corps, at the same time representing to such recruiting officers that the slaves so enlisted by their direction and concurrence were freemen; and it appearing further to this Assembly, that on the expiration of the term of enlistment of such slaves that the former owners have attempted again to force them to return to a state of servitude, contrary to the principles of justice, and to their own solemn promise, (and since, the law continued, such Negroes, by their service) have thereby of course contributed towards the establishment of American liberty and independence,

the Attorney General was instructed to see to it that those Negroes were confirmed in their freedom.

Certain it is that several thousand Negroes, a minimum estimate would be 5,000, served as regular soldiers in the American Revolutionary Army. Certain it is, also, that others, probably a greater total, served that army as teamsters, cooks, guides, and what were then called pioneers—or are known today as combat engineers.

VI

The record of the Negroes' service to the Army and the Navy as fighters and workers does not complete the account of their direct aid to the military effort in the Revolution. For excellent evidence exists proving that Negroes also performed valiantly as spies.

For example, an unnamed Negro contributed significantly to the overwhelming defeat inflicted upon a British force at the Battle of Edenton, N.C., December 8, 1775. The Negro, acting under the direct orders of the American commander, Colonel Fordyce, entered the British camp and told, in such a convincing fashion, of a weak, disorganized American force, that the English hastily attacked what in reality was a well-prepared and strategically-placed American force. The result was one hundred British casualties contrasted with one American killed. Of this engagement, the late distinguished historian, William E. Dodd, wrote: "It was a godsend to the revolutionists of Virginia; it stirred drooping spirits as they had not been stirred since the news of Lexington."

Anthony Wayne's surprise attack upon and relatively easy capture of the fort at Stony Point, New York, in July, 1779, was materially assisted by Pompey, a Negro slave belonging to the American Captain Lamb. Pompey obtained the British password and used this in aiding an American detachment to overcome the British guards, thus leading to the surprise and seizure of the strategic stronghold, together with considerable supplies, and 600 prisoners. For this, Pompey was given his freedom.

Rhode Island, in 1782, freed a Negro, Quaco Honeyman, as a reward for important spying activity; South Carolina, in 1783, freed the wife and child of a deceased Negro whose spying efforts had been valuable. Virginia, in 1786, freed James, slave of William Armistead, because he had, in 1781 at the seige of Yorktown, as the act of emancipation declares, entered "into the service of the Marquis La Fayette, and at the peril of his life found means to frequent the British camp, and thereby faithfully executed important commissions entrusted to him by the Marquis." On liberation, James became James Lafayette; in 1819, the Virginia legislature awarded him $100, with an annual pension thereafter of $40.

VII

The evidence shows that the activities of that 20 per cent of the population in Revolutionary America who were Negroes is of fundamental importance for an understanding of the Revolution. On the labor power of those 600,000 rested to a very large degree the economic viability of the nascent Republic and without it the new nation could not have been conceived.

Further, the organized activities of the Negro masses themselves, where any possibility of such activities existed—the court actions, petitions, plots and uprisings, the flight and guerrilla warfare, the service in and for the navy and army as pilots, seamen, laborers, soldiers, spies—always had as their fundamental motivation the achievement of freedom, the realization, in fullest practice, of the Declaration of Independence.

Some fairly considerable advances in this direction were made, particularly in the North, during the Revolution (and as part of that Revolution); these, together with service in the armed forces, did lead to the emancipation of several thousand slaves. But the movement fell short and, in part because of such compromise, tens of thousands of slaves sought freedom by flight or rebellion. That the movement for emancipation did fall short came close to bringing victory to the British; it is, moreover, quite possible that the British would have won had not their own position made it impossible for them to wage a real war of Negro liberation.

It seems safe to say that this failure to free the Negro people led to the postponement of the final victory of the American forces. It is certain that the failure to root out slavery produced, in less than 80 years, a very bloody Civil War before the Second American Revolution could complete this task neglected by the First.

Chapter XIV

The Social Effects of the Revolution

HISTORIANS DIFFER in their overall estimates of the effects of the American Revolution. Some, who tend to deny the revolutionary qualities of its origin and conduct, naturally tend to deny that it induced any significant revolutionary results; others, holding contrary views as to its roots and course, see different results.

I

One of the pivots about which the debate turns is the volume produced by the late J. Franklin Jameson, *The American Revolution Considered as a Social Movement,* published by Princeton University Press in 1926, a year after its substance had been delivered in a series of lectures at that university. We shall have more to say of this work shortly, but its theme is clearly conveyed in its title. To indicate the content of the debate, one may contrast two recent statements by Richard B. Morris of Columbia University and Frederick B. Tolles of Swarthmore College.

Tolles, offering "a re-evaluation" of Jameson's book in *The American Historical Review* (October, 1954), and summarizing some of the corrections and exceptions taken to it, concluded:

> Still, a historian who fashions so useful a conceptual tool, who popularizes so fruitful a hypothesis, who enlarges so notably

our understanding of a significant era in American history, can be forgiven a few oversights, a few overstatements. Basically, the "Jameson thesis" is still sound, and, what is more important, still vital and suggestive, capable of still further life, still greater usefulness.

Morris, on the other hand, concludes an essay on "The Confederation Period" (*William and Mary Quarterly*, April, 1956), with this sentence: "Despite the efforts of J. Franklin Jameson to consider the American Revolution as a social movement, the fact is that the great internal social reforms lay ahead."

The evidence, I think, supports Jameson—and Tolles—and not Morris. There is a note of ambiguity in Professor Morris' mode of expression; *i.e.*, the fact that great internal social reforms were to occur after the American Revolution is not something that justifies discarding Jameson. For, of course, the question is what were the changes achieved during and under the impetus of the Revolution; not what reforms other eras might feel were still needed.

There is another area of confusion about the impact of the Revolution that needs tackling. This is in part indicated in the title of Jameson's work; it is a certain compartmentalizing of the Revolution's results—into political, economic, social, etc.—as though each was really distinct from the other. There is, surely, distinction among changes, as those which effect suffrage requirements, and those that effect the instiutional forms of religious organizations, or those that give an impulse to manufacturing and those that alter the status of slaves. There are, of course, significant qualitative differences in such results which justify their being categorized. But such distinctions and categories must not obscure the interpenetration of these results; they must not hide the fact that each impinged upon the other, that all were part of one national and societal fabric, and that all are significant in any effort at an overall estimate of the Revolution's effects.

Indicative of the confusion, it seems to me, is the concluding chapter in the valuable study by Elisha P. Douglass, *Rebels and Democrats* (1955). The chapter's title, "Democracy and Liberalism," suggests the confusion for it posits two distinct and even partially contrasting entities; the text of the chapter spells out this confusion. Professor Douglass asks:

> Why did democracy make so little progress in the nation as a whole during the Revolution? . . . Why did the protest against political privilege, often heard in the years before the war, not lead to widespread social revolution when the confusion and dislocations attendant upon civil strife offered an opportunity to do so?

He does not leave his question with no answer. He sees a high degree of social elasticity as part of the answer; finds the existing government, during the Revolution, to have been such and to have acted in such a way that "its impositions were not keenly felt"; sees the abundance of cheap land as assuaging social bitterness and tending to allay potential ferment; observes an overwhelmingly agrarian society, such as Revolutionary America was, as one where widespread and really antagonistic social conflicts and contradictions tended to be minimal; and finally, he remarks that "the degree to which the ideals of the Revolution were achieved was sufficient to remove most of the incentive for social revolution."

But is not much of this significant democratic progress, rather than an explanation as to why there was "so little progress"? Douglass tends to equate 20th century popular demands, which often have an economic and social content quite different from those of 250 years ago, with progress in democracy in general— *i.e.*, rule by, for, and of the people. But, of course, different centuries and different locales pose different questions.

Thus, when Douglass notes the changes which he does summarize, he is describing very significant democratic progress. Further, where he defines the "liberalism" portion of his chapter, in terms of protections against governmental arbitrariness, the insistence upon officials operating in accordance with stated law, the care with which individual freedoms are safeguarded, the effort to establish the concept of government as serving the people and not dominating them, he is also, I think, describing real progress in democracy, confined as that is and must be, within the limitations of the 18th century.

Contemporaries saw the tremendous revolutionary and democratic meaning of a successful colonial liberation effort in the first place; that a nationality could rip itself away from the domination of imperial Britain, despite the forcible efforts at repression by that power, was no small democratic advance. And contemporaries—Thomas Paine, for instance—saw that not only had this historic achievement been recorded but also that in achieving it, there had been at home "a revolution in the principles and practice of government." Contemporaries, living in Europe "under arbitrary power," as Benjamin Franklin wrote on May 1, 1777, "read the translations of our separate Colony constitutions with rapture." They were enraptured by democratic progress, not of the same kind, perhaps, as would similarly effect them in the mid-20th century, but that, of course, is an anachronistic, not an historical test.

The best brief evaluation of this question, so far as I know, occurs in one of the last works of that preeminent scholar of the American Revolution, the late Evarts Boutell Greene. In his *Revolutionary Generation* (1943), Greene declared: "From an eighteenth century European standard the American states had gone far toward equalitarian democracy."

In essential agreement with this appraisal is the argument of a leading contemporary authority on the same period, Merrill Jensen. Jensen's work has come in for rather intensive criticism in the very recent past—some of it seems to be well taken—but the main conclusions of that work, so far as this period is concerned, are, I believe, sound. In his volume, *The New Nation* (1950), Jensen wrote:

> The spirit of optimism, of belief in America as a refuge for the oppressed of the Old World, as a place of democratic equality, all show that the American Revolution, in result if not in origin, was far more than a movement for independence. Planted in it were seeds that promised the fruit of democracy. The breakdown of old political controls and the creation of new governments, however similar in form and substance to the old, carried with it the possibility of the democratization of American society.

Further on, he declared:

Whatever we may think today, the men of the eighteenth century thought that "democracy" was a vital force unleashed by the Revolution. Democracy as they saw it found expression in the revolutionary constitutions of the states and in the refusal to grant coercive powers to a central government under the Articles of Confederation. The Revolution had altered the whole theoretical foundation of American government . . . however often the theory has been disregarded since then, the idea that the people may create and destroy their government at will has been the theoretical starting point for all governments in the United States.

Jensen also emphasized—overemphasized, I think—that another result of the Revolution, "the removal from the American scene of a central government with coercive power," was held by contemporaries to be of the greatest consequence in furthering democracy.

Jensen makes a significant point when he insists that the Revolution advanced the potential for democratization.[1] This is of consequence when one considers the social advances which, as Professor Morris observed, came *after* the Revolution. In the sense of preparing the ground, the fact that important social reforms followed the Revolution may help confirm rather than refute Jameson's thesis.

II

Specifically, what are the developments which may be fairly ascribed to the Revolution? So far as general political and social impact is concerned, historians before Jameson had commented upon it. This was true of Carl Becker writing in 1909, of Edward Channing in 1912, and, particularly, Allan Nevins, in his *American States During and After the Revolution,* first published in 1924. From their work and the work of later writers, who have generally dealt with more limited subjects, as well as an examination of contemporaneous material, it becomes manifest that notable and numerous changes were made and steps taken to give reality to the idea of the people's sovereignty.

I would say, first of all, with Jensen, that the promulgation of popular sovereignty (no matter how much in practice this might

be limited, by considerations, for example, of sex, property ownership, race, etc.) as the only legitimate basis for governmental
power was a basically revolutionary event and one fundamental
to a democratic society.

The Revolution represented not only a fundamental break in
the theory of government; it resulted in a fundamental change in
the form of government. This change was least notable where, as
in Connecticut, the colonial charter was retained as the frame-
work for state government. But this was exceptional; in 11 of the
13 states, the revolutionists remade the structure of the state, as
they terminated their allegiance to monarchy.

In the 18th century, given adherence to the sanctity of contract
and the private ownership of the means of production, political
theory projected three possible state forms, resting upon and bulwarking this material basis. These were: Hereditary monarchy
with aristocratic accompaniments, personal tyranny or individual
dictatorship, and a republic. Of the three, the last was exceptional in mankind's experience, and where it had existed, was
restricted to very narrow territorial limits. The democratic essence
of the American Revolution shows itself in the rejection of the
two traditional forms of political rule and the adoption of the
third. And this choice was made despite the vastness of the territory involved. The unprecedented nature of a republican form
for so vast an area argued in favor of a decentralized and rather
loosely federated national government; the unhappy experiences
suffered by the colonies with the centralization of power in Westminster served to reinforce support for such decentralization and
federalism.

But it is of major historical significance that the American
Revolution results, because of its popular nature, in the republican form being adopted, first by the State governments and then,
in the Constitution, by the national government. It is somewhat
surprising, in view of its consequences, that this development has
received little notice in the historical literature. A notable exception is an essay by George M. Dutcher (*Political Science Quarterly,* June, 1940).

In his work, Dutcher points out that the United States was the
"first fully republican modern nation—the first republic clearly

on a basis broader than municipal." While this is actually the accomplishment of the Constitution (to be discussed in a subsequent volume) and while it is true that none of the revolutionary State constitutions uses the word "republic," it is also true that their form was republican and was so understood by contemporaries. It is also a fact that three of the original thirteen states—Virginia, Pennsylvania, and Massachusetts—in their constitutions referred to themselves as commonwealths, and that Vermont, in its first and second constitutions, similarly defined itself.

When the Constitution in article 4, section 4, declares that, "The United States shall guarantee to every State in this Union a Republican Form of Government," it was actually confirming that which had been established, though not in words, in each of the States. This establishment was the work of the Revolution; it marked a significant political transformation and provided great potential for further progressive advance.

III

The achievement of the republican *form* was momentous, but more decisive was the popular *content* placed within that form. The form itself reflects popular pressure and carries with it the potential of real development; hence its adoption was momentous. But what of the *content* achieved, in terms of enhancement of popular political power?

In the first place, certain great principles aimed at guaranteeing a considerable degree of popular sovereignty and at inhibiting the development of tyranny were incorporated within the State governments and both in the Articles of Confederation and the Constitution. These principles included: (1) legitimate government requires popular consent; (2) oppressive government is to be undone, by revolutionary action, if necessary; (3) civil power is superior to and must be dominant over military power; (4) the separation of the legislative, executive and judicial arms of government inhibits the concentration of power and thus helps frustrate the growth of tyranny; (5) the powers of government are limited and therefore are subject to being specified in written constitutions; (6) government operates through stipulated rules, known to all, and broken only by traitors and oppressors, *i.e.,* stated laws and procedures must be observed by the government in the course of its doing those things the Fundamental Law allows it to do; (7) generally speaking, office-holders are elected; those of lesser power may be appointed, but as a rule office-holders are looked upon with suspicion, surrounded by limitations, the most notable being that on the duration of their tenure—but, in any case, hereditary possession of office or of political power is forbidden; (8) while the three branches of government are separated, the legislative is favored over the executive in terms of the locus of power, and care is exercised to institutionalize the independence of the judiciary; (9) provision for amendment of the Fundamental Law is present and is there as an expression of democratic bias: *i.e.,* the dead are not to bind the living; error, of commission and omission, is human and therefore rectification is inevitable, not invidious; societies grow and change and social needs alter, wherefore social and political institutions must be subject to alteration. To provide the constitutional means for this, beforehand, is wise and democratic; (10) geographical centralization of power may be as dangerous and harmful as political centralization; hence, the dispersing of power-potential in terms of local or statewide powers serves the cause of enhancing popular control and of restraining the appearance of tyranny; (11) the sovereignty of the people makes logical the idea of limited, specified governmental power. But this carries with it not only an enumeration of what the government may legally do; it also carries with it an enumeration of what the government may not do—*i.e.,* of those rights and freedoms which are inviolable, of a Bill of Rights.

Before offering a sampling of details to substantiate the above generalizations on the impact of the Revolution upon political institutions, it is important to note that that era greatly furthered what Charles A. Barker has called "the politics of protest." In his valuable study, *The Background of the Revolution in Maryland* (1940), Barker pointed to the development, in the decade of the 1770's, of the regularized appearance of "election pledges, instructions to delegates, mass meetings, committees and associations," all of which from outside legislative doors, widened popular participation in politics and enhanced the influence of such participation upon political decision.

It is activities of this kind that, during Revolution, result in significant and numerous democratic innovations in political structure.

In the first place, the electorate was broadened considerably in this period. Exactitude in this connection is not possible; the comment of the Beards as to the number of voters just before the Revolution, in their *Rise of American Civilization,* written a generation ago, remains substantially in accordance with current historical findings:

> The various limitations on the suffrage excluded from the polls a large portion of the population—just how large a percentage cannot be ascertained from any records now available. Certainly in the country districts of Pennsylvania, half the adult males were denied the ballot; in Philadelphia, the restrictions disfranchised about nine-tenths of the men, a sore point with a growing class of artisans, and an interesting side light on the concentration of property in that urban area. On the other hand, it is estimated that about four-fifths of the men in Massachusetts were eligible to vote, so numerous were the owners of small farms.

Subsequent research, especially that of Robert E. Brown, has indicated that it is likely that less males were legally disfranchised up to the Revolution than had hitherto been believed. But even here, the Beards' estimate of 80 per cent as eligible to vote in Massachusetts might be raised some four or five per cent; certainly in the remainder of the country, prior to the Revolution, a much larger percentage—probably exceeding half—of the adult white male population was disfranchised by law. Of course, all other inhabitants were without the vote.

There developed during the Revolution demands for the extension of the suffrage, not excluding proposals that all adults, regardless of sex or color or property, be enfranchised. Such proposals, however, were exceptional. More common were those which held that, in the face of the fundamental revolutionary slogan, "no taxation without representation," it was paradoxical for the Revolutionary Governments to allow the disfranchisement of taxpayers. Typical was the letter from a New Jersey resident,

in September, 1775, published in the press at that time, objecting
to the current mode of confining the vote only to freeholders:

> By the mode, many true friends of their country, who are
> obliged to pay taxes, are excluded from the privilege of a vote
> in the choice of those by whom they are taxed, or even called
> out to sacrifice their lives. This is a real grievance . . . [if this
> is changed] our enemies will be cut off from one of their most
> plausible arguments against us.

Characteristic were the suffrage developments in New Jersey;
these changes came because of the total impact of the Revolution,
and specifically because through letters, petitions and meetings,
public demand for such changes was registered. The suffrage basis
established in New Jersey's Constitution of July, 1776, provided
that every adult person,[2] who had resided in the state for a minimum of one year, and who possessed property—whether real or
personal—worth at least £50, had the right to vote.

There is some difference among students as to the actual impact of this legislation upon the numbers of the Jersey electorate,
but the most recent of these students agree that it extended the
suffrage very considerably. R. P. McCormick, in his *Experiment
in Independence* (1951) stated: "The practical effect of the
change was unquestionably a great increase in the number of
eligible voters." J. P. Pole, in a later study (1956) adds that the
inflation of the currency, incidental to the Revolution, "annihi-
lated the remaining property qualifications for the suffrage" so
that in that era universal male suffrage existed in the state.

In an immediate sense, the most significant determinant of the
number of voters was the availability of polling places. Here, too,
a decided improvement came with the Revolutionary era. Thus,
McCormick, in the aforementioned study, states:

> Alternate locations [for voting] were provided in three coun-
> ties [in N.J.] in 1779, in six counties in 1782, in eight counties
> in 1783, and in all thirteen counties in 1788. There were in 1779
> only eighteen places where voters might cast their ballots for
> members of the legislature; a decade later there were fifty.

The Revolutionary constitutions of Delaware, New Hampshire,
North Carolina and Pennsylvania provided that all adult males,
meeting modest residence requirements, were to have the right to

vote, regardless of property ownership, if they were taxpayers. Georgia, which by an act of 1761 confined the vote to white adult males possessing at least 50 acres of land, revised this set of requirements in its 1777 Constitution. There the ownership of land as a prerequisite was abandoned; it was necessary only that the white adult male possess £10 worth of property of any kind, or, if unable to meet this, to be engaged in any kind of a mechanical occupation. This 1777 Constitution also barred multiple voting by an individual (as had occurred before on the basis of extensive property and land ownership); forbade anyone claiming a title of nobility to vote; and provided for fining (not in excess of £5) a qualified voter who, without sound excuse, failed to exercise the privilege.

There were many other acts significantly extending the popular control over the functioning of government during the Revolutionary era. This included increasing the number of offices to be filled by election rather than appointment—from the Governor of New York, in 1777, and of Massachusetts in 1780, to the election of judges in several states; it included putting the origination of appropriation bills in the hands of the most popular branch of the legislature; subordinating the executive to the ultimate will of the legislature; moving the state capitals (of Virginia, Pennsylvania, New York, Georgia, the Carolinas) westward so that the eastern aristocracy and moneyed power was less overawing. While most of the states maintained important property or religious qualifications for officeholding—and the more exalted the office, the more restrictive the qualification—still even here certain reductions and changes were introduced. Thus, in Pennsylvania it was affirmed that all free men were to have the right to hold any public office; Delaware prohibited all religious tests for officeholding.

Another significant feature of the political structure erected in Revolutionary America was that of the separation of powers in government. This has frequently been treated as a device aiming at the protection of the interests of a well-to-do minority, but this by no means exhausts its meaning. It is true that with a republican form of government and with the theory of popular sovereignty triumphant, the rich did fear that concentrating power within that branch of the government most directly subject to popular control, opened the door to levelism and democratic "excesses." This certainly was a motive among some of the supporters of separation of powers.

But, in addition, it is to be observed that separation of powers *may* serve to protect the rights of dissident and radical minorities, as well as rich ones. It is also to be noted that separation of powers was one way of avoiding or inhibiting personal tyranny, certainly one of the main aims of the Revolution. Furthermore, the absence of separation of powers, under England's aegis, had resulted in plural officeholding and this, during the colonial period, had been one of the main devices of Royal control. Ellen E. Brennan, in her study of *Plural Office-Holding in Massachusetts, 1760-1780* (1945), demonstrated the connection between the battle for separation of powers and the battle against plural office-holding as one of the main attributes of anti-popular government. The success of this effort, then, during the Revolutionary period, is another evidence of the politically democratizing impact of that Revolution.

Among the most momentous of the democratic moves in political structure was the enactment of Bills of Rights as separate sections in the revolutionary constitutions of eight states—Virginia, Pennsylvania, Delaware, Maryland, North Carolina, Vermont, Massachusetts, New Hampshire (1784)—and their incorporation in separate provisions of the constitutions in Georgia, South Carolina, New Jersey and New York.

The first of the separate Bills of Rights, which influenced all that followed, was that of Virginia, adopted June 12, 1776. It affirmed the inherently free and independent quality of men; the sovereignty of the people; government as the people's servant; the right of revolution; opposition to inherited office; the wisdom of separation of powers; the need for frequent, regular elections; no taxation without representation; no suspension of popular sovereignty due to "emergency"; the right of the accused to know the nature of the accusation, to confront accusers and witnesses, call for evidence in his favor, to a speedy trial by impartial jury, not to be compelled to testify against himself; that neither excessive bail nor cruel punishments exist; that no general search or arrest warrents be issued; that freedom of the press be guaranteed; that the military be subordinate to the civil power; and that the state never interfere in matters of religion, since such questions were properly amenable only to "reason and conviction," never to "force or violence."

Each of the States adopted similar provisions. Rights and immunities, in addition to those contained in the Virginia law, which appear in one or more of the Revolutionary constitutions of other states include: (1) no one is to be twice in jeopardy for the same offense; (2) no one is to be held for a serious crime except upon indictment by a grand jury; (3) owners of private property, if taken for public use, were to receive compensation; (4) the right to travel freely from and to the State was guaranteed; (5) quartering of troops in homes during peace was forbidden; (6) monopolies were forbidden (by Maryland and North Carolina); (7) neither ex post facto laws nor bills of attainder were to be passed; (8) accused were to have the right of counsel.

Surely all of the preceding, which summarizes the main enactments by the revolutionary state governments in the area of political institutions, adds up to an impressive accomplishment in the direction of democratization.

IV

Church-state relationships were fundamentally altered by the American Revolution. We have indicated, in preceding paragraphs, some results in this area in the elimination in one state of any kind of religious test as a qualification for voting, the Virginia Bill of Rights explicitly declaring that matters of conscience should be and were to be outside the ken of the State.

The changes in church-state relations that appear during the Revolution, as in other areas, were culminations of a process that had marked American colonial life. William W. Sweet, an outstanding authority on the history of religion in the United States, has pointed out that until well into the 18th century a very small percentage of the colonial population were church members—that, indeed, there were "more unchurched people in America, in proportion to the population, than was to be found

in any country in Christendom." The revivalism of the Great
Awakening helped change this, but that movement won over to
the evangelical churches much of the nominal membership of
the established, Anglican Church, and, in New England, bound
together the Congregational and Presbyterian Churches against
the Anglican.

The late Evarts B. Greene, who was particularly interested in
church-state relations, after describing colonial conditions, concluded that: "The time was ripe for more radical departures
from the prevailing theory and practice of the early colonial era.
The impact of revolution was soon to bring further advance in
the same direction."

The Revolution saw the hastening of the breakaway from the
Anglican (Tory) Church, a development of dissenting churches
and an upsurge in liberal religious ideology. This, plus the general equalitarian and libertarian features of the Revolution, enhanced the movement for dis-establishment and for religious
freedom; the tendency received special impetus because of the
wartime alliance with Catholic France, and the comradeship that
developed among the predominantly Protestant Americans—
civilian and military—and the thousands of French Catholic
officers and men on military and naval duty here.

The most advanced position of the time on this question, as
on so many others, is expressed cogently by Thomas Jefferson. As
may be seen by his reasoning in the matter, the revolutionary
objection to religious intolerance was grounded in the generalized
concept of freedom of thought, expression and association. In his
Notes on Virginia, Jefferson considers the man who may be in
error and argues:

> Constraint may make him worse by making him a hypocrite,
> but it will never make him a truer man. It may fix him ob-
> stinately in his errors, but will not cure them. Reason and free
> enquiry are the only effectual agents against error. Give a loose
> to them, they will support the true religion, by bringing every
> false one to their tribunal to the test of their investigation. They
> are the natural enemies of error, and of error only.

The most advanced piece of legislation in this area was the
Statute of Religious Freedom, which Jefferson introduced into

the Virginia legislature in 1779, but which was only adopted in January, 1786, after a very bitter struggle.

As Jefferson's Declaration of Independence classically elucidates the finest tenets of the Revolution's roots, so his Statute of Religious Freedom beautifully distills the best of that Revolution's impact. The human mind, it holds, must not be constrained nor intimidated, for "all attempts to influence it by temporal punishments or burdens, or by civil incapacitations, tend only to beget habits of hypocrisy and meanness." It denounces "the impious presumption of legislators and rulers, civil as well as ecclesiastical, who being themselves but fallible and uninspired men, have assumed dominion over the faith of others"; it specifically condemns any established church or any formal church-state tie. It insists "that our civil rights have no dependence on our religious opinions, any more than our opinions in physics or geometry"; it adds that "to suffer the civil magistrate to intrude his powers into the field of opinion, and to restrain the profession or propagation of principles on supposition of their ill tendency, is a dangerous fallacy." The preamble of this great Act closes with these words:

> It is time enough for the rightful purposes of civil government, for its officers to interfere when principles break out into overt acts against peace and good order; and finally, that truth is great and will prevail if left to herself, that she is the proper and sufficient antagonist to error, and has nothing to fear from the conflict, unless by human interposition disarmed of her natural weapons, free argument and debate, errors ceasing to be dangerous where it is permitted freely to contradict them.

Hence, said the statutory section of this Law of 1786:

> no man shall be compelled to frequent or support any religious worship, place or ministry whatsoever, nor shall be enforced, restrained, molested, or burthened in his body or goods, nor shall otherwise suffer on account of his religious opinions or belief; but that all men shall be free to profess, and by arguments to maintain, their opinions in matters of religion, and that the same shall in no wise diminish, enlarge or affect their civil capacities.

This represented the ultimate accomplishment in church-state relations, and in terms of civil rights, of the Revolutionary era;

while introduced in 1779, it was not enacted until seven years of effort passed. During the Revolution, disabilities based upon religion were onerous and common. Thus, New Hampshire, Massachusetts, New Jersey, and the Carolinas forbade any but Protestants to hold public office; Pennsylvania and Delaware required that they be Christians. But the negative way of putting this is non-historical, for it is the elimination of religious disqualifications, not their retention, which is characteristic of the *developments* during the Revolution and in the generation that followed.

It was momentous that eight states during the Revolution acted to permit Catholics to hold public office and that four states advanced to the point of granting this right to Jews. Strictly religious prohibitions tended to be relaxed, also, not only in the disestablishment of the Anglican Church in Maryland, the Carolinas, Georgia and Virginia, but also in such acts as that in the Massachusetts Constitution of 1780 allowing public worship by Catholics.

The generally nationalizing, as well as democratizing, influence of the Revolution reflected itself in the sphere of religion. Thus, the Anglican Church in the United States, severing its organic ties with the Church in England, emerged as the Protestant Episcopal Church with (in 1789) a bicameral assembly, like the nation itself, made up of a House of Bishops and a House of Lay and Clerical Deputies. Similarly, the Dutch and the German Reformed Churches became completely independent of ecclesiastical authorities in the Old Countries, while the Catholic Church in the United States was severed from the jurisdiction of the English Vicar Apostolic.

Thus, while it is true that by the end of the Revolutionary era only two states, Rhode Island and Virginia, had achieved full religious freedom and total separation of church and state, it is also true that in the era great strides were made in terms of democratizing, liberalizing and nationalizing religious aspects of life.

V

The Revolution gave significant impetus to progressive development in many other areas of social life. Prominent among these were: the position of women; the field of education; the treatment of criminals.

As we have tried to show, the vast majority of the American population supported the Revolutionary effort. This support most certainly extended to the women; indeed, contemporaries reported that the women were more ardent in their desire for change and separation from England than were the men.

Women actively supported the popular demonstrations and participated in all of the activities, notably of boycott, which preceded and accompanied the Revolution. They were towers of strength in terms of morale and supply throughout the years of fighting. And they were especially prominent in the struggles against corruption and profiteering that so seriously sapped the strength of the Revolutionary forces. Notable in this regard was the action of a considerable group of women in Boston, in 1777, who broke into the warehouses of a hoarding and speculating merchant, dumped the businessman into a cart and divided his supplies among themselves. Women elsewhere, desperate for food or clothing, acted similarly, as in East Hartford, Connecticut, also in 1777.

The real beginnings of industry in the United States date from the Revolutionary period and in this women played a part. Thus, the American Manufactory of Philadelphia, established in 1775, employed as many as 400 women. With the origins of wage-earners went the origins of their struggles against the employers. Hence during the Revolution work-stoppages occurred, especially as the swift increase in living costs ran ahead of the rise in pay, and as this condition was aggravated by runaway inflation. Notable was the strike in Virginia in 1777 of women laboring as shirtmakers, for an increase in their piece-rate.

During the Revolutionary period the power of parents over youngsters, especially in connection with "arranged" marriages, was seriously questioned, and the practice went into decline.

The same reasoning which saw affection and mutual esteem as necessary preconditions for the contracting of marriage, would see their absence as the justification for the termination of marriage. As a result, it was considerably easier to obtain a divorce in the newly-revolutionized United States than it was in Europe, and five states—New Hampshire, Massachusetts, Rhode Island, New Jersey, and Pennsylvania—enacted laws for this purpose.

This was in line with Abigail Adams' well-known complaint to her husband John, that while Americans were rebelling against the King's tyranny, they ignored the tyranny exercised by husbands towards wives. Mrs. Adams does not seem to have had in mind so much the lack of political rights for women, as she did women's complete absence of adulthood so far as common law was concerned, and especially her being denied effective property rights. Mrs. Adams denounced, also, as she wrote in 1778, "the trifling, narrow, contracted education of the females of my own country."

It is a fact, however, that the question of political rights, and particularly of propertied widows being taxed without any representation, was raised by women, whose objections evoked sympathetic response, though moderately phrased, from men like John Adams, Thomas Jefferson and Richard Henry Lee. Some men—outstanding in this connection was Thomas Paine—did support the idea of enfranchising women. It is significant that the question: "Whether women ought to be admitted into the Magistracy and Government of Empires and Republics," was debated by Yale students during the Revolution; presumably the affirmative side was represented as well as the negative. In any case, clearly, th posing of the question reflects the impact of the Revolution upon this area of life.

During the Revolution, property and inheritance rights of women were enhanced and especially notable progress was made in furthering the idea that "trifling" education for women was not sufficient. The establishment of schools for girls was common in the era and manifested a distinct trend towards the equalization of the status of women in the United States.

VI

The Revolution, with its emphasis upon reason, popular sovereignty and human equality, naturally tended to further a renovation in the whole theory and practice of education. The trend in the United States, very much reinforced, if not inspired, by the

Revolution was towards secular, scientific, humanistic, democratic, universal education. The reactionary idea of education as the exclusive privilege of the rich, and as an instrumentality for their continued domination, was challenged, though by no means overthrown, by the American Revolution.

Thomas Paine, in "A Serious Address to the People of Pennsylvania," first printed in December, 1778, declared that "there are two ways of governing mankind"; one, was "by keeping them ignorant," the other, "by making them wise." He continued: "The former was and is the custom of the old world. The latter of the new." Developing this theme, Paine wrote:

> It has been the constant practice of the old world to hold up a government to the people as a mystery, and of consequence to govern them through their ignorance. And on the contrary it is the practice of the new world, America, to make men as wise as possible, so that their knowledge being complete, they may be rationally governed.

More precisely, the Revolutionary idea was to have an educated populace not so that they might be governed rationally, but rather that, since the aim of the Revolution was to establish an independent Republic where the people were sovereign, to assure an educated populace so that they might govern themselves rationally. Somewhat subtler questions—as to the class nature of the State, and the consequent essential domination of its educating structure by the rulers of the State—did not present themselves as major matters of concern, or, at least, of public discussion.

Later, in his *Rights of Man,* Paine made explicit the logical connection between a Republic and universal education, for: "A nation under a well regulated government should permit none to remain uninstructed. It is monarchical and aristocratical governments, only, that require ignorance for their support."

Thomas Jefferson was especially impressed with the necessity for public and thorough education, if government was to be democratic, and if it was to remain democratic. Hence did he favor universal education and public libraries, galleries, museums and other depositories of learning and culture for the enlightenment of the populace. Jefferson viewed public enlightenment as a protection against the corruption of government and as a vital accompaniment of popular participation in government.

That future generations were to discover complexities in education and its relation to government, not clearly foreseen by Jefferson—nor, it may be believed, yet fully comprehended by those future generations—does not detract from the transforming essence of the American Revolution so far as the theory and, to a large degree, the practice of education are concerned.

Writing from Paris in August, 1786, to the distinguished Virginia jurist, George Wythe, Jefferson declared "the diffusion of knowledge among the people" was the only "sure foundation . . . for the preservation of freedom and happiness." In France he saw the people "loaded with misery," due to the exactions and oppressions of "kings, nobles, and priests," wherefore he urged "a crusade against ignorance":

> Let our countrymen know, that the people alone can protect us against these evils, and that the tax which will be paid for this purpose, is not more than the thousandth part of what will be paid to kings, priests and nobles, who will rise up among us if we leave the people in ignorance.

Frederick Tolles, in his already-mentioned essay on Jameson's ideas concerning the social impact of the Revolution, correctly points out that: "Curiously, Jameson found little evidence of educational advance in the Revolutionary era, except for the founding of new colleges." Tolles then goes on, taking "a broader view of education," to summarize "a number of important developments directly or indirectly related to wartime experience." These he presents as follows:

> the improvement of medicine (including dentistry) and of medical education; the emergence of civil engineering from military engineering; the founding of Judge Tapping Reeve's "law school" at Litchfield, Connecticut, in 1784; the diffusion of scientific knowledge through the revived activity of the American Philosophical Society and the founding [in 1780] of the American Academy of Arts and Sciences; and—not least important—the informal education, the widening of horizons, that resulted from wartime mobility, from the fact that, for the first time, many Americans rubbed elbows—and minds— not only with Europeans but with other Americans.

Certainly part of the educational impact of the Revolution, as Dixon Ryan Fox and Evarts B. Greene especially remarked, was the overcoming of a regionalism and a provincialism that had marked colonial life. With this went a nationalizing and democratizing content to educational and intellectual life during the Revolution, which scholars like Merle Curti and Harvey Wish have documented.

Further, the Revolutionary constitutions of five states—Massachusetts, Pennsylvania, North Carolina, Georgia, Vermont—affirmed the public responsibility for the education of its citizenry. Money and land realized during the Revolution by the confiscation of loyalist estates and the acquisition of crown lands were used directly for educational purposes in New York, Connecticut, Virginia, the Carolinas and Georgia. Thus, Transylvania University in Lexington, Kentucky (then Virginia) was founded on the basis of 8,000 acres of land, confiscated from Tories. Again, states made definite, and often generous, provisions for assisting elementary and higher levels of education—notable was the Georgia act of 1783 granting 1,000 acres to every county for the support of its schools.

Indicative of changes in quantity and quality of educational activity, prior to, and during and immediately after the Revolution, is the fact that while of ten colleges established by 1776 but one was non-sectarian, during the next 20 years 14 colleges were founded, of which only four were denominational.

George Wythe in Virginia and James Wilson in Pennsylvania, in launching professorships in law did so quite consciously in terms of vindicating American independence in jurisprudence as well as in national terms. Similarly, Benjamin Waterhouse, pioneer instructor in medicine at the Harvard Medical School (established in 1782), felt that "a country so completely independent in other respects as the United States . . . should blush to be indebted to foreign seminaries for *first principles of professional instruction.*" Noah Webster in spelling and Jedidiah Morse in geography were intent upon producing American textbooks, emphasizing national and democratic values.

The war itself, in its physical impact and necessities, led to notable advances in the organization and standardization of medical practice. The first medical handbooks, pharmacopoeia, and general tests for proficiency made their appearance with the Revolution. At the same time there appeared, especially in the work of John Morgan and Benjamin Rush, an effort to develop an American approach to the theory and practice of public health, rather than an exclusive dependence upon European authority.

The interrelation of these values and their challenge for American education and scholarship were made quite explicit by Jefferson, writing from Paris in March, 1789, to Dr. Joseph Willard, President of Harvard. Proudly describing the scientific contributions of "two of our countrymen," Thomas Paine and James Ramsey, he went on:

> What a field have we at our doors to signalize ourselves in! The Botany of America is far from being exhausted, its Mineralogy is untouched, and its Natural History or Zoology, totally mistaken and misrepresented. . . . It is for such institutions as that over which you preside . . . to do justice to our country, its productions and its genius. It is the work to which the young men, whom you are forming, should lay their hands. We have spent the prime of our lives in procuring them the precious blessing of liberty. Let them spend theirs in showing that it is the great parent of *science* and virtue; and that a nation will be great in both, always in proportion as it is free.

Jefferson in 1776 attempted to get Virginia to establish a system of public libraries. Three years later, and for several years thereafter, Jefferson tried—in vain, at that time—to have Virginia adopt what would have been a close approximation to the modern school systems: The state to be divided into districts, each with a public school, where all children of free parents might receive without cost a minimum of three years instruction in history and the "three R's," with provisions for talented, though poor, students to be educated, without cost to themselves, all the way through college. Though it was not until 1796 that Virginia enacted a public education law—even then it was but a very pale imitation of Jefferson's proposal—still that proposal belongs in the history of the Revolution's transforming impact.

Momentous was the educational provision, inspired by Jefferson, in the Land Ordinance adopted May 20, 1785, by the

Congress of the Confederation. The Ordinance, following Virginia's somewhat belated cession of its Western lands to the federal government (December 20, 1783), laid the foundations for the public land system as it continued for another 80 years. It contained the following clause: "There shall be reserved the lot No. 16, of every township, for the maintenance of public schools within the said township."

Again, in the Northwest Ordinance, enacted July 13, 1787, the Confederation Congress, prodded by land speculators combined in the Ohio Company of Associates, provided the administrative structure for the governing of this vast area. In the course of establishing a system founded on "the fundamental principles of civil and religious liberty," basic to the American republics (*i.e.,* states), the Ordinance, in its third Article, provided: "Religion, morality, and knowledge, being necessary to good government and the happiness of mankind, schools and the means of education shall forever be encouraged."

We have already seen that the Revolution's impact upon the Negro people and upon the thinking of whites concerning Negroes was marked and generally salutary. It is to be observed that, as part of the era's atmosphere there appeared various economic, social and religious organizations among Negroes. Accompanying this went collective demands from Negroes for various forms of relief ranging from an end to slavery, to the right to vote and to receive an education.

The foregoing establishes that the American Revolution, as part of its social impact, had a clear and important influence upon democratizing the theory and practice of public education.

A word of caution, however, is needed. Democratization was the *tendency* in educational theory and practice produced by the Revolution. This tendency did not, of course, achieve its goal— not even by the mid-20th century, let alone the late 18th. The predominant view on education, natural to a class-stratified society, was expressed in an unsigned article, "An Examination of the Question: Whether the Children of the Poor Should Receive a Literary Education or Not?" in the influential Philadelphia magazine, *American Museum,* September, 1789.

The query is answered in the negative. This is explained on

the grounds that some who are poor must always be with us;
that being poor meant working hard and getting little in return,
and that:

> As nothing but early habit can render it tolerable, therefore
> to give to the meanest of the people an education beyond that
> station which providence has assigned them, is doing them a
> real injury. . . . We may pity the state of such, but we seldom
> hear them complain. Having never known better things, they
> are contented with their lot. . . . If their industry affords them
> only the plainest food and clothing, it is some compensation
> that they are perplexed with no other care.

Nevertheless, the need to pose the question and to "answer" it,
is something of a tribute to the generally democratic impulse
which the Revolution gave to education.

VII

In the areas of criminology and penology, also, the Revolution
served as an innovator and accelerator of humanist and democratic ideas and conduct. Again, as in the cases of education,
slavery, women's rights, so here the application was organic to the
Revolutionary outlook. The democratic emphasis upon equali-
tarianism and the repudiation of man's innate and ineradicable
depravity, called for attention to social and environmental conditions where individual failure appeared. Nothing was more
starkly indicative of such failure than criminality; perhaps, given
Revolutionary postulates, the criminal was more sinned against
than sinning? And, perhaps, reform rather than punishment
should be the central emphasis in penology?

Moreover, the whole concept of criminality was attacked from
another angle, especially suggesting itself to Revolutionists. This
was the fact that one era's crime was another's glory; that had
George III caught Washington, Adams and Jefferson, they would
have ended their days abruptly on a gibbet as damnable criminals, rather than living out long lives filled with numerous and
high honors. A whole series of crimes—conspiracy, sedition, libel,
treason, heresy—had had strange careers and sharp alterations

within the lifetime of any mature American living in 1780. Surely, this was cause for thought as to the nature of crime, its mutability, its dependence upon social convention and organization; clearly, criminology, as penology, was to be transformed by the Era of the Revolution.

As the American Revolution properly may be viewed as a grand result of the Age of Reason, so many of the social innovations stimulated by that Revolution were inherent in the Age itself. We have seen this to be true in such matters as education and enslavement; it was true, too, in the area of crime, and punishment therefor.

Thus it is that in the years just preceding the Revolution, several European leaders of the Age of Reason turned their attention to penology, moved thereto not only by the logical assumptions of rationalism, but also by the abominations committed everywhere in Europe against those—men, women and children—who ran afoul of the Draconian systems of law. Outstanding in this connection were the Italian jurist and economist, Cesare Beccaria (1738-1794), and the English reformer, John Howard (1726-1790).

In this same period, concern with the welfare of prisoners— especially, but not exclusively, those jailed for indebtedness— appears in the American press. Beginning no later than 1749, notices appear, for example, of affairs being conducted "for the benefit of the poor prisoners" (New York *Post Boy,* October 30, 1749), while in the 1760's the Sons of Liberty made it a practice to donate food to those held in New York City jails.

By 1776 there appeared, in Philadelphia, a Society for Assisting Distressed Prisoners, and individuals like Franklin, Jefferson, Madison and Benjamin Rush were actively involved in organizational and legislative efforts at prison reform.

Indicative of the advance in thinking on this matter is the fact that the 1776 Pennsylvania Constitution urged the reform of the criminal code so that punishments might be "less sanguinary, and in general more proportionate to the crime." Again, in 1777, the State Council of Delaware appointed a committee to investigate prisons; the theme of its report appears in this sentence from it: "It is frequently found by experience, that ignominious and disgraceful punishments harden more offenders than they reclaim."

In Virginia, beginning in 1776, the barbarous criminal code —copied from the British, which at that time made 160 offenses subject to capital punishment—was reformed, and death as a penalty was abolished for all crimes but murder and treason. Jefferson fought against the chain gang and was influential in getting the State to build the Richmond Prison which separated its inmates according to sex and crime. Pennsylvania, where 53 individuals had been executed from 1779 to 1789 for crimes other than murder, finally (in 1794) after the agitation of the Revolutionary era, abolished capital punishment for all crimes other than murder. In New York City and in Philadelphia important reforms in prison management—separation of inmates, salaried jailors, prohibition of dispensing of liquor to prisoners, etc.—were accomplished in the same general period.

In 1787 was formed the first organization in the world devoted to the reform of penological practices (as distinct from charity for prisoners). This—the work of Franklin, Rush, William Bradford and Caleb Lownes—was the Philadelphia Society for Alleviating the Miseries of Public Prisons. Harry Elmer Barnes, in his *Evolution of Penology in Pennsylvania* (1927), has summarized the results of the movement which led to this Society and which was invigorated by it. Barnes wrote:

> In 1775 there was little or no imprisonment as a normal punishment for crimes. Felonies were almost exclusively punished by death and the lesser offenses by fines or brutal forms of corporal punishment, such as whipping, branding, mutilating, and exposure in the stocks and pillory. There was no unified state prison system. The local county and municipal jails were the typical penal institutions of the period. In them there was no classification or separation of convicts on any basis. No labor was provided. There was no moral nor educational instruction. No attention was given to the possibilities of reforming the offenders. The only aim of criminal jurisprudence and penal procedure was the utter extinction of serious offenders and the deterence of others by brutal, painful and humiliating penalties.

Within a generation—and most of it accomplished from 1776 to 1794—this whole theory and system was transformed and, in Pennsylvania, there existed a penal system more advanced than any other in the world. "The outstanding feature of the change," said Barnes, "was that the combination of an elimination of most of the capital crimes and of a wide use of imprisonment in the repression of crime, necessitated for the first time the provision of a complete system of penal institutions and a systematic regulation of their administration."

The most remarkable contributions to the theory of penology in the United States at this time were made by the great revolutionary patriot, Dr. Benjamin Rush. In 1787 was published his *Inquiry into the Effects of Public Punishments upon Criminals and upon Society;* in 1792 appeared his *Considerations on the Injustice and Impolicy of Punishing Murder by Death.*

Here Rush related crime to mental imbalance or illness, and stressed that the aim of penal institutions should be the cure or the rehabilitation of the inmates. To this end, he proposed that such institutions assume more the character of communities, with homes and gardens and churches. He was particularly indignant at the use of physical punishment and torture and demanded, in the name of "reason and humanity," their elimination. He insisted, too, that "murder is propagated by hanging for murder"; Rush was one of the first to condemn capital punishment in toto and *per se.*

These views on penology were related to Rush's remarkable insights into psychological and psychiatric problems. Albert Deutsch, in his *The Mentally Ill in America* (1937), devoting a chapter to Rush, quite properly entitled it "Father of American Psychiatry." This concern with mental illness, in which the Revolution also provides initial impetus, similarly reflects the humane, democratic and rational kernel of that great social upheaval.

VIII

There was one group of criminals in the 18th century for whom arrest and imprisonment (sometimes confinement to an area rather than a building), not execution or physical punishment was the rule: the insolvent debtor. Imprisonment or arrest for debt was very common in America at this time and involved many thousands of victims.[3] Thus, for example, half the inmates of Philadelphia jails in 1785 were imprisoned for debt; in New York City from January, 1787, to December, 1788, almost 1,200 persons had been confined to the city prison for debt; in many instances their indebtedness did not exceed 20 shillings.

The movement to eliminate debt imprisonment, while not generally successful until the Jacksonian era, was launched during the Revolutionary period. Again this reflected the egalitarian and democratic content of the Revolution. Thus it was, that Yale seniors in 1786 argued affirmatively to the question: "Whether Imprisonment for Debt ought to be abolished in all civilized States?" and that a "Friend of Liberty" writing in the New Jersey *Brunswick Gazette,* September 9, 1788, declared the imprisonment of insolvent debtors to be unreasonable and cruel.

The radical Pennsylvania Constitution of 1776 provided that there was to be no imprisonment for debt where presumption of fraud was not strong, and where all assets had been turned over to creditors. The North Carolina Constitution of the same year contained a similar provision. In New York, a legislative effort in 1776 to prohibit debt imprisonment was vetoed by the Council of Revision. In 1784, however, a law was passed, based on colonial precedent, permitting an insolvent debtor to win release from jail by going through a bankruptcy proceeding, if creditors holding a minimum of 75 per cent of the indebtedness approved.

The dependence upon the creditors' benevolence did not result in wholesale liberation of debt prisoners; the post-Revolutionary economic downturn added to their number. Inflation was one expedient resorted to by several states to help debtors; in addition, New York, by an act passed in April, 1787, discharged from jail all debtors held therein for debt less than £15. Such relief followed public discussion, numerous petitions from debtors and their families, and from organized representations, as reflected in the appearance, for example, of the New York Society for the Relief of Distressed Debtors (formed January, 1787).

In 1789, New York passed a law restricting to not more than

30 days' jail confinement, debtors newly convicted where the indebtedness did not exceed £10. Complete abolition of debt imprisonment in New York, however, was not to come for another generation. This was stimulated not only by mass pressure, but also by the business community's desire for effective bankruptcy law and more rational protection of creditors' interests than the jailing of debtors—especially when, as happened beginning in the 1790's, laws were passed (for example, in Pennsylvania in 1792) requiring that creditors contribute to the cost of feeding jailed debtors.

One of the most enlightened of the immediate post-Revolutionary acts on debt imprisonment was that passed by Massachusetts, in 1788, stimulated by Shays' Rebellion. This law provided for the release of debtors who swore that they could not pay either their debts nor their prison expenses, and creditors were forbidden to continue the incarceration by paying the board.

Chapter XV

The Economic Effects
of the Revolution

IN ADDITION TO significant advances in particular areas of social iniquity—as slavery, the inferior status of women, educational inadequacies, religious intolerance, barbarous criminal procedures,—the Revolution stimulated action on the broadest front of economic domination. Just as the Revolution resulted in significant changes in political organization, so it led to a re-examination of, and some alteration in, the basic economic postulates and forms of the old society.

Something of the intention in this matter, and the dimensions of accomplishment, as viewed by contemporaries, comes through in a letter from one not ordinarily associated with radicalism, John Adams. In 1777, Patrick Henry wrote Adams telling him of the patriots' efforts in Virginia to democratize their southern society so that it more nearly approximated that of New England. John Adams gave Henry every encouragement, and then generalized with these words:

> The dons, the bashaws, the grandees, the patricians, the sachems, the nabobs, call them what name you please, sigh, and groan, and fret, and sometimes stamp, and foam, and curse, but all in vain. The decree is gone forth, and cannot be recalled, that a more equal liberty than has prevailed in other parts of the earth, must be established in America. That exuberance of pride which has produced an insolent domination in a few, a

very few, insolent and monopolizing families, will be brought down nearer to the confines of reason and moderation than they have been used to.

At the same time, astute contemporaries, realizing the dual aspect of the Revolution—internal and external, with the two interpenetrating—sought to push forward, or to restrain (depending upon their views) changes in basic social relationships. Jefferson put the feelings of the Left concerning this matter with his customary lucidity in a letter written in 1780, as the war was coming to a close:

> It can never be too often repeated, that the time for fixing every essential right on a legal basis is while our rulers are honest, and ourselves united. From the conclusion of this war we shall be going down hill. It will not then be necessary to resort every moment to the people for support. They will be forgotten therefore and their rights disregarded.

I

An important component of the American Revolution was a commitment against monopolization of economic power and resources; a dedication to the task of building a fluid, equitable, prosperous society, without exclusive privileges, legal or caste-frozen advantages. Basically, in the Revolution, one had significant progress in removing or weakening obstacles to capitalist development, and for that era everything that helped release capitalist development represented progressive economic change.

There was, during the Revolution, a fervent desire to maintain and build a society without the extremes of poverty, and luxury that characterized England and France. This was joined with the conviction that, given the new nation's extraordinary expanse, enormous resources, republican government—and, given the basic ideological groundwork of the Revolution, a confidence in rationality and the unconquerable power of scientific inquiry—it would be possible in the United States to create really a new social order which would inspire the oppressed of the world as much as its new political order inspired the enthralled.

Such fundamental social and economic transformation was

not possible. Relationships based upon the private ownership of the means of production—in the hands of manufacturers, merchants, real-estate operators, farmers—not only could not then be altered, or seriously challenged, but were rather in the process of consolidation and development during the era of the Revolution. But what one does have are attacks upon anything conflicting with, inhibiting, or challenging this property relationship; and one has this when this relationship was young, fresh and progressive. The relationship was one having within it the capacity of infinitely advancing productivity and of aligning itself with efforts to eliminate obstacles to its fullest development.

Where property relationships were foreign to the "free enterprise" essence of young capitalism, they came under attack and, in almost all cases, were significantly altered, if not eliminated. To some extent, this applied even to the slave system and the slave-trade feeding it—as we have seen. But here the attack fell far short, and the following factors explain the failure. (1) The predominant nature of the economy based on free labor was either mercantile—in which case there was a complementary, not competing, relationship between the merchants and the planters—or was agricultural, in which again, at that time, the grounds for compatibility were greater than those for hostility. (2) The slave system was confined to one area, in which it predominated; this tended to abate and delay the conflict between classically developing capitalist society with plantation slavery, while it made very formidable the power of the slave system within its zone of concentration. (3) Racism was virulent and widespread, rooted in the rape of Africa, the genocidal policy toward the Indian peoples, and the ideological requirement of the slave system itself; this tended to vitiate significant political or moral opposition, by whites, to the existence of "the peculiar institution."

While then there was some advance in the anti-slavery cause during the Revolution, it was not nearly so great as the advances made in extirpating remnants of feudalism. Here the vested interests involved, while potent and tenacious, were much weaker than the slaveowners; and here, too, the legal and economic ramifications more clearly and immediately conflicted with rising American capitalism, largely landed and mercantile as it was.

Thomas Jefferson, in his *Autobiography*, stated that in Virginia there were four laws passed during the Revolutionary period which formed "a system by which every fibre would be eradicated of ancient or future aristocracy; and a foundation laid for a government truly republican." Two of these—separation of church and state, and the efforts at establishing public education—have already been sufficiently described. The other two may be indicated in Jefferson's words:

> The repeal of the laws of entail would prevent the accumulation and perpetuation of wealth, in select families, and preserve the soil of the country from being daily more and more absorbed in mortmain. The abolition of primogeniture, and equal partition of inheritances, removed the feudal and unnatural distinctions which made one member of every family rich, and all the rest poor, substituting equal partition, the best of all agrarian laws.[1]

The significance of these feudal laws and institutions so far as colonial Virginia was concerned, and the revolutionary motivation for their repeal, again are described authoritatively by Jefferson, in his *Autobiography:*

> In the earlier times of the colony, when lands were to be obtained for little or nothing, some provident individuals procured large grants; and, desirous of founding great families for themselves, settled them on their descendants in fee tail [i.e., not subject to alienation.] The transmission of this property from generation to generation, in the same name, raised up a distinct set of families, who, being privileged by law in the perpetuation of their wealth, where thus transformed into a Patrician order, distinguished by the splendor and luxury of their establishments. From this order, too, the king habitually selected his counsellors of State; the hope of which distinction devoted the whole corps to the interests and will of the crown.

Jefferson continued:

> To annul this privilege, and instead of an aristocracy of wealth, of more harm and danger, than benefit, to society, to make an opening for the aristocracy of virtue and talent, which nature has wisely provided for the direction of the interests of society, and scattered with equal hand through all its conditions, was deemed essential to a well-ordered republic.

Jefferson declared that to effect this change, "no violence was necessary, no deprivation of natural right, but rather an enlargement of it by a repeal of the law." One may certainly agree that the elimination of primogeniture and entail enhanced freedom, but it seems somewhat disingenuous of Jefferson to remark that to secure this "no violence was necessary"; for the point is that it was the Revolution which offered the opportunity and produced the Legislature—with Jefferson a member—which in fact, repealed these laws. The repeal of these feudal land laws was as much a result of the Revolution as was independence from Great Britain.

It is, moreover, worth noting, as Jefferson does, that even in the Revolutionary legislature the opposition to repeal, led by Edmund Pendleton, was bitter and prolonged and came "within a few votes" of success.

That under capitalist law, land engrossing has been possible and does exist, does not invalidate the decisive advance in terms of releasing the economy and adding social fluidity that the attack upon entail, primogeniture and other features of feudal law meant.

Thomas P. Abernethy, in his stimulating book, *From Frontier to Plantation in Tennessee* (1932), added another, and related, motive for the attack upon feudal land laws. He did this in describing the work of the predominantly conservative North Carolina legislature of 1784 which, while it enacted a law basing land taxation upon quantity, rather than value—thus favoring the rich easterners—also abolished entail and primogeniture. Wrote Abernethy, of the latter legislation:

> It was in accord with the spirit of the times that this should have been done, but it would not so easily appear to have been in accord with the temper of the body which did it. However, the contradiction is hardly so great as it might seem. Speculators require a fluid medium in which to work, not a stable one. They are engaged in the building up of fortunes, not in the preservation of those already accumulated. Primogeniture and entail can easily be dispensed with by such men.

In addition to the elimination of entail and primogeniture in Virginia and North Carolina, significant legislation of a similar nature, at times with additional details, was enacted elsewhere. Thus, primogeniture was terminated in Georgia (1777), Maryland (1785) and in South Carolina (1790). In the New Jersey legislation of 1780 ending primogeniture, it was provided, however, that the share of male heirs was to be double that of females. Entail of property was prohibited in New Jersey in 1784 and in New York two years later. Further, in New York, the lordships and manorial privileges which had been held by the Hudson River patroons since the days of the Dutch, were terminated by Revolutionary legislation. Here, however, the failure to eliminate all special privileges—in the terms of leasing land possessed by these families—caused social turmoil, reaching insurrectionary proportions, well into the 19th century.

One of the payments that developed as feudalism declined was quit-rent. This derived its name from its function; *i.e.,* it was a payment reserved in grants of land, by meeting which the tenant was freed from—quit of—all other services. This persisted, long after its original purpose had any real significance, as little more than a tax accruing to proprietors on the basis of a feudal vestige. Quit-rents were annoyances during the colonial era, and were real burdens in two colonies in particular—Maryland and North Carolina. In the single year 1774, proprietors realized in quit-rents, largely from these two areas, a total of $100,000. This obligation was voided by the Revolution.

II

Of great significance, in terms of the availability of land and the mode of its distribution, consequent upon the Revolution, in addition to what has already been stated, were: the confiscation of the King's forests; the confiscation of the estates of Tories; the termination of the rights of Proprietors, especially important in Pennsylvania and Maryland; the granting of land as soldiers' bounties; and the elimination of the authority of Great Britain over the enormous land mass from the Appalachians to the Mississippi River. It is true that in the latter case one had *de facto* possession by several scores of thousands of Indians, but neither their property rights nor their lives were permitted seriously to impede the greed for land on the part of the Americans.

In some states, the Revolution brought a deeper and more rapid socio-economic transformation than in others, largely because of differences in reference to land distribution. Of Maryland, for example, Charles Barker, in his already-cited study, wrote:

> The sloughing off of the old—especially the feudal—aspects of the Maryland system was to mark the victory, at last, of the anti-proprietary movement. The demands of 1739, and more than those demands, were to be fulfilled by the Revolution in Maryland. Proprietary offices and fees, the duties and prerogatives, the old land system, the collection of quit-rents, and the tax-supported church—all these were to fall during the Revolution: Their destruction was to be the completion of generations of Assembly protest.

In Pennsylvania, the ungranted proprietary lands were taken over by the State—the Penn family was given a modest compensation—and quit-rents were abolished. In New York, the matter is best summarized by E. B. Greene, who wrote that "the confiscation and sale of Tory estates brought a considerable redistribution of land ownership and undoubtedly had a certain leveling effect, partially offset, however, by new concentrations of property in the hands of speculative purchasers."

In North Carolina, also, where repression of Tories was notably severe and prolonged, there was considerable re-distribution of the confiscated estates of Loyalists. An outstanding example was that of the enormous holdings of Henry E. McCulloch, appropriated by the State and sold by it to about 80 separate families.

Similarly in New Jersey, property shifts due to the Revolution were sufficient to cause Richard P. McCormick to write that there, too, "the structure of society had not gone unscathed." Spelling this out, McCormick wrote of the general democratization in politics in the States and the elimination of entail and primogeniture, to which reference has already been made. He also noted that, "Altogether the estates of at least 500 active loyalists were confiscated and disposed of by New Jersey in the decade after 1778." True it is, that a disproportionate share of the bonanza was taken by newcomers like William Paterson, Abraham Clark and John Neilson, but the overall result of the Revolution in New Jersey was to broaden considerably the ownership of land.

Although, then, it is true that much of the enhanced opportunity for land ownership, consequent upon the Revolution, was usurped and monopolized by well-heeled and strategically placed "patriots," it is also a fact that everywhere the enhanced opportunity did result in a wider distribution of land ownership than had existed before the Revolution. Further, the Revolution opened up the development of a generous land-granting system, extended in the post-war era; it encouraged a constant westward movement of land-hungry Easterners, and of others fresh from Europe. The significance in American history of the availability of relatively cheap, if not completely free, land ever westward was enormous; a basic result of the American Revolution was to assure and encourage such availability.

On all these grounds, then, it may be affirmed that the developments in land tenure and distribution consequent upon the Revolution had a significant impact upon the political, social and economic history of the United States.

III

We have already considered the Revolution's impact upon slavery; what of its effect upon the other widespread form of formed labor, indentured servitude? This was destined to survive the Revolution, in diluted form, for a generation. Clearly its decline and disappearance are attributable to the relatively rapid industrialization of the northern part of the country accelerating after the Revolution and the consequent preference for a free, wage-earning class of workers, to the generous land policy befitting a fabulous empire of public land, and to the fastening upon the southern part of the country of a plantation system in which chattel-slave labor was decisive.

Nevertheless, the Revolution itself did have some influence upon indentured servitude. Something of this story is told in Abbot E. Smith's excellent study, *Colonists in Bondage* (1947):

... at the time of the Revolution, American opinion was either entirely opposed to the enlistment of servants in the provincial army, or at least it was insistent that compensation be paid [to the master]. We have evidence of several soldiers being discharged upon testimony that they were servants, and the Assembly of Pennsylvania in 1778 granted money to those whose servants had enlisted. This act was in answer to such sentiments as those expressed by a committee from Cumberland County, which sounded oddly in the midst of the battle for freedom, "Resolved that all Apprentices and servants are the Property of their masters and mistresses, and every mode of depriving such masters and mistresses of their Property is a violation of the Rights of mankind. . . ." The Provincial Congress of New York instructed its officers not to enlist servants, but by 1784 sentiment had altered, for in that year a group of the citizens of New York, beholding a newly-arrived cargo of servants, declared that the "traffick of White People" was contrary to the idea of liberty, and voted to pay their passages and set them free, reimbursing themselves by a small rateable deduction from the immigrants' wages.

William Miller, in a study of the Revolution's impact upon indenture in Pennsylvania, reported no discernible influence; possibly he did not exhaust the evidence in that state. Elsewhere, as in New York, a direct connection between Revolutionary needs and sentiments and the institution of indenture, does appear.

Furthermore, it is a fact that many indentured servants throughout the rebellious area did enlist in the Army and Navy —legally or illegally; as a result some gained their freedom— generally with government compensation for the masters. It is because of this that Elizabeth Cometti was able to report that "the war provided a path to freedom for many indentured servants, both male and female." Something specific and apparently not exceptional, appears in the experience of a printer and his apprentice from Worcester, Massachusetts. In 1780, Isaiah Thomas was served with a draft call for six months' service in the Army. In his place he sent his indentured apprentice, who faithfully performed his military duties; but upon his return, the young man demanded and obtained an earlier release from his apprenticeship.

Louis Hartz, furthermore, in a study of Pennsylvania, while citing the essay by Miller already mentioned, added: "The Revolution did, however, produce serious practical problems for the maintenance of the indentured service system." These problems derived not only from the wirespread (illegal) enlistment of servants, but also from the attacks upon the theory and practice of imprisonment for debt. These attacks we have detailed elsewhere; here it is necessary to observe their relation to the weakening of the indenture system. Writing of revolutionary Pennsylvania, Hartz declared:

> But it is of some significance to observe that the state did, indirectly, strike a fatal blow at indentured service, and that with little consideration for the vested rights involved. That blow was the abolition of imprisonment for debt. The institution of debtor imprisonment was the legal rock upon which indentured service rested.

Moreover, during and immediately after the Revolution in Pennsylvania, New York and Maryland, there were formed societies, particularly among the German immigrants, to protect the interests and the health of indentured newcomers. Pennsylvania, through its Register of German Passengers, also undertook some form of government supervision of their conditions upon landing; Maryland, by law, reduced the period of maximum servitude of all indentured workers to four years.

Available evidence shows, then, that the American Revolution significantly stimulated the process of destroying the system of indentured servitude.

IV

The Pennsylvania Resolution of 1778 condemning the liberation of indentured servants as "a violation of the rights of mankind," is a striking forerunner of the Decree of June 14, 1791, passed during the classical French bourgeois revolution outlawing trade unions as "an attack upon liberty and upon the Declaration of the Rights of Man." Both are characteristic of the tendency among possessors of property to identify the rights of property with the rights of humanity. Where forms of property relationship are progressive, historically considered, this identification may not be wholly amiss; but it is indicative of the fundamentally exploitative nature of the bourgeois property relationship that it severely inhibits attacks upon chattel and indentured servitude and illegalizes, where it can, combinations among workers even when it stands in conflict against colonial and feudal bonds.

It is, however, important to observe that in both the American and French Revolutions there already appeared the sharp posing of the conflict between human and property rights, and that in both there were elements who questioned the whole foundation of the private ownership of the means of production. So far as the American Revolution is concerned, this idea represented a pressing forward of the quite advanced concepts of Jefferson, who tended to view fundamental human freedoms as part of one's property in oneself, and who also opposed the concentration of property control in the hands of a few.

A presentation of the attacks upon or questionings of private property ownership during the American Revolution is necessary to a comprehension, in a rounded way, of its social and political content. What follows is offered as indicative, not exhaustive, of this evidence.

Class feelings were intensified by the Revolution. Colonel Randolph of Virginia complained in 1780 that "the spirit of independency was converted into equality." The Tory, Jonathan Boucher, reported: "Both employers and the employed . . . no longer live together with anything like attachment and cordiality on either side; and the laboring classes, instead of regarding the rich as their guardians, patrons, and benefactors, now look on them as so many overgrown colossuses, whom it is no demerit in them to wrong."

Another contemporary reported from Massachusetts "alarming symptoms of the abatement in the mind of the people of the sacredness of private property." "Agricola," in the *Virginia Gazette* in 1779, went so far as to suggest: "Take the whole trade of the continent out of the hands of individuals and let it be carried on for the benefit of the public by persons authorized by the legislature under stated but liberal salaries."

Less extreme, but related, was the idea Benjamin Franklin

expressed four years later. He held that property ownership might well be included under man's "natural rights," but he severely circumscribed the quantity, if not the kind, of such property that might be so described. Only that property necessary to a man, in terms of his conservation and the propagation of children, "is his natural right, which none can justly deprive him of." All in excess is actually public property, for public laws have permitted its production; hence, the public (presumably, the state) may, by law, otherwise dispose of such property whenever it decides that the general welfare requires this.

The views of Thomas Jefferson, on property distribution, were similar to those of Franklin and were markedly equalitarian. A rather full development of these views is contained in a letter Jefferson wrote to Madison from France in October, 1785. It is this letter which contains the oft-quoted line, "The small land-holders are the most precious part of a state"; but the preceding remarks, though less often cited or quoted, are necessary if the particular sentence itself and if Jefferson's views on property distribution are to be comprehended. The relevant material, in full, is as follows:

> I am conscious that an equal division of property is im-practicable. But the consequences of this enormous inequality producing so much misery to the bulk of mandkind, legislators cannot invent too many devices for subdividing property, only taking care to let their subdivision go hand in hand with the natural affections of the human mind. The descent of property of every kind therefore to all the children, or to all the brothers and sisters, or other relations in equal degree is a politic meas-ure, and a practicable one.
>
> Another means of silently lessening the inequality of property is to exempt all from taxation below a certain point, and to tax the higher portions of property in geometrical progression as they rise. Whenever there is in any country uncultivated lands and unemployed poor, it is clear that the laws of property have been so far extended as to violate natural right. The earth is given as a common stock to man to labor and live on. If, for the encouragement of industry we allow it to be appropriated, we must take care that other employment be permitted to those excluded from the appropriation. If we do not, the fundamental right to labor the earth returns to the unemployed.

> It is too soon in our country to say that every man who can-
> not find employment but who can find uncultivated land, shall
> be at liberty to cultivate it, paying a moderate rent, but it is
> not too soon to provide by every possible means that as few as
> possible shall be without a little portion of land. The small
> landholders are the most precious part of a state.

The sentiment in favor of a more or less radical economic outlook was stimulated not only by the radicalism natural to revolutionary endeavor; it was stimulated also by the unscrupulous and
selfish activity of many among the rich. This activity was dangerous to the cause as well as despicable, and provoked attacks and
proposals for remedy which supplemented general assaults upon
economic inequality such as have already been quoted. Furthermore, the conditions of the laboring portions of the population
were worsened during the fighting; from many of them came
action aimed at reversing this trend and this, too, stimulated
attacks upon property concentration and economic exploitation.

It was the unconscionable behavior of many among the
wealthy that led the Rev. Thomas Allen, a radical Massachusetts patriot, to say in a sermon delivered in February, 1776:

> It concerned the people to see to it that whilst we are fighting
> against oppression from the King and Parliament, that we did
> not suffer it to rise up in our own bowels, that he was not so
> much concerned about carrying our point against Great Britain,
> as he was of having usurpers rise up against ourselves.

There was fantastic profiteering at the expense of starving
civilians and soldiers; there was the sale of shoddy blankets, de-
fective weapons, inedible food—all threatening military disaster;
there was widespread trading with the enemy. In a word, there
was the normal behavior of so many among the rich seeking to
become richer during a nation's emergency; their "patriotism"
was then, as always, first and foremost to their own aggrandize-
ment. "Speculation, peculation, engrossing, forestalling with all
their concomitants," wrote Washington, "afford too many melan-
choly proofs of the decay of public virtue; and too glaring instances of its being the interest and desire of too many who would
wish to be thought friends, to continue the war."

War and thievery have been, historically, basic methods for

the "primitive accumulation of capital"; these fitting character-istics of bourgeois development are the hallmark of the class in the United States, at its birthing time.

Opposition to profiteering and to monopolistic practices was intense during the Revolution. Hence it is that the original draft —not, however, the final version—of the Bill of Rights for the 1776 Constitution of Pennsylvania contained this paragraph:

> An enormous proportion of property vested in a few indi-viduals is dangerous to the rights and destructive of the com-mon happiness of mankind; and therefore every free state hath a right to discourage possession of such property.

Maryland's revolutionary Constitution did denounce monop-olies as "odious, contrary to the principles of a free government, and the principles of commerce." In 1779 this State—goaded on by the particularly outrageous attempt of Samuel Chase, a mem-ber of Congress, to corner the market on wheat—enacted a law forbidding merchants to represent it in Congress.

In several states serious thought was given to laying special taxes upon wartime profits; this was done, however, only in Con-necticut. Everywhere concern was given to controlling prices, whose runaway increases were far outstripping increases in wages. 'A bushel of corn sold for seven shillings in 1777 and for $80 two years later; in the same period a pound of beef rose in cost from eight pence to eight shillings.

Interstate conferences were held on the matter, beginning late in 1776. By the next year the Continental Congress was urging similar conventions. At the same time, local congresses met to control—as a county-wide meeting in Massachusetts, in May, 1777, said—the "avarice and extortion, which, like a resistless current, has overspread the land."

Connecticut, adopting price-fixing legislation in November, 1776, said "the rapid and exorbitant rise upon the necessaries and conveniencies of life . . . is chiefly occasioned by monopo-lizers, that great pest of society, who prefer their own private gain to the interest and safety of their country." Yet the fact is that the price-fixing was more successful in holding down wages (for the price of labor was also fixed) than commodities. Even strikes, demonstrations and near civil wars (as that by many Philadelphia workers, in 1779, aimed against Benedict Arnold and his profiteering friends) did not succeed in halting the wartime process whereby a very few gained fabulous fortunes, and the many suffered increased privation.

Then, too, the attempt was made to fasten the blame for the inflation upon the "excessive" demands of working people, despite the fact, as we have stated, that prices far outdistanced wages and the profits of the merchants and traders were fantastically high. Actually, the absence of an effective taxing system, of effective borrowing of capital and of a sufficiently bold program of confiscating enemy property stimulated the resort to the printing press as the source of money.

By the Spring of 1780 the Continental Congress confessed bankruptcy and repudiation ensued. On March 18, 1780, Congress retired outstanding bills at a ratio of 40 to 1, thus cutting an obligation of $200,000,000 to $5,000,000. The fall continued; in February, 1781, outstanding bills were retired at a ratio of 75 to 1; by 1783, it stood at 1,000 to 1.

But intimately connected with the inflationary process was speculation, profiteering and monopolization. James Madison analyzed Revolutionary inflation in a paper written in 1779 (but not published until 1792). There he did not find the fundamental cause to be, as in the orthodox view, the excessive printing of money, hence its cheapening and hence the rise of prices. Rather, Madison reversed the explanation; he saw monopolizers and profiteers creating "an artificial scarcity of commodities wanted for public use; the consequence of which has been an increase of their price, and of the necessity, emissions."

In addition to taxing excessive profits and fixing prices, other modes of confining the profit motive or curbing monopolization were considered seriously. Thus, Jefferson, in his proposals for the Virginia Constitution of 1776 suggested land distribution by the State, so that every adult free male be in possession of at least 50 acres. John C. Miller, in his *Triumph of Freedom* (1948), accurately summarized an additional phase of the battle against profiteering, when he wrote that, at Congress' recommendation:

The states themselves engaged in the export of provisions and the import of war supplies, and even undertook to manufacture powder and saltpeter. Several states, notably Pennsylvania and Virginia, operated their own armament factories; and Congress itself established foundries for the manufacture of brass cannon in Pennsylvania and Connecticut. North Carolina bought ore lands, and erected furnaces and slitting mills which supplied the army with guns and bullets; and this state also took occasion to proclaim the principle that these enterprises, in every well-founded commonwealth, ought to be owned and operated by the people.

As a result it was already in the Continental Congress that a representative, John Jay of New York, propounded the intimidating question, which has since seen such repeated service: "Shall we shut the door against private enterprise?"

V

The impact of the Revolution upon the American economy was very great; it summed up to a notable stimulus for the development of capitalism.[2] The elimination of feudal practices and laws —such as quit rents, entail, primogeniture—served to provide the flexibility so necessary for the flourishing of young capitalism. The elimination of Crown ownership over forests and minerals and the tendency to turn these great natural resources over to the rapacious appetites of entrepreneurs also stimulated this development.

Of course, as already suggested, the war itself provided vast opportunities for the quick accumulation of great fortunes—by more or less legitimately meeting the demands of the war-market, and by profiteering, trading with the enemy, grafting, and other kinds of business thievery.

Further, the cancellation of indebtedness to the British served as an important release for investment funds elsewhere, especially among Southern planters, particularly in land speculation and fur-trading. Meanwhile, not only did the war naturally stimulate manufacturing (especially in textiles and metals), but, in addition, the whole process of governmental subsidizing of ventures for private profit began during the Revolution.

Somewhat ironically, though the American bourgeoisie have been outstanding in their insistence upon "rugged individualism," they have, at the same time, seen to it that the state actively assisted them—via bounties, grants and immunities—in their profit-making. This practice was quite notable during the Revolution and, especially, in the immediate post-Revolutionary era. Thus, several States exempted from taxation for varying periods many different kinds of manufacturing; land was granted in other instances; bounties in still others; and loans, at very low interest rates, were also not uncommon. Meanwhile, through tariffs and other kinds of restrictive legislation, States further assisted capitalist enterprise.

During the war "there was an outburst of domestic production unlike anything that had gone before," as Arthur H. Cole wrote in his study of wool manufacture. By 1790 Pennsylvania equalled Great Britain as the South's source of manufactured goods; by the same year the American demand for glass and paper was being met by American factories.

The break from England had several significant economic results of a direct character. The United States, no longer bound by British mercantile regulations, sought and gained entry, commercially, into Southern European, West Indian, South American and Asian ports hitherto more or less unknown or barred to American ships. While the severance of the English tie brought some hardships (as the closing of trade with the British West Indies) this was more than made up for in the opening of new opportunities.

Further, the ending of a colonial subordination was the result of and stimulated national development. One of the results of the establishment of actual national sovereignty was the opening up to the unimpeded exploitation by the American bourgeoisie of the resources of the country, with trade, travel and investment encouraged, rather than impeded.

Commercial and financial institutions to service this national economic renaissance soon appeared—as the Bank of North America in 1780, the Bank of New York and the Bank of Boston, both in 1784.

Robert A. East, in his pioneering study, *Business Enterprise in the Revolutionary Era* (1938), pointed out that prior to the Revolution, where surplus capital was not invested in commerce, it was devoted to processing and secondary industries, as distilleries, sugar refineries, flour mills, pot and pearl ash work, etc., with but the barest beginnings of iron foundries and bloomeries. Further, the reliance on British commercial credit, together with imperial restrictions, made group investment mechanisms unknown before the Revolution. With the Revolution and immediately thereafter, the economy began notable shifts in all these respects. A spurt in manufacturing, especially in textiles and metals appeared; a significant reduction in complete dependence upon British credit began; banks and other pooled commercial efforts started, through joint-stock methods, in turnpike, bridge and canal building, in manufacturing and in land speculation.

By way of summary, East writes: "In contrast with the half dozen American business charters granted in the entire colonial period, eleven were issued in the United States between 1781 and 1785, twenty-two between 1786 and 1790, and one hundred and fourteen between 1791 and 1795."

The American Revolution—its conduct and impact—helped American capitalism emerge from infancy to childhood. In its greater extent, wider diversification, developing impersonalization, worldwide spread, the economy of the United States in 1790 was notably different from that of 1770. In this, as Professor Ver Steeg has suggested, the "American Revolution considered as an economic movement," was quite as significant as it was in social, or political or national terms. Indeed, the developments in all these respects were intertwined; together they demonstrate the effects of that Revolution to have been so momentous as to justify the superlative term, "revolution."

VI

We choose to conclude our presentation of the American Revolution with quotations from two distinguished personages connected with it. One is Benjamin Franklin. On May 1, 1777, in a letter from Paris addressed to Samuel Cooper, Franklin wrote:

All Europe is on our side of the question, as far as applause and good wishes can carry them. Those who live under arbitrary power do nevertheless approve of liberty, and wish for it; they almost despair of recovering it in Europe; they read the translations of our separate Colony constitutions with rapture; and there are such numbers everywhere, who talk of removing to America, with their families and fortunes, as soon as peace and our independence shall be established, that 'tis generally believed we shall have a prodigious addition of strength, wealth, and arts, from the emigrations of Europe; and 'tis thought that, to lessen or prevent such emigrations, the tyrannies established there must relax, and allow more liberty to their people. Hence 'tis a common observation here, that our cause is *the cause of all Mankind* [italics in original], and that we are fighting for their liberty in defending our own. 'Tis a glorious task assign'd us by Providence; which has, I trust, given us spirit and virtue equal to it, and will at last crown it with success.

The other contemporary is David Hartley, a friend of Franklin, a scientist and inventor of some distinction, a Whig member of Parliament, opponent of the war against America, and a negotiator and signer of the 1783 Treaty of Paris formally ending the war. Hartley prepared a memorandum for the consideration of the British Government, January 9, 1785, in which—pointing to its enormous resources and availability of colossal land area— he stated that it was certain this new United States of America was destined to be, in the not very remote future, one of the greatest powers in the world. But of the first importance, in terms of the future of the new nation and in terms of its impact upon the world's future, David Hartley emphasized the freedom of the individual and the sovereignty of the people which, because of the Revolution's success, might be hall-marks of American development. Wrote Hartley:

It is a new proposition to be offered for the numerous common rank of mankind in all the countries of the world, to say that there are in America fertile soils and temperate climates in which an acre of land may be purchased for a trifling consideration, which may be possessed in freedom, together with all the natural and civil rights of mankind. The Congress have already proclaimed this, and that no other qualification or name is necessary but to become settlers without distinction of Country or Persons. The European peasant who toils for his scanty sustenance in penury, wretchedness and servitude, will eagerly fly to this Asylum for free and industrious labor. The tide of emigration may set strongly outwards from Scotland, Ireland and Canada to this new land of promise.

A very great proportion of men in all countries of the world are without property, and generally are subject to governments of which they have no participation and over which they have no control. The Congress have now opened to all the world a sale of landed settlements where the liberty and property of each individual is to be consigned to his own custody and defense. . . . These are such propositions of free establishment as have never yet been offered in the future progress of things.

How well or ill these prospects were to be fulfilled will form the substance of ensuing pages in this work. But that these were the promises (or forebodings, depending upon one's viewpoint) of the American Revolution and of the new nation whose sovereignty it created, so far as contemporaries were concerned, cannot be denied. In the continuing struggle for the creation of a social order wherein the people as a whole direct their own destinies, in all spheres of human existence, the American Revolution stands as a momentous landmark.

Reference Notes

CHAPTER II

[1] Vincent T. Harlow fully presents this momentous development in *The Founding of the Second British Empire, 1763-1793,* vol. I, *Discovery and Revolution* (London, 1952, Longmans, Green).

[2] These considerations are at least a partial answer to O. M. Dickerson's demand: "Whoever seeks to explain the Revolution must show why thirteen colonies joined in the revolt while seventeen remained loyal"—in *Canadian Historical Review,* March, 1942. In Jamaica, in 1774, there were about 13,000 whites and over 192,000 slaves; serious slave uprisings occurred there in 1765, 1769, 1776.

CHAPTER III

[1] In their very useful *The Making of American Democracy: Readings and Documents* (2 vols., Rinehart, N.Y., 1950) I, p. 72.

CHAPTER V

[1] A leading Irish-born Whig member of Parliament, Isaac Barré, referred to the Americans as "Sons of Liberty" when arguing against the Stamp Act. He, and John Wilkes, were Parliamentary leaders of pro-American sentiment which was very widespread among the British people, as we shall see later. Their names are immortalized in the city of Wilkes-Barre, Pennsylvania. Despite the publication of some good studies of this organization, as that by Herbert M. Morais, these are all very limited essays. There is great need for a detailed, book-length examination of the Sons of Liberty.

[2] The legislatures of New Hampshire and Georgia sent assurances of support to the Congress; the Royal Governors of Virginia, North Carolina and Georgia had refused to permit the Assemblies to gather in order to select delegates.

[3] There is need for a modern, full-length study of the whole phenomenon of committee organization and the making of the American revolution. There are two brief works, of some value, but both are over fifty years old: Edward D. Collins, "Committees of Correspondence of the American Revolution," in *Annual Report of the American Historical Association,* 1901, pp. 245-271; Agnes Hunt, *The Provincial Committees of Safety of the American Revolution* (Cleveland, 1904). There is useful material in Margaret B. Macmillan's *The War Governors in the American Revolution* (N.Y., 1943), especially pp. 15-25.

[4] Officially it was simply "The Congress," but there were several provincial congresses and so a distinction was necessary. At first the term General Congress was used, but Continental Congress soon received general usage.

Officially, with the adoption of the Articles of Confederation, 1781, Congress became "The United States in Congress Assembled." Despite conservative bias, Edmund C. Burnett's *The Continental Congress* (N.Y., 1941) is a definitive work. It should be supplemented by the *Journals* of the Congress, edited by W. C. Ford, and the eight-volume collection, *Letters of Members of the Continental Congress,* edited by Burnett.

⁵ Joseph Galloway became a Tory—civil administrator of British-occupied Philadelphia—and moved to England in 1778. Deane was a leading Revolutionary diplomat in France, but, faced with charges of financial irregularities, he resigned. Some evidence of disaffection on his part becoming public, Deane was denounced as a traitor. He spent his life from 1778 to his death in 1789 abroad virtually in exile. Evidence later appearing that the charge of treason was excessive, Congress voted $37,000 to his heirs as restitution in 1842, because of the earlier "gross injustice." Still later evidence shows Congress to have been over-generous.

CHAPTER VI

¹ It is noteworthy that only one of the Signers repudiated his signature. This was Richard Stockton of New Jersey, who did so late in 1776, when the British had over-run his State.

CHAPTER VII

¹ Strictly speaking the document was submitted by the Committee appointed to write it; but Jefferson was its author. The Committee members made very few changes—John Adams' were most numerous, and even his were altogether minor.

² This had reference mainly to Lord Dunmore's proclamation in Virginia, issued Nov. 7, 1775, offering freedom to all *male* slaves of *rebels* reaching his troops. Plots among slaves—with charges of British inspiration—were reported from Massachusetts and Georgia in 1774, and from New York, South Carolina, Virginia, and—most serious—North Carolina, in 1775.

³ Locke's idea was used by him explicitly in an anti-slavery sense; that is, the effort to enslave or the fact of enslavement, was declared by Locke to be a "state of war." It is interesting to note that, on Lockeian thinking, later Abolitionists justified militant resistance to slavery. John Brown, for example, insisted the slaves were "prisoners of war."

CHAPTER VIII

¹ An important exception was the Burgoyne campaign, 1777-78. Here the base was Canada, but the southern anchor was supposed to have been New York. Liaison, however, between Howe and Burgoyne was faulty, bringing catastrophe to the latter.

² The first professional study of partisan warfare was published in two volumes in Germany in 1786; it was the work of a Captain Johann Ewald who had served with the Hessians in America—later, as von Ewald, a lieutenant-general in the Danish Army.

CHAPTER IX

¹ As late as 1790—the first census—Virginia, with 750,000 people, had as large a population as New York and Pennsylvania taken together. New

England then had one million people; half lived in Massachusetts, a state outnumbered only by Virginia.

CHAPTER X

¹ Shelburne became Prime Minister in 1782, when the failure of the effort to repress the Americans had become clear even to the King. It was his Government which signed the Treaty of Paris, in 1783, recognizing the independence of the United States. Richard Price was a close personal friend and adviser; Joseph Priestley was his librarian for several years.

² The post-North parliamentary reforms provided: (1) government contractors were excluded from the House of Commons; (2) the pension list was limited and many sinecures were abolished; (3) revenue officers, hitherto required to vote for government candidates, were disfranchised.

CHAPTER XI

¹ In addition to very stringent "normal" trade restrictions, in 1777 England placed an embargo on the exportation of linen from Ireland with the purpose of keeping supplies out of American hands. The impact of this measure was disastrous; within months there were 20,000 unemployed in Dublin alone.

² In a belated effort to win over Canada, Congress sent a top-level Commission there early in 1776. Its members were the leading American Catholic rebel, Charles Carroll of Maryland, Father John Carroll (later the first Catholic Bishop in the U.S.), Samuel Chase, and Benjamin Franklin.

³ In 1779 a formidable insurrection in India nearly drove the British to the sea; at the same time the Anglo-French war, that had started over the American question in 1778, extended to India. In 1784 Britain completely over-hauled her mode of dominating and exploiting India.

CHAPTER XII

¹ There were five members of this committee: Benjamin Harrison of Virginia, Benjamin Franklin of Pennsylvania, Thomas Johnson of Maryland, John Dickinson of Pennsylvania, and John Jay of New York. The Committee was succeeded, in April, 1777, by the Committee of Foreign Affairs, and, in 1781, by Congress selecting Robert R. Livingston of New York, as its Secretary for Foreign Affairs. While these bodies are the ancestors of the present Department of State, it is to be noted that all of them were created by and functioned as arms of the Congress.

² Typical was John Adams' letter to James Warren, May 3, 1777, warning against America's becoming "entangled in the quarrels of Europe." This is, of course, an important theme in Paine's *Common Sense*. Prof. Bemis says that American Revolutionary statesmen felt "that one of the most significant things which they might hope for in independence was comparative disentanglement from European international convulsions." The deeds of these statesmen demonstrate, however, that they certainly were not "isolationists" as that term is now understood. I agree with W. A. Williams: "The Founding Fathers sought time to gain strength, which they hoped to use eventually in whatever manner they saw fit. They did not want isolation; they wanted freedom of action."

³ Over 12,000 Germans never returned home. About 1,200 were killed in

action; over 6,000 died of illness and accident; about 5,000 went over to the Americans.

[4] By the end of 1776 Spain had given, in loans and subsidies, a total of about $650,000; France, by the same period, a total of about $8,500,000.

[5] Rodney's pre-occupation with St. Eustatius made it possible for Admiral de Grasse to move north from the West Indies and participate, decisively, in the seige of Cornwallis at Yorktown. The English concluded a separate treaty with the Dutch in 1784 which resulted in gains for Great Britain in India and in the Moluccas.

[6] This is the characterization of Dr. J. Presser in a letter to me, dated Amsterdam, January 9, 1956. Dr. Presser, a distinguished Dutch historian, is the author of a massive history of the United States, *Amerika, van Kolonie Tot Wereldmacht* (Amsterdam, Brussel, 1951, Elsevier).

[7] The settlement with Holland, signed in 1784, has been referred to earlier. France made some slight gains in Africa and in India; the clause in the Treaty of Utrecht forbidding her to build fortifications at Dunkirk was repealed; she was granted important fishing rights off the Newfoundland coast. (The latter ended in 1904, in exchange for which England gave France 14,000 square miles of territory in West Africa.) Spain recovered Minorca and East Florida, but she restored the Bahamas to England and confirmed British lumber rights in Honduras.

CHAPTER XII

[7] As a matter of fact British soldiers occupied, until 1796, eight American posts—Detroit, Michellemackinac, Fort Erie, Niagara, Oswego, Oswegatchie (now Ogdensburg), Pointe Au Fer, and Dutchman's Point on Lake Champlain. These were important for the Indian trade and in terms of British aspirations to weaken the United States. Related also were the earnest efforts to get Vermont to affiliate to Canada.

CHAPTER XIV

[1] After writing this section, the essay, "Democracy and the American Revolution," by Professor Jensen (published in *The Huntington Library Quarterly*, Aug. 1957, XX, pp. 321-42) became available. Here Jensen re-affirms his position and meets some of the criticism of his work. On the whole he strengthens his case in this paper; some of the exaggerated terminology of his earlier work is modified. He concludes that, "the American Revolution was a democratic movement, not in origin, but in result." I think his posing of this sharp distinction between origin and result is wrong, though it is true that the actual fighting did enhance some of the democratic inspiration and content present from the beginning.

[2] A literal reading of the enactment resulted in voting by Negroes, and women, from 1790 to 1807.

[3] This is said with full awareness of the corrective—itself quite exaggerated—on the question of debt imprisonment offered by E. T. Randall in his provocative essay, "Imprisonment for Debt in America: Fact and Fiction," in the *Mississippi Valley Hist. Rev.*, June 1952, XXXIX, 89-102.

CHAPTER XV

[1] *Entail:* the settlement of a landed estate on a particular line or succession of individuals in such a way that none of them can alienate it—thus tending to freeze land ownership.

Mortmain: the possession of lands by those who cannot alienate—either by sale or will; i.e., an inalienable possession, and the necessary result of the law of entail.

Primogeniture: the right, in law, by which the eldest son inherits the entire estate of the father.

All these provisions were basic tenets of feudal law, ensuring the stability and concentration in possession of land so vital to feudalism.

[2] After the original draft of this section, the writer found encouraging corroboration and illuminating suggestions in Clarence L. Ver Steeg's, "The American Revolution Considered as an Economic Movement," in *The Huntington Library Quarterly,* (Aug. 1957).

Bibliography

The literature relevant to the Revolutionary Era is enormous. When one considers the international ramifications, the sources, conduct, impact, the relationship to areas of economics, diplomacy, politics, culture, ideology, it becomes clear that a mastery of this literature probably is outside the competence of any one person. Certainly, the present writer makes no claim to having even nearly exhausted the literature on this subject.

The sources which were studied are listed below; those marked with an asterisk were found to be of particular importance. The best full-length, one-volume study of the subject remains the third volume in Edward Channing's *History of the United States;* this has been amended and supplemented by many later scholars, but it has not been displaced.

The following abbreviations are used:

AHR: American Historical Review
CaUP: Cambridge University Press
CHR: Canadian Historical Review
COP: Cornell University Press
CUAP: Catholic University of America Press
CUP: Columbia University Press
DUP: Duke University Press
GPO: Government Printing Office
HUP: Harvard University Press
JHUP: Johns Hopkins University Press
LUP: Louisiana State University Press
MVHR: Mississippi Valley Historical Review
NYUP: New York University Press
OUP: Oxford University Press
PUP: Princeton University Press
RUP: Rutgers University Press
UCaP: University of California Press
UCP: University of Chicago Press
UNCP: University of North Carolina Press
UOkP: University of Oklahoma Press
UPP: University of Pennsylvania Press
UWP: University of Wisconsin Press
YUP: Yale University Press

CONTEMPORARY SOURCES

The letters, diaries, and writings of outstanding participants in the Revolution have been published in great abundance. Among those of special

284

consequence are the collections dealing with: John Adams, Thomas Jefferson, George Washington, Richard Henry Lee, Benjamin Franklin, Benjamin Rush, James Madison, and Thomas Paine.

Collections of newspapers dating back to the Revolution are abundant; those in the Library of Congress and in the Library of Columbia University were used by the writer. Large selections from these newspapers are printed in certain state archival collections; especially strong in this are the Archives of Pennsylvania and New Jersey. The works edited by Frank Moore and Peter Force, noted below, also contain numerous extracts from the contemporary press.

Other source collections of the greatest importance are those edited by Albert B. Hart, Edmund C. Burnett, and Merrill Jensen, to which full references will be found below.

APTHEKER, HERBERT, ed., *A Documentary History of the Negro People in the United States* (N.Y., 1951, Citadel)

BECCARIA-BONESANA, CESARE, *An Essay on Crime and Punishments* (1819, Phila. edit. reprinted by Academic Reprints, Stanford, 1953)

BELOFF, MAX, ed., *The Debate [in Parliament] on the American Revolution, 1761-1783* (London, 1949, Kaye)

BILLINGTON, R. A., LOEWENBERG, J. B., BROCKUNIER, S., eds., *The Making of American Democracy: Readings and Documents* (2 vols., N.Y., 19 Rinehart), Vol. I

BURNETT, EDMUND C., ed., *Letters of Members of the Continental Congress* (8 vols., Washington 1941, Carnegie)

COMMAGER, HENRY S., ed., *Documents of American History* (4th edit., N.Y., 1948, Appleton-Century-Crofts) I, pp. 42-124

COMMAGER, H. S., ed., *America in Perspective: The U.S. Through Foreign Eyes* (N.Y., 1947, Random)

COMMAGER, H. S. and MORRIS, R. B., eds., *The Spirit of 'Seventy-Six: The Story the American Revolution as Told by Participants* (2 vols., Indianapolis, 1958, Bobbs-Merrill). This work appeared after the final draft of the present volume was completed. Containing over 1,300 pages, it is the fullest overall documentary account of the Revolution available. Notable is the fact that though its index is very full, no reference to the Negro appears. Six pages are devoted to documents on the theme, "How Reconcile Freedom to Slavery?"; this may be compared with eleven pages given to documenting "The Carlisle Commission."

CRANE, VERNER W., ed., *Benjamin Franklin's Letters to the Press,* 1758-1775 (Chapel Hill, 1950, UNCP)

FORCE, PETER, ed., *American Archives* . . . (9 vols., Washington, 1839-98)

FORD, PAUL L., ed., ISRAEL MAUDUIT, *A Handbill Advocating American Independence* . . . *London, 1778* (Brooklyn, 1890, Hist. Printing Club)

HACKER, LOUIS M., ed., *The Shaping of the American Tradition* (2 vols., N.Y., 1947, CUP) Vol. I

HART, ALBERT B., ed., *American History Told by Contemporaries,* Vol. II *1689-1783* (N.Y., 1898, Macmillan)

HISTORICAL MANUSCRIPTS COMMISSION: *Report of American MSS in the Royal Institution of Great Britain* (2 vols., London, 1904)

JENSEN, MERRILL, ed., *American Colonial Documents to 1776* (being Vol. IX of *English Historical Documents,* N.Y., 1955, OUP)

LINCOLN, WILLIAM, ed., *The Journals of Each Provincial Congress of Massachusetts in 1774 and 1775* (Boston, 1838, Dutton & Wentworth)

MCILWAINE, H. R., ed., *Official Letters of the Governors of Virginia* (Richmond, 1929), Vol. III

MENG, JOHN J., ed., *Despatches and Instructions of Conrad Alexandre Gerard, 1778-1780* (Baltimore, 1939, JHUP)

MOORE, FRANK, ed., *Diary of the American Revolution from Newspapers and Original Documents* (2 vols., N.Y., 1865)

NELSON, WILLIAM, ed., *Documents Relating to the Revolutionary History of New Jersey* (Vol. III, Trenton, 1906, Murphy Pub.)

SCHEER, GEORGE F. & RANKIN, HUGH F., eds., *Rebels and Redcoats: The Living Story of the American Revolution* (Cleveland, 1957, World Pub.)

SCOTT, JAMES B., ed., *The Armed Neutralities of 1780 and 1800* (N.Y., 1918, OUP)

SMITH, ADAM, *The Wealth of Nations* (E. Cannan, ed.) (N.Y., 1937, Random)

SPARKS, JARED, ed., *Correspondence of the American Revolution; being letters of eminent men to George Washington* (4 vols., Boston, 1853, Little, Brown)

STEVENS, BENJAMIN F., ed., *Facsimiles of Manuscripts in European Archives Relating to America, 1773-1783* (25 vols., London, 1889)

STRYKER, WILLIAM, ed., *Documents Relating to the Revolutionary History of New Jersey* (Trenton, 1901, vol. I, Murphy Pub.)

UHLENDORF, BERNHARD A., ed., *Revolution in America: Confidential Letters and Journals, 1776-1784 of Adjutant General Major Baurmeister of the Hessian Forces* (New Brunswick, 1957, RUP)

VAN DOREN, MARK, ed., *The Voice of America* (Cleveland, 1942, World Pub.) Book III

WHARTON, FRANCIS, ed., *The Revolutionary Diplomatic Correspondence of the United States* (6 vols., Washington, 1889, GPO)

WILLARD, MARGARET, ed., *Letters on the American Revolution, 1774-76* (Boston, 1925, Houghton, Mifflin)

SECONDARY WORKS

ABERNETHY, THOMAS P., *From Frontier to Plantation in Tennessee* (Chapel Hill, 1932, UNC)

ABERNETHY, T. P., *Western Lands and the American Revolution* (N.Y., 1937, Appleton-Century)

ADAMS, RANDOLPH G., *The Political Ideas of the American Revolution* (Durham, 1922, Trinity College Press)

*ALDEN, JOHN R., *The American Revolution: 1775-1783* (*New American Nation* Series, N.Y., 1954, Harper)

ALVORD, CLARENCE W., *The Mississippi Valley in British Politics* (2 vols., Cleveland, 1917, A. H. Clark)

*ANDREWS, CHARLES M., *The Colonial Period of American History* (4 vols., New Haven, 1934-38, YUP)

APTHEKER, HERBERT, *The Negro in the American Revolution* (N.Y., 1940, International Publishers)

APTHEKER, H., *American Negro Slave Revolts* (N.Y., 1943, CUP)

AUGUR, HELEN, *The Secret War of Independence* (N.Y., 1956, Duell, Sloan & Pearce)

AXELRAD, JACOB, *Patrick Henry: The Voice of Freedom* (N.Y., 1947, Random)

AZOY, A. C., *Patriot Battles, 1775-1781* (Washington, 1943, Infantry Journal)

BAILEY, THOMAS A., *A Diplomatic History of the American People* (N.Y., 1950, 4th edit., Appleton-Century-Crofts)

BAKELESS, JOHN, *Turncoats, Traitors and Heroes* (Phila., 1959, Lippincott). This appeared after the present volume was in proofs. It is the fullest account available of espionage and military intelligence work conducted by both sides within the battle-zones.

*BALDWIN, ALICE M., *The New England Clergy and the American Revolution* (Durham, 1928, DUP)

BANCROFT, GEORGE, *A History of the United States* (Boston, 1860, Little Brown), Vol. VIII

BARKER, CHARLES A., *The Background of the Revolution in Maryland* (New Haven, 1940, YUP)

BARNES, HARRY E., *The Evolution of Penology in Pennsylvania* (Indianapolis, 1921, Bobbs-Merrill)

BEARD, CHARLES A. AND MARY R., *The Rise of American Civilization* (2 vols., in 1, N.Y., 1936, Macmillan) Vol. I

*BECKER, CARL L., *The History of Political Parties in the Province of New York, 1760-1776* (Madison, 1909, UWP)

BECKER, C. L., *The Declaration of Independence* (N.Y., 1922, Harcourt, Brace)

BECKER, C. L., *The Heavenly City of the 18th Century Philosophers* (New Haven, 1932, YUP)

BECKETT, J. C., *A Short History of Ireland* (London, 1952, Hutchinson)

BEER, GEORGE L., *British Colonial Policy, 1754-1765* (N.Y., 1907, Macmillan)

BELCHER, HENRY, *The First American Civil War* (2 vols., London, 1911, Macmillan)

BEMIS, SAMUEL F., "British Secret Service and the French-American Alliance," AHR (April, 1924), XXIX, 474-95

BEMIS, S. F., "Canada and the Peace Settlement of 1782-83," CHR (Sept., 1933), XIV, 265-84

*BEMIS, S .F., *The Diplomacy of the American Revolution* (N.Y., 1935)

BEMIS, S. F., *A Diplomatic History of the U.S.* (N.Y., 1936, Holt)

BENSON, ADOLPH B., *Sweden and the American Revolution* (New Haven, 1926, Tuttle, Morehouse & Taylor)

*BENSON, MARY S., *Women in 18th Century America* (N.Y., 1935, CUP)

BODKIN, M. M., *Grattan's Parliament* (London, 1912, Unwin)

BOLTON, CHARLES K., *The Private Soldier Under Washington* (N.Y., 1902, Scribner's)

BOND, BEVERLEY W., JR., "Some Political Ideals of the Colonial Period as Realized in the Old Northwest," in *Essays in Colonial History Presented to Charles M. Andrews by his Students* (New Haven, 1931, YUP)

BOORSTIN, DANIEL J., *The Genius of American Politics* (Chicago, 1953, UCP)

BOORSTIN, D. J., *The Americans: The Colonial Experience* (N.Y., 1958, Random)

BOWMAN, ALLEN, *The Morale of the American Revolutionary Army* (Washington, 1943, American Council on Public Affairs)

BOYD, JULIAN P., "The Declaration of Independence," in E. N. Saveth, ed., *Understanding the American Past* (Boston, 1954, Little Brown)

BRENNAN, ELLEN E., *Plural Office-Holding in Massachusetts, 1760-1780* (Chapel Hill, 1945, UNC)

BROWN, ROBERT E., *Middle-Class Democracy and the Revolution in Massachusetts* (Ithaca, 1955, COP)

BROWN, WELDON A., *Empire or Independence* (Baton Rouge, 1941, LUP)

BROWNE, CHARLES A., "Joseph Priestley and the American 'Fathers'," *American Scholar* (Spring, 1935), IV, 133-47

BREBNER, JOHN B., *The Neutral Yankees of Nova Scotia* (N.Y., 1937, CUP)

*BREBNER, J. B., *North Atlantic Triangle: The Interplay of Canada, the United States, and Great Britain* (New Haven, 1945, YUP)

*BURNETT, EDMUND C., *The Continental Congress* (N.Y., 1941, Macmillan)

BURNS, ALAN, *History of the British West Indies* (London, 1954, Allen & Unwin)

*BURT, ALFRED L., *The Evolution of the British Empire and Commonwealth* (Boston, 1956, Heath)

BURT, A. L., *The United States, Great Britain, and British North America from the Revolution to the Establishment of Peace after the War of 1812* (New Haven, 1940, YUP)

BUTTERFIELD, HERBERT, *George III, Lord North, and the People* (London, 1949, G. Bell)

CALDWELL, ROBERT G., *The Penitentiary Movement in Delaware, 1776-1829* (Wilmington, 1946, Hist. Soc. of Del.)

CAMPBELL, MILDRED, "English Emigration on the Eve of the American Revolution," *AHR* (Oct., 1955), LXI, 1-15

Canadian Historical Review (March, 1942), XXIII, 1-39: "The American Revolution: A Symposium"

CARTER, CLARENCE E., "The Office of Commander in Chief," in R. B. Morris, ed., *The Era of the American Revolution*

CASSIRER, ERNST, *The Philosophy of the Enlightenment* (Princeton, 1951, PUP)

*CHANNING, EDWARD, *A History of the United States,* Volume III, 1761-1789 (N.Y., 1912, Macmillan)

CLARK, DORA M., *British Opinion and the American Revolution* (New Haven, 1930, YUP)

CLARK, WILLIAM B., "John the Painter," *The Pa. Mag. of Hist. & Biog.,* (Jan., 1939), LXIII, 1-23

COLE, ARTHUR H., *The American Wool Manufacture* (2 vols., Cambridge, 1926, HUP), Vol. I

COLEMAN, J. M., "The Treason of Ralph Morden and Robert Land," *Pa. Mag. of Hist. & Biog.* (Oct., 1955), LXXIX, 439-51

COLEMAN, KENNETH, "The American Revolution in Georgia, 1763-1789," unpublished Ph.D. thesis, Univ. of Wisconsin, 1952 (since published, Chapel Hill, 1959, UNCP)

COLLINS, EDWARD D., "Committees of Correspondence of the American Revolution," *Annual Report of the American Hist. Ass'n., 1901* (Washington, 1902, GPO)

COMETTI, ELIZABETH, "Women in the American Revolution," *New England Quarterly* (Sept., 1947), XX, 329-46

CONE, CARL B., *Torchbearer of Freedom: The Influence of Richard Price in 18th Century Thought* (Lexington, 1952, UKP)

COOLEY, TIMOTHY, *Sketches of the Life and Character of the Rev. Lemuel Haynes* (N.Y., 1837, Harper)

CORWIN, EDWARD S., *French Policy and the American Alliance of 1778* (Princeton, 1916, PUP)

*COUPLAND, REGINALD, *The American Revolution and the British Empire* (London, 1930, Longmans Green)

CREIGHTON, DONALD G., *The Commercial Empire of the St. Lawrence, 1760-1850* (Toronto, 1937, Ryerson)

CREIGHTON, D. G., *Dominion of the North: A History of Canada* (Boston, 1944, Houghton Mifflin)

CROWL, PHILIP A., *Maryland During and After the Revolution* (Baltimore, 1943, JHUP)

CURTI, MERLE, *The Growth of American Thought* (2nd edit., N.Y., 1951, Harper), chapters I-VII

CURTI, M., *Probing Our Past* (N.Y., 1955, Harper)

*DARLING, ARTHUR B., *Our Rising Empire, 1763-1803* (New Haven, 1940, YUP)

DAVIDSON, PHILIP, *Propaganda and the American Revolution, 1763-1783* (Chapel Hill, 1941, UNCP)

DeMOND, ROBERT O., *The Loyalists in North Carolina during the Revolution* (Durham, 1940, DUP)

DEUTSCH, ALBERT, *The Mentally Ill in America* (Garden City, 1937, Doubleday, Doran)

DICKERSON, OLIVER M., *The Navigation Acts and the American Revolution* (Phila., 1951, UPP)

DICKERSON, O. M., "Writs of Assistance as a Cause of the Revolution," in R. B. Morris, ed., *The Era of the American Revolution*

*DORFMAN, JOSEPH, *The Economic Mind in American Civilization* (2 vols., N.Y., 1946, Viking) Vol. I

*DOUGLASS, ELISHA P., *Rebels and Democrats: The Struggle for Equal Political Rights and Majority Rule during the American Revolution* (Chapel Hill, 1955, UNCP)

DOWNES, RANDOLPH C., "Indian War on the Upper Ohio, 1779-1782," *Western Pa. Hist. Mag.* (June, 1934), XVII, 93-115

DRAKE, THOMAS E., *Quakers and Slavery in America* (New Haven, 1950, YUP)

DUMBAULD, EDWARD, *The Declaration of Independence* (Norman, 1950, UOkP)

DUNBAR, LOUISE B., "The Royal Governors," in R. B. Morris, ed., *The Era of the American Revolution*

*EAST, ROBERT A., *Business Enterprise in the American Revolutionary Era* (N.Y., 1938, CUP)

ECKENRODE, H. J., *The Revolution in Virginia* (Boston, 1916, Houghton Mifflin)

EGERTON, HUGH E., *A Historical Geography of the British Dominions: Canada,* Part II, *The History from 1763-1921* (Oxford, 1923, Clarendon Press)

EGERTON, H. E., *The Causes and Character of the American Revolution* (London, 1931, OUP)

EINSTEIN, LEWIS, *Divided Loyalties: Americans in England during the War of Independence* (Boston, 1933, Houghton Mifflin)

EKIRCH, ARTHUR A., JR., *The Civilian and the Military* (N.Y., 1956, OUP)

EYCK, ERICH, *Pitt versus Fox: Father and Son, 1735-1806* (London, 1950, G. Bell)

FALKINER, C. L., *Studies in Irish History and Biography* (London, 1903, Longmans, Green)

FISHER, SYDNEY G., *The Struggle for American Independence* (2 vols., Phila., 1908, Lippincott)

FOX, DIXON R., *Ideas in Motion* (N.Y., 1935, Appleton-Century)

FRIEDENWALD, HERBERT, *The Declaration of Independence* (N.Y., 1904, Macmillan)

GANTER, HERBERT L., "Jefferson's 'Pursuit of Happiness' and Some Forgotten Men," *William & Mary Coll. Q* (July, October, 1936)

GARNER, JOHN, "The Enfranchisement of Roman Catholics in the Maritimes," CHR (Sept., 1953) XXXIV, 203-218

GILLIS, D. HUGH, *Democracy in the Canadas, 1759-1867* (Toronto, 1951, OUP)

GINZBERG, ELI, *The House of Adam Smith* (N.Y., 1934, CUP)

GIPSON, LAWRENCE H., *Jared Ingersoll* (New Haven, 1920, YUP)

GIPSON, L. H., *The Coming of the Revolution, 1763-1775* (N.Y., 1954, Harper)

GOLDER, FRANK A., "Catherine II and the American Revolution," *AHR,* (Oct., 1915), XXI, 92-96

GOODMAN, NATHAN G., *Benjamin Rush* (Phila., 1934, UPP)

GRAHAM, GERALD S., *British Policy and Canada, 1774-1791* (London, 1930, Longmans Green)

GREEN, FLETCHER M., *Constitutional Development in the South Atlantic States, 1776-1860* (Chapel Hill, 1930, UNCP)

GREENE, EVARTS B. AND HARRINGTON, V. D., *American Population Before 1790* (N.Y., 1932, CUP)

GREENE, E. B., *The Foundations of American Nationality* (N.Y., 1935, rev. edit., American Book)

GREENE, E. B., *Religion and the State: The Making and Testing of an American Traditional* (N.Y., 1941, NYUP)

*GREENE, E. B., *The Revolutionary Generation, 1763-1790* (vol. IV of *A History of American Life,* N.Y., 1943, Macmillan)

GREENE, JOHN C., "The American Debate on the Negro's Place in Nature, 1780-1815," *The Journal of the History of Ideas* (June, 1954), XV, 384-96

GREENE, LORENZO J., *The Negro in Colonial New England, 1620-1776* (N.Y., 1942, CUP)

GROCE, GEORGE C., JR., *William Samuel Johnson* (N.Y., 1937, CUP)

GUTTMACHER, MANFRED S., *America's Last King: An Interpretation of the Madness of George III* (N.Y., 1941, Scribner's)

GUTTRIDGE, GEORGE H., *David Hartley, M.P., An Advocate of Conciliation* (Berkeley, 1926, UCaP)

*GUTTRIDGE, G. H., *English Whiggism and the American Revolution* (Berkeley, 1942, UCP)

HACKER, LOUIS M., *The Triumph of American Capitalism* (N.Y., 1940, Simon & Shuster)

HACKER, L. M., *Alexander Hamilton in the American Tradition* (N.Y., 1957, McGraw, Hill)

HALEVY, ELIE, *The Growth of Philosophical Radicalism*, M. Morris, tr., (Boston, 1955, Beacon)

HANDLIN, OSCAR AND MARY F., *A Study of the Role of Government in the American Economy: Massachusetts, 1774-1861* (N.Y., 1947, NYUP)

HARDY, JACK, *The First American Revolution* (N.Y., 1937, International)

HARLOW, RALPH V., "Aspects of Revolutionary Finance," AHR (Oct., 1929), XXXV, 46-68

*HARLOW, VINCENT T., *The Founding of the Second British Empire, 1763-1793: Discovery and Revolution*, Vol. I (London, 1952, Longmans Green)

HARPER, LAWRENCE A., "The Effect of the Navigation Acts on the 13 Colonies," in R. B. Morris, *The Era of the American Revolution*

HARRELL, ISAAC S., *Loyalism in Virginia* (Durham, 1926, DUP)

HARTZ, LOUIS, *Economic Policy and Democratic Thought: Pennsylvania, 1776-1860* (Cambridge, 1948, HUP)

HARTZ, L., *The Liberal Tradition in America* (N.Y., 1955, Harcourt Brace)

*HASKETT, RICHARD C., "Prosecuting the Revolution," *AHR* (April, 1954) 578-87

HATCH, LOUIS C., *The Administration of the American Revolutionary Army* (N.Y., 1904, Longmans Green)

HAWORTH, PAUL L., "Frederick the Great and the American Revolution," *AHR* (April, 1904), IX, 460-78

HENDERSON, ARCHIBALD, "A Pre-Revolutionary Revolt in the Old South-West," *MVHR* (Sept., 1930), XVII, 191-212

HILL, BRIDGET, "The Emancipation of Women and the Women's Movement," *The Marxist Quarterly* (London, Jan., 1956), III, 40-57

*HINDLE, BROOKE, *The Pursuit of Science in Revolutionary America, 1735-1789* (Chapel Hill, 1956, UNCP)

Historians Group, Communist Party of Great Britain, "Party Politics in the 18th Century," pamphlet No. 15 (mimeographed) of *Our History*, Autumn, 1959. This is an important critique of the work of Sir Lewis Namier; it appeared after the final draft of this volume was prepared.

HOFFMAN, PHILIP G., "Australia's Debt to the American Revolution," *The Historian* (Spring, 1955), XVII, 143-56

HOFFMAN, ROSS J. S., *Edmund Burke, New York Agent, with his letters to the New York Assembly* . . . (Phila., 1956, Amer. Phil. Soc.)

HUNT, AGNES, *The Provincial Committees of Safety of the American Revolution* (Cleveland, 1904, Clark)

*JAMESON, J. FRANKLIN, *The American Revolution Considered as a Social Movement* (Princeton, 1926, PUP)
JENSEN, MERRILL, *The Articles of Confederation* (Madison, 1940, UWP)
*JENSEN, M., "Democracy and the American Revolution," *The Huntington Library Quarterly* (Aug., 1957), XX, 321-42
*JOHNSON, ELMER D., "The War of the Regulation: Its Place in History," unpublished master's thesis, Univ. of N.C., 1942
JOHNSON, EMORY R., *et al.*, *History of Domestic and Foreign Commerce of the U.S.* (2 vols., Washington, 1915, Carnegie Inst.), Vol. I
JOHNSON, WILLIAM, *Sketches of the Life and Correspondence of Nathanael Greene* (2 vols., Charleston, 1822, A. E. Miller)
JONES, HOWARD M., *The Pursuit of Happiness* (Cambridge, 1933, HUP)

KAPLAN, SIDNEY, "Rank and Status among Massachusetts Continental Officers," *AHR* (Jan., 1951), LVI, 318-26
KAPLAN, S., "Pay, Pension, and Power," *Boston Public Library Quarterly* (Jan. and April, 1951). This article deals with the economic grievances of Massachusetts Revolutionary officers.
KEPPEL, THOMAS, *The Life of Augustus Viscount Keppel* (2 vols., London, 1842, Colburn)
KERR, WILFRED B., *The Maritime Provinces of British North America and the American Revolution* (Sackville, N.B., n.d., Busy East Press)
KERR, W. B., *Bermuda and the American Revolution, 1760-1783* (Princeton, 1936, PUP)
KIDDER, FREDERICK, *History of the Boston Massacre* (Albany, 1870, Munsell)
KIMBALL, MARIE, *Jefferson: The Road to Glory, 1743-1776* (N.Y., 1943, Coward, McCann)
KNOLLENBERG, BERNHARD, *Washington and the Revolution* (N.Y., 1940, Macmillan)
KOCH, G. A., *Republican Religion: The American Revolution and the Cult of Reason* (N.Y., 1933, Holt)
*KRAUS, MICHAEL, "America and the Irish Revolutionary Movement in the 18th Century," in R. B. Morris, ed., *The Era of the American Revolution*
KULL, IRVING S., ed., *New Jersey: A History* (4 vols., N.Y., 1930, Amer. Hist. Soc.), Vol. II

LABAREE, LEONARD W., *Royal Government in America: A Study of the British Colonial System before 1783* (New Haven, 1930, YUP)
LABAREE, L. W., *Conservatism in Early American History* (N.Y., 1948, NYUP)
LANCTOT, GUSTAV, "The Founding of French Canada," in George W. Brown, ed., *Canada* (Berkeley 1950, UCaP)
LASCELLES, E. C. P., *Granville Sharp and the Freedom of Slaves in England* (London, 1928, OUP)
LEVENE, RICARDO, *A History of Argentina* (Chapel Hill, 1937, UNCP)
LINCOLN, ANTHONY, *Some Political Ideas and Social Ideas of English Dissent, 1763-1800* (London, 1938, CaUP)

*LINCOLN, CHARLES H., *The Revolutionary Movement in Pennsylvania, 1760-1776* (Phila., 1901, UPP)

LOVELAND, CLARA O., *The Critical Years: The Reconstitution of the Anglican Church in the U.S., 1780-89* (Greenwich, Conn., 1956, Seabury)

*LOWELL, EDWARD J., *The Hessians and the Other German Auxiliaries of Great Britain in the Revolutionary War* (N.Y., 1884, Harper)

*MACCOBY, SIMON, *English Radicalism, 1762-1785* (London, 1955, Allen & Unwin)

MACFARLANE, R. O., "The Loyalist Migrations: A Social and Economic Movement," in R. C. Lodge, ed., *Manitoba Essays* (Toronto, 1937, Macmillan)

MACMILLAN, MARGARET B., *The War Governors in the American Revolution* (N.Y., 1943, CUP)

MALCOLM-SMITH, E., *British Diplomacy in the 18th Century, 1700-1789* (London, 1937, Williams & Norgate)

MALONE, DUMAS, *Jefferson The Virginian* (Boston, 1940, Little Brown)

MANUEL, FRANK E., *The Age of Reason* (Ithaca, 1951, CoUP)

*MARK, IRVING, *Agrarian Conflicts in Colonial New York, 1711-1775* (N.Y., 1940, CUP)

MARTIN, CHESTER, *Empire and Commonwealth: Studies in Governance and Self-Government in Canada* (London, 1929, OUP)

*MARTIN, C., *Foundations of Canadian Nationhood* (Toronto, 1955, UTP)

MAXWELL, CONSTANTIA, *Country and Town in Ireland Under the Georges* (London, 1940, Harrap)

MAYS, DAVID J., *Edmund Pendleton* (2 vols., Cambridge, 1952, HUP)

McCORMAC, EUGENE I., *Colonial Opposition to Imperial Authority during the French & Indian War* (Berkeley, 1911, UCaP)

McCORMICK, RICHARD P., *Experiment in Independence: New Jersey in the Critical Period, 1781-1789* (New Brunswick, 1950, RUP)

McCRADY, EDWARD, *The History of South Carolina in the Revolution* (N.Y., 1901, Macmillan)

McILWAIN, CHARLES H., *The American Revolution: A Constitutional Interpretation* (N.Y., 1923, Macmillan)

McINNIS, EDGAR, *Canada: A Political and Social History* (N.Y., 1947, Rinehart)

McLAUGHLIN, ANDREW C., *A Constitutional History of the U.S.* (N.Y., 1935, Harper)

MENG, JOHN J., *The Comte de Vergennes: European Phases of his American Diplomacy (1777-1780)* (Washington, 1932, CUAP)

MENG, J. J., "French Diplomacy in Philadelphia: 1778-79," *The Catholic Hist. Rev.* (April, 1938), XXIV, 39-57

MILLER, JOHN C., *Sam Adams: Pioneer in Propaganda* (Boston, 1936, Little, Brown)

*MILLER, J. C., *The Origins of the American Revolution* (Boston, 1943, Little, Brown)

*MILLER, J. C., *Triumph of Freedom: 1775-1783* (Boston, 1948, Little, Brown)

MITCHELL, BROADUS, *Alexander Hamilton: Youth to Maturity* (N.Y., 1957, Macmillan)

MOHR, WALTER H., *Federal Indian Relations, 1774-1788* (Phila., 1933, UPP)

MONAGHAN, FRANK, *John Jay: Defender of Liberty* (N.Y., 1935, Bobbs-Merrill)

MONTROSS, LYNN, *The Reluctant Rebels: The Story of the Continental Congress, 1775-1783* (N.Y., 1952, Harper)

*MONTROSS, L., *Rag, Tail and Bobtail: The Story of the Continental Army, 1775-1783* (N.Y., 1952, Harper)

MOORE, GEORGE H., *Historical Notes on the Employment of Negroes in the American Army of the Revolution* (N.Y., 1862, Evans)

MORAIS, HERBERT M., *Deism in 18th Century America* (N.Y., 1934, CUP)

*MORAIS, H. M., "The Sons of Liberty in New York," in R. B. Morris, ed., *The Era of the American Revolution*

*MORAIS, H. M., *The Struggle for American Freedom* (N.Y., 1944, International)

MORGAN, EDMUND S. AND HELEN M., *The Stamp Act Crisis* (Chapel Hill, 1953, UNCP)

MORGAN, E. S., *The Birth of the Republic, 1763-89* (Chicago, 1956, UCP)

*MORGAN, E. S., "The American Revolution: Revisions in Need of Revising," *William & Mary Q.* (Jan., 1957), XIV, 3-15

MORRIS, RICHARD B., "Labor and Mercantilism in the Revolutionary Era," in R. B. Morris, ed., *The Era of the American Revolution* (N.Y., 1939, CUP)

*MORRIS, R. B., *Government and Labor in Early America* (N.Y., 1946, CUP)

MORRIS, R. B., *The American Revolution: A Brief History* (N.Y., 1955, Van Nostrand)

MUIR, RAMSAY, *A Short History of the British Commonwealth* (2 vols., N.Y., 1927, World)

MULLETT, CHARLES F., *Fundamental Law and the American Revolution, 1760-1776* (N.Y., 1933, CUP)

NAMIER, LEWIS B., *Structure of Politics at the Accession of George III* (London, 1929, Macmillan)

*NAMIER, L. B., *England in the Age of the American Revolution* (London, 1930, Macmillan)

NETTELS, CURTIS P., *The Roots of American Civilization* (N.Y., 1931, Crofts)

*NETTELS, C. P., *George Washington and American Independence* (Boston, 1951, Little, Brown)

*NEVINS, ALLAN, *The American States During and After the Revolution, 1775-1789* (N.Y., 1924, Macmillan)

NEWCOMER, LEE N., *The Embattled Farmers: A Massachusetts Countryside in the American Revolution* (N.Y., 1953, King's Crown Press)

NYE, RUSSELL B. AND J. E. NORPURGO, *A History of the United States* (2 vols., London, 1955, Penguin), Vol. I

PADOVER, SAUL K., *The Mind of Alexander Hamilton* (N.Y., 1958, Harper)

PARES, RICHARD, *King George III and the Politicians* (Oxford, 1953, OUP)

PARKES, HENRY B., *The American Experience* (N.Y., 1947, Knopf)

PEARSON, HESKETH, *Tom Paine: Friend of Mankind* (N.Y., 1937, Harper)

PELL, JOHN, *Ethan Allen* (Boston, 1929, Houghton Mifflin)

PERKINS, JAMES B., *France in the American Revolution* (Boston, 1911, Houghton Mifflin)

PERRY, RALPH B., *Puritanism and Democracy* (N.Y., 1944, Vanguard)

PHILLIPS, PAUL C., *The West in the Diplomacy of the American Revolution* (Champaign, 1913, UIP)

PLUMB, J. H., *England in the 18th Century* (Harmondsworth, 1950, Penguin)

POLE, J. R., "Suffrage Reform and the American Revolution in New Jersey," *Proceedings of the N. J. Hist. Soc.* (July, 1956), LXXIV, 173-94

PRATT, JULIUS W., *A History of U.S. Foreign Policy* (N.Y., 1955, Prentice-Hall)

*RITCHESON, CHARLES R., *British Politics and the American Revolution* (Norman, 1954, UOkP)

ROBBINS, CAROLINE, *The Eighteenth-Century Commonwealthman: Studies in the transmission, development and circumstances of English Liberal Thought from the Restoration of Charles II until the War with the Thirtteen Colonies* (HUP, Cambridge, 1959). This work appeared after the final draft of the present volume was completed. Its chapter IX contains important additional material on English radicalism during the reign of George III.

ROBSON, ERIC, *The American Revolution in its Political and Military Aspects* (N.Y., 1955, CUP)

ROCHE, JOHN F., *Joseph Reed: A Moderate in the American Revolution* (N.Y., 1955, CUP)

ROOT, W. T., "The American Revolution in New Books and New Light," CHR, (Sept., 1942), XXIII, 308-15

*ROSSITER, CLINTON, *Seedtime of the Republic* (N.Y., 1953, Harcourt, Brace)

RYERSON, STANLEY B., *French Canada* (N.Y., 1943, International Publishers)

*SAVELLE, MAX, *Seeds of Liberty: The Genesis of the American Mind* (N.Y , 1948, Knopf)

SAVELLE, M., "The American Balance of Power and European Diplomacy," in R. B. Morris, ed., *The Era of the American Revolution*

SAVELLE, M., "The Appearance of an American Attitude toward External Affairs," *AHR*, (July, 1947), LII, 655-66

SAVELLE, M., "Road to Revolution," in R. W. Leopold and A. S. Link, eds., *Problem in American History* (N.Y., 1952, Prentice-Hall)

SCHACHNER, NATHAN, *Thomas Jefferson* (N.Y., 1957, Yoseloff)

*SCHLESINGER, ARTHUR M., *The Colonial Merchants and the American Revolution, 1763-1776* (N.Y., 1918, CUP)

SCHLESINGER, A. M., *Prelude to Independence: The Newspaper War on Britain, 1764-1776* (N.Y., 1957, Knopf)

SCHUYLER, ROBERT L., *Parliament and the British Empire* (N.Y., 1929, CUP)

SCHUYLER, R. L., *The Fall of the Old Colonial System* (N.Y., 1945, OUP)

SELSAM, J. PAUL, _The Pennsylvania Constitution of 1776: A Study in Revolutionary Democracy_ (Phila., 1936, UPP)

*SMITH, ABBOT E., _Colonists in Bondage: White Servitude and Convict Labor in America, 1607-1776_ (Chapel Hill, 1947, UNCP)

SMITH, CHARLES P., _James Wilson Founding Father_ (Chapel Hill, 1956, UNCP)

SMITH, JUSTIN H., _Our Struggle for the 14th Colony: Canada and the American Revolution_ (2 vols., N.Y., 1907, Putnam)

SPAULDING, E. WILDER, _His Excellency George Clinton_ (N.Y., 1938, Macmillan)

STEPHEN, LESLIE, _History of English Thought in the 18th Century_ (2 vols., London, 1927, Murray)

STEPHENS, ALEXANDER, _Memoirs of John Horne Took_ (2 vols., London, 1813, Johnson)

STOCK, LEO F., "The Irish Parliament and the American Revolution," _Historical Records and Studies,_ XXX, 11-29 (U.S. Catholic Hist. Soc., 1939)

THAYER, THEODORE G., _Pennsylvania Politics and the Growth of Democracy, 1740-1776_ (Harrisburg, 1953, Pa. Hist. & Museum Comm.)

THOMSON, DAVID, "Scientific Thought and Revolutionary Movements," _Impact of Science on Society_ (March, 1955), VI, no. 1 (published by UNESCO)

ᵗTOLLES, FREDERICK, "The American Revolution Considered as a Social Movement: A Re-Evaluation," AHR, (1954), LX, 1-12

TREVELYAN, GEORGE O., _The American Revolution_ (4 vols., N.Y., 1899-1913, Longmans, Green)

TURNER, FREDERICK J., "The Policy of France toward the Mississippi Valley . . . ," AHR, (Jan., 1905), X, 249-79

VAN DOREN, CARL, _Benjamin Franklin_ (N.Y., 1938, Viking)

VAN DOREN, C., _Secret History of the American Revolution_ (N.Y., 1941, Viking)

VAN TYNE, CLAUDE H., _The Loyalists in the American Revolution_ (N.Y., 1902, Macmillan)

VAN TYNE, C. H., _The War of Independence_ (Boston, 1929, Little, Brown)

ᵗVER STEEG, CLARENCE L., "The American Revolution Considered as an Economic Movement," _The Huntington Library Quarterly_ (Aug., 1957) XX, 361-72

ᵗWADE, MASON, _The French Canadians, 1760-1945_ (Toronto, 1955, Macmillan)

ᵗWALLACE, WILLARD M., _Appeal to Arms: A Military History of the American Revolution_ (N.Y., 1951, Harper)

WARD, CHRISTOPHER, _War of the Revolution_ (2 vols., N.Y., 1952, Macmillan)

WARREN, CHARLES, _The Making of the Constitution_ (Boston, 1929, Little, Brown)

WEAVER, EMILY P., "Nova Scotia and New England during the Revolution," AHR (Oct., 1904), X, 52-71

WERTENBARKER, THOMAS J., *Father Knickerbocker Rebels: New York City during the Revolution* (N.Y., 1948, Scribner's)

WILKES, JOHN W., "British Politics Preceding the American Revolution," *The Huntington Library Quarterly* (August, 1957), XX, 301-20

WILLIAMS, DAVID, *A History of Modern Wales* (London, 1950, Murray)

WISHY, BERNARD, "John Locke and the Spirit of '76," *Political Science Quarterly* (Sept., 1958), LXXIII, 413-25

WITTKE, CARL, *A History of Canada* (N.Y., 1941, 3rd edit., Crofts)

WRIGHT, LOUIS B., *Culture on the Moving Frontier* (Bloomington, 1955, IndUP)

WRONG, GEORGE M., *Canada and the American Revolution* (N.Y., 1935, Macmillan)

ZEICHNER, OSCAR, *Connecticut's Years of Controversy, 1750-1776* (Chapel Hill, 1949, UNCP)

ADDITIONAL BIBLIOGRAPHY

BARTON, H. A., "Sweden and the War of American Independence," *William & Mary Q.*, July, 1966, XXIII, 408-30

CHAPIN, BRADLEY, *The American Law of Treason: Revolutionary and Early National Origins*, (Seattle, 1964, Univ. of Wash. Press)

COLBOURN, H. TREVOR, *The Lamp of Experience: Whig History and the Intellectual Origins of the American Revolution* (Chapel Hill, 1965, UNCP)

HIGGINBOTHAM, DON, "American Historians and the Military History of the American Revolution," *American Historical Review*, Oct. 1964, LXX, 18-34

LACY, DAN, *The Meaning of the American Revolution* (N.Y., 1964, New American Library)

LEIBY, ADRIAN C., *The Revolutionary War in the Hackensack Valley: The Jersey Dutch and the Neutral Ground, 1775–1783* (1962, RUP)

MACKESY, PIERS, *The War for America, 1775–1783* (Cambridge, 1964, HUP)

MAIN, JACKSON T., *The Social Structure of Revolutionary America* (Princeton, 1965, PUP)

MASON, BERNARD, *The Road to Independence* (Lexington, 1966, Univ. of Ky. P.) (This volume deals with New York, 1773-1777.)

——, "Entrepreneurial Activity in N.Y. during the American Revolution," *Business History Review*, Summer, 1966, XXIII, 33–59

MIDDLEKAUF, ROBERT, *Ancients and Axioms: Secondary Education in 18th Century New England*, (New Haven, 1963, YUP)

MORAIS, HERBERT M., "Doctors and the American Revolution," *Schriftenreihe für Geschichte der Naturwissenschaften, Technik und Medizin* (Leipzig), 1965, VI, 99–120

NELSON, W. H., "The Revolutionary Character of the American Revolution," *American Historical Review*, July, 1965, LXX, 998–1014

QUARLES, BENJAMIN, *The Negro in the American Revolution*, (Chapel Hill, 1961, UNCP)

WOOD, GORDON S., "A Note on Mobs in the American Revolution," *William & Mary Q.*, October, 1966, XXIII, 635–42

Index